When Kenan was first diagnosed with leukaemia, I had no idea that it was the most common of all childhood cancers. I felt helpless and alone, as did the rest of my family. But we are stubborn East Enders, so we put on a good front, especially to each other, and this book reveals the pains, the laughs and the rows we went through and, in many ways, are still going through.

It is, of course, about Kenan's brave struggle against leukaemia, and we have so much pride in the way he carried on living his life, despite many setbacks. My friend Karen, whom I met soon after I moved to Spain, helped me to write 'Oi Oi, Saveloy!', and our hope is that it lends a shoulder to families who find themselves in a similar place, yet hides nothing about the journey of cancer. This book is my tribute to Kenan and it is my way of letting his brothers, Angelo and Louis, know and remember him forever.

Gina

Oi Oi, Saveloy!

Gina Gatoli-King
Karen Mullally

U P Publications
2010

First published in Great Britain in 2010 by
U P Publications Ltd
25 Bedford Street, Peterborough, UK PE1 4DN

A CIP Catalogue record of this book is available
from the British Library

ISBN 978-0-9557447-9-2

Printed in England by The MPG Book Group

FIRST EDITION

www.uppublications.ltd.uk
www.oioisaveloy.info

For
Kenan,
Angelo
and Louis

Publisher's Note

...not only have some names been changed but some people in the book are semi-fictitious 'combination characters' made from several people and several events and are there as a foil to convey Gina's feelings and the sequences of events and attitudes etc with which she had to deal – without stopping the flow of the book or by including any person who might be offended...

Foreword

Before I first met Gina, I knew her story; I had read the raw manuscript and had thoroughly lost myself in her journey. But knowing this was a journey it was right to share, did not stop me from worrying that the slow and rigorous demands of publishing would be too stressful for her.

There is an intensity and raw emotion in 'Oi Oi, Saveloy!' that makes you want to cry through the low moments, while you laugh through the highs.

Above anything there is an honesty in the writing that has helped me to see a little way into her world, through her eyes.

Gina is amazing, her drive is phenomenal and her boundless enthusiasm for life, while it has been knocked, is still vibrant. Through this book she has given Angelo, Louis and us a chance to get to know Kenan. Through her strength, she has allowed us to glimpse his.

Kenan leaps off the pages with the same boundless and brave enthusiasm that he used to leap through his life.

At our last meeting to agree the final edit, I asked if I could have the honour of writing the foreword to the First Edition.

I know it was unfair of me to steal the place that should have been filled by a celebrity, but, I wanted to say thank you to Gina and Lev for giving me a little bit of Kenan and letting me play a part in helping them to bring him to you.

Unexpectedly, as our meeting finished, Kenan had the last word. The lyrics from his special song drifted past where we were sitting and out across the sunlit bay behind us... We hope that they reach you too.

Gaile

Gaile M Griffin Peers MBA FCMI
Managing Director
U P Publications Ltd
Peterborough

When Kenan was seven years old he sometimes came to work with me in the West End of London, like during the holidays and stuff.

Even at that age he was a real little grafter – for a price of course! He earned his money though, because laying floors is no picnic and he'd put in a whole day, picking up the off-cuts until the room was clean.

I used to sit him just behind me and the lads in the van as we drove through town and we would get him to shout, "Oi Oi, Saveloy!" out the window, at all the nice bits of West End 'totty'. The girl would turn around and instead of some tired old git, she'd see Kenan – he always got a smile.

Must take after his old man eh!

Lev

Chapter One

"Happy anniversary, Babe," Lev says, pretending not to notice the waitress, young and pretty, who brings our drinks, a chilled beer for him and a Martini and lemonade for me.

"All this time you've put up with me, eh!" He raises his glass in a toast and I smile at the well worn joke. A flutter, that has nothing to do with the beachside setting or the soft sea breeze, runs across my skin, because we've been lucky. The years have been good to us mostly.

Today is 2nd April, 2005 and it's our eleventh wedding anniversary. For the first time in a long time Lev and me are out enjoying dinner without the kids. I can hardly believe eleven years have passed.

"Happy anniversary to you too," I reply, tilting my glass back towards his, my smile breaking into a grin. "We've done alright 'aven't we?"

Don't get me wrong, we have our moments Lev and me. I'm half-Italian, he's half-Turkish and we both grew up in the East End of London, so when I say we enjoy a good row, I mean we *really* enjoy a good row. But we're happy right now, and I confess to a feeling of smug contentment since we quit our busy lives in Essex, for a less hectic one here in Spain, six months ago. Then, life revolved around work for him and for me, well indulging in the latest must-have handbag about sums it up.

Lev still commutes to and from England to run our flooring business – that was part of the deal in moving here – but even that is working out.

"Gina," Lev had said. "People leave their brains behind at Dover. They make a few quid on their drums back in the UK and then piss it all up the wall. We're not going to be in the sun and skint."

And he's right. Finding work that makes money is hard even if you speak the lingo, especially within the craggy coastline of Javea on the Costa Blanca where we live. It's a small, undeniably beautiful, fishing port, where the sun shines ten months of the year and loads of people move here to 'live the dream', thinking it'll be easy because the place is full of expats. But Javea relies mostly on the tourist season, and it's amazing how many people get it wrong and lose everything.

The main resort area is called the Arenal, which means sand, and it's where we are now, in one of the many stylish restaurants along the beach front. We order nightcaps after our meal and then idly linger, talking about the kids, yet relishing our time without them vying for attention.

Our youngest, Louis, was born only four months ago bringing our tally to three boys. There's Kenan, who's eight, Angelo, three and now my lovely Louis who, I admit, I was hoping was going to be my little girl. I've always longed for a girl I could pass pretty things on to, but that's life, you can't pick and choose. Maybe we'll try again, although I best not say anything to Lev about that just yet!

It's getting late so Lev knocks back his drink, we nod our thanks to the staff and leave for home, which is a large, modern house about ten minutes drive from the beach. My mum and dad, who moved to Spain with us, are babysitting the boys, so we briefly consider going on to a club, but Kenan hasn't been feeling well this week and I'd rather get back.

Usually I can tell what's up with the kids, but I haven't been able to put my finger on what's wrong with him. It's nothing obvious like a tummy ache, a cold or an earache – his 'symptoms' are a bit vague really. He gets out of breath easily and all day he complains of being tired. No, more than tired – exhausted. He's struggling to do the stuff he normally does without thinking, like play football or ride his bike up and down the hill outside our house with his friend Jaime.

Strange, small, black bruises have appeared like thumbprints all over his body, even though he hasn't bumped himself. He says they don't hurt but it's a bit weird. I guess kids are always picking things up, but I just feel somehow this is different. Kenan does too, but he can't tell me how exactly. He does say he's too tired to go to school, but he's the new boy so perhaps he's making that bit up. Most of the other kids are Spanish, and he's still learning the language so it's not easy for him.

The boys are all fast asleep in bed when we get home. Mum says that Kenan enjoyed the evening playing with Jaime until about nine o'clock, but was getting so tired they had to help him on and off his bike.

"It's not right," I say, turning to Lev. "I can't figure it out. He must have some sort of virus. Or maybe he's not happy here. What do you think?" I want Lev to come up with an answer, but instead he just shrugs. "He's so sensitive," I carry on, "and knowing Kenan, he's probably laying it on a bit thick 'cos he doesn't want to go to school."

Lev looks worried, but says it could be anything, so we leave it at that, say goodbye to Mum and Dad and go to bed. It's not the perfect end to our evening I'd hoped for.

The next day, Sunday, Kenan wakes feeling lethargic and miserable. The sun is shining again so Lev and me try to chivvy him up a bit, make him do something to enjoy the day, but he is so tired and low that it's obvious our efforts are misguided. In the end we leave him be and all spend the day at home, worrying why Kenan just wants to lounge around on the sofa all the time. We talk about why he's behaving like he is, but decide only that if he doesn't feel better in the morning, I'll take him to the paediatrician with Louis, who has a routine vaccination booked.

Come Monday morning, Kenan wakes up feeling even worse. More tired, more aches and more bruises. Lev is concerned about going back to work in England for the week.

"Don't worry," I tell him, finishing off a cup of tea with my mum and dad, who've come around early because Dad is going back to England with Lev. "You know what kids are like. He's bound to be over whatever it is in a few days, he'll be fine. I'll call you later, OK?"

Reluctantly, Lev kisses us all goodbye before walking over to the sofa where Kenan is resting and gives his head an affectionate 'Daddy ruffle'. He leaves for the airport then with my dad who, unlike Lev, is really excited because he's been homesick and it's his first visit back since he moved here seven months ago. He can't wait to catch up with his old mates.

We wave until they're out of sight from the *naya*[1] in our garden which overlooks the road outside, and then Mum and me lock up and load the kids in my car before setting out on the half-hour drive to Acuario hospital, in a small town called Beniarbeig.

This was where Louis was born on 18th December, 2004, memorable also, because snow fell for the first time in Javea for fifty years. His water birth was as good as it gets, and after two previous attempts, I managed at last to do it without pain relief. I was so proud of myself. In truth, the gas and air I'd pleaded for never appeared which meant I found out the hard way that *mañana, mañana*[2] really is Spain!

I drive, chatting away as always, through the familiar sweet smelling orange groves that line the way to the hospital. A tractor and a couple of lorries amble along the winding road, each one unconcerned that it's causing a bloody great queue behind. It's that kind of place. While I curse the delay, I consider that, at worst, that Kenan is going to be given a course of antibiotics. It doesn't cross my mind that he might be seriously ill. Why should he be?

[1] *Terrace - covered balcony*
[2] *maybe tomorrow, or the day after - or whenever*

"Do you fancy going shopping after this as your dad is away?" Mum asks, cutting short my thoughts.

"Yeah, I'd love to. What do you want to get?" I say. We pass the time talking about shopping. We both love shopping and it doesn't occur to either of us that whatever is up with Kenan might be bad enough to stop us going.

It's still early when we arrive at the hospital and we enter the small building to a sense of calm. I'm more worried about how Louis is going to react to his jab than about Kenan, so wanting to get it out of the way, I take Louis in to see Anne, the paediatrician, first (he's really good – only a few tears), before Mum takes him out and I ask her about Kenan.

As we sit together in the chairs in front of Anne's desk, I take a moment to look at Kenan and it strikes me that he does look quite poorly – pale and withdrawn. I explain his 'symptoms' and then Anne examines him, taking him gently to lie on the white paper-covered bed. I feel the first pangs of anxiety crawl over me. She's too quiet. Usually Anne talks whilst she works, explaining all the while what she's doing, but now, as she checks Kenan's temperature and lifts his slim arms to look at the unusual bruises around his body, her face is impassive. She takes some blood – no I'll rephrase that, she takes a lot of blood and I watch her tick off at least eighteen different tests to be done, on the form. Anne offers nothing, just a half-smile, and tells us we can go. She'll ring with the results later today.

"Blimey, that's quick," I say to Mum as I pay the huge bill on the way out. "Must be 'cos it's private. I wonder what she thinks it is?"

I'm a bit disappointed that Anne hasn't even hinted as to what may be wrong. Although she wants to wait for the test results, I have a sense that deep down she does know why Kenan isn't feeling well. For the first time I wonder if Kenan might have something more serious than a mild virus. I still can't think what; it's nothing I've come across before.

We drive home more subdued than during the drive there, all thoughts of shopping now forgotten. For once, I don't appreciate the wonderful views around our beautiful, new home in our smart, hilly urbanisation as I park up. Me and Mum say nothing. We get out of the car and go through the routine of unloading the kids. I unfasten Angelo's safety straps and he runs off as fast as his short, three year old, little legs can shift him, up the sloping path to our front door. Next, I take a sleeping Louis out of his car seat and together me and Mum help Kenan walk slowly into the house. His legs hurt again, which I now understand to mean they ache and feel weak. I put Louis in his cot and switch the TV on to Cartoon Network for Angelo and wait for civil war to break out between him and Kenan, who prefers to watch the Discovery Channel. But Kenan is too tired to bother, which worries me because it is so out of character. Instead he goes and lies down on the sofa.

Mum calls from the kitchen. "Do you want a cup of tea, Gina?" and I hear her switch the kettle on. Kenan is starting to drift off to sleep, so I go and cover him gently with a blanket.

"Yeah, love one, thanks," I call back. Even though the sun is growing warm now outside, placing a blanket over Kenan feels the right thing to do. I notice that his face has started to change colour from pale to jaundiced. I touch it; his skin is soft and silky beneath my fingers. I then stroke his straight, mousy hair and I smile, because, as always, it is neatly brushed. Kenan likes to look smart. His big, brown eyes are already closed, almost hidden by the long, dark lashes that I've always imagined any girl would be proud of. He looks as tranquil as I've ever seen him. How can he be ill?

I stand up and go to join Mum in the kitchen for a much needed cuppa, casting an eye towards Angelo as I go. He's fine watching the telly. Louis is fine, sleeping in his cot; therefore I tell myself Kenan is fine too. The house doesn't feel right though – not enough noise. I'm used to Kenan and Angelo squabbling and lots of running around.

I sit down next to Mum at the kitchen table with a sigh, not sure of what to say, and clutch my mug of tea between my hands. We stick to small talk, and my tea grows cold while we wait for the doctor to ring.

Normally, on a beautiful, sunny day like today I'd be pushing the pram along the beachfront with Louis. Angelo would be at nursery and Kenan at school in the port area of town. We'd probably be heading off to a café after collecting him. The kids like to do that; sit with a drink and watch the fishermen unload their catch, before starting work on tidying their nets again ready for the next morning. It's a world away from our old life in Essex, where we'd probably be setting out on some after-school activity. But instead of watching the fishermen, I'm watching the clock.

Occasionally, we broach the subject of what may be wrong with Kenan. I'm imagining all sorts of things now, but nothing *really* awful. Still, I have this nagging feeling in the pit of my stomach that something isn't right. We conclude that, at worst, it might be hepatitis. They have to do a blood test to tell that, don't they?

Time is creeping by, yet I notice it's been less than two hours since we got home. It's driving me crazy. I'm an active person and sitting around the house like this is doing my head in. So, I pace the floor and pick the nail varnish off my perfectly painted finger nails. For Christ's sake, come on ring!

I jump when the phone does just that. The time is half-past twelve on Monday, 4th April, 2005. Mum comes and stands next to me as I reach for it. It's Anne, the doctor. My head starts to throb, but I'm not expecting her to tell me anything devastating, now I've convinced myself that it is hepatitis. However, Anne says, without preamble, that she has bad news. Goosebumps spring up on my arms and the room spins round. How bad can bad possibly be? She tells me she is sorry, but Kenan has leukaemia.

He has what? I don't say anything. Her words don't register because I know nothing about leukaemia.

She continues. "The tumorous cancers in his blood…" Cancer? I can't take it in.

"Cancer! What do you mean?" Mum is staring at me, her eyes wide in disbelief.

Numbness starts to curl around my body but I hear a distant voice down the phone calling my name, telling me to come back to the hospital immediately to collect a letter.

I must then take Kenan to a specialist cancer hospital called *Universitario*[3] *La Fe* in the city of Valencia, an hour and a half away. Where the hell is Lev?

"Cancer, cancer, cancer," I repeat over and over into the phone. I have to keep saying it because my mind won't let it go in: can't let it go in. At last, I put the phone down and then do something only ex-smokers will understand... I reach for my mum's cigarettes and, in a daze, light one and drag the smoke deep into my lungs. The tobacco hit helps. Shit, now what? I need to see Lev, because that one phone call has thrown my happy, normal little life into one of panic, chaos and change.

Lev

When I left Javea, the morning Kenan was diagnosed, to catch my usual ten-thirty EasyJet flight out of Alicante, the sun was shining. A feeling of 'summer is just around the corner' was in the air, and to anyone watching, I had no cause to have a care in the world. But I just had a feeling that whatever was wrong with Kenan was bad, which I couldn't shake. Tony, Gina's dad, was trying to be upbeat about it all saying things like, "He'll be OK, probably just needs a tonic," and I knew he meant well but I sensed he was wrong.

Usually, I get a couple of hours kip on the plane, but this time all I could think about was my little boy. He'd been so quiet over the weekend and I

---

[3] *Universitario - University*

hated being on the plane travelling away from him, I wanted to be with him.

We landed into clouds at Stansted Airport, at about twelve-thirty and I switched my phone on straight away as I was anxious to hear about Kenan's visit to the doctor. I was secretly very worried, although I didn't let on of course.

No missed calls, so I tried Gina but couldn't get hold of her. I got to my work van in the car park, calling Gina all the while but no answer. Tone and me didn't say much. I don't think he was as worried as me; he genuinely thought it was a virus or something. Still, it pissed me off when, during our drive from Stansted, he got on the phone to his mates and arranged to meet for a pint at the pub later.

My 'old man' was there to meet us when we got to my mum's house in Chingford, Essex. I'd told him over the blower that Kenan wasn't well and although he was a bit more concerned than Tony he didn't think it was anything to worry about either. It must be their age I thought to myself, think they know it all, bless 'em.

I remember standing in the kitchen making coffees when the phone rang. It was Gina. She told me straight away, no messing.

"They think he's got leukaemia!" I could tell from her voice she was scared. I knew right away how serious this was. I started to shake and I couldn't think straight, but I told her not to worry and that I'd get the first plane back home to Spain. Then my 'old man' came through the doorway with Tony and young Dave, who worked for me. Coffees forgotten, I broke the news to them. My dad immediately cuddled me and I started to cry, something I hadn't done since I was a kid. My dad and Dave were welling up too. Tony was silent. All I could think about was Kenan and getting home to him. He needed me. I couldn't stop myself thinking over and over,

"What the hell are they doing to my kid?"

Chapter Two

"Why do women bother to have babies?" I scream out, as I enter my fifteenth hour of labour at Whipps Cross Hospital in East London.

Mum and my best friend, Floria continue to mumble words of encouragement I don't hear, while Lev stays quiet, having finally decided that he can't do or say the right thing anyway. He can't! Until a few minutes ago, my mother-in-law, Maureen, who arrived unannounced and uninvited into the, already crowded, delivery room, had also been watching my, so far futile, effort to give birth, but apparently she'd found it too gruelling and left again. Do what? I'm the one going through sheer physical hell!

Neither the epidural nor the pain relief is doing its job as far as my nerve receptors can tell. But I keep on pushing, effing and blinding, and eventually Kenan Gatoli-King emerges into this world, and smiles of relief break out all around.

The date was 9th May, 1996 and he weighed a respectable seven pounds, eleven ounces. I'm always tempted to tell everyone he was three pounds heavier, because then I'd have an excuse for how much it hurt.

My overwhelming memory of that precious moment, when the midwife placed him gently, a bit blue but healthy, on top of my still rounded, jelly belly, was not one of overwhelming love, or even thanks that it was all over, but why. Why, why, why do we women do it to ourselves?

Giving birth wasn't anything like I'd imagined it to be you see. For me, it was a huge disappointment and for that I blame my birth plan. Somebody – on one check-up or another – had suggested I write one, but it didn't quite work. The main bits were as follows (I've left the graphic stuff out!):

> Q. Who would you like to be with you?
> A. Husband Lev, Mum, friend
>
> Q. Preferred position?
> A. Moving around, birth ball etc
>
> Q. Preferred position for delivery?
> A. Not lying down
>
> Q. Preferred pain relief?
> A. None, or gas and air
>
> Q. Do you want immediate skin to skin contact with the baby?
> A. Of course!

My *dream* was to be the perfect Earth Mother, sharing the moment with my loved ones, needing minimal gas and air, and sailing through delivery with a well rehearsed push or two. So when I ended up being pumped full of drugs, absolutely knackered on a bed, my hair sweaty and matted, it left me in a state of shock. I share the blame with, clearly, watching too much television whilst growing up because, somehow, I honestly thought that within a few minutes I'd be resting on plumped-up pillows, a slick of make-up on, holding my sleeping baby just like someone out of *Dynasty*.

Well why not? Women are always being told how 'natural' it is to have a baby (as long as we stick to the breathing rules), and I did try, but instead of the glowing Earth Mother, I'd been exposed as a wimp. With my dream shattered, I didn't know what to do with Kenan in those first few minutes. I had no desire to feed him, not even any rush of affection – certainly not unequivocal love. But I hid it and no one in that small, overfilled delivery room, ever guessed that at that stage, Kenan was simply something that had given me hours of the worst pain I'd ever known. Lev on the other hand was elated – he had a son.

Leaving hospital the next day, my feelings towards Kenan hadn't changed much, which troubled me. I wasn't bothered now by how painful his birth had been, or even by the ridiculous disappointment I'd felt at ending up more like *Waynetta Slob* than *Crystal Carrington*. Instead, what concerned me was a strange feeling of almost no interest in him.

Of course I said the right things and smiled while the nurses peeked through Kenan's soft, baby blanket. But stepping outside into the light, May wind, I recall feeling oddly empty. Even at that early stage I suspected something more than new 'Mummy blues' might be challenging me, but I kept quiet, hoping my feelings would change when we got home.

They didn't, and a few days later, whilst sitting in our bedroom looking at Kenan all cosy in his cot, I decided that giving birth to him had been easy compared to the emptiness I felt now. I was desperate to take my perfect, much-wanted beautiful son into my heart, but I just couldn't.

Physically, I was exhausted and struggled to muster up the energy to care for him, and although I tried, I wasn't able to breastfeed (another black cross on my perfect Earth Mother list.) Mentally, I was like a zombie, more robot than a mother; I just couldn't function as normal.

The only part I enjoyed was dressing him in the fancy, baby clothes I'd bought and that was only because, as a born shopper, I loved the clothes. It was devastating because I had always wanted a baby, but now he was here I was barely aware of him.

Lev was the one who bonded first with Kenan, the one who bathed him at night, fed him his milk and rocked him off to sleep. I kept thinking it was just a phase that I'd snap out of, but instead of getting better, I felt more distant and useless with each day that disappeared. Mum and Dad came over to help out and a few weeks passed before my dad said to my mum, "She's just not right, Brenda," which Mum rubbished.

"She's just had a baby, Tony," she reminded him in my defence.

But I wasn't right. Finally Mum agreed with Dad and suggested I see a doctor. The doctor came round and, after a quick chat, he said I was suffering from postnatal depression. What? Me?

I'd heard about postnatal depression at my prenatal classes of course, but by nature I'm a happy, organised, optimistic person so I never imagined it could – let alone would – happen to me. It was a real blow, but now I look back I think, why not? No one can tell you who might get postnatal depression or why it happens, only that some women are victims to it. I think I was lucky that my doctor took my problems seriously, because many women go undiagnosed. He left me clutching a prescription for Prozac; the wonder drug for aiding depression at the time, and within a few weeks my mood started to lift and my confidence came back.

I no longer feared looking into mirrors because I hated myself so much and I stopped torturing myself that because I was so hopeless, Lev might leave me. I can't pretend it happened overnight, it didn't, but the Prozac did work well for me, and six months later I felt I was back in control of both my family and my life again.

The most magical part about getting better was being able to fall in love with Kenan. It happened on a rare warm day for that year, while I was watching him play with a toy on his pram, in our small garden. An unexpected flood of tenderness ran through me, and I knew then that I could finally start to get to know my precious baby.

Lev

Man, I was over the moon when Kenan came along. My own little, 'mini me'. I didn't care how long he took to come out – thirteen hours I think it was, but Gina would know the exact time. Boy it was hard work, what a mission. I always wind Gina up about it and tell her I don't know what all the bleeding fuss was about. She says "When you can pass a cannon ball through the end of your Jap's eye then you'll know what it feels like." Sounds painful! Well however long it took, Kenan was there, and I was so proud of him.

Gina had postnatal depression for the first few months, and we were all worried about her because we didn't know what was wrong for ages. She was a different person and the mood around home wasn't like it should have been after the birth of a 'pukka', new baby. I didn't know what to do to help Gina, except look after Kenan, which turned out to be special because we really got on together.

I carried him everywhere when I was home, dressed him like a teenager which made Gina do her nut. I used to do the night feeds, watching MTV with my can of Stella. She'd come down because the telly was too loud and I'd be 'a kip' with Kenan sucking on his bottle in my arms. Sod me I'd soon wake up then!

I even used to get up at five o'clock in the morning and wake him up so I could video him making noises. I wanted to catch his first word you see, couldn't bear to miss it. What a nutter eh!

When I think back now though, after everything that happened, I'm glad that I was an over-the-top dad. I was proud of him, even then.

Chapter Three

"Mum, will you sort the k is out?" I ask, seconds after putting the phone down from the doctor. I draw down again on my cigarette, thinking fast.

"Pack some bags for all of us, but whatever you do try not to alarm Kenan."

I stub out the ciggie and look over at him, my baby, lying covered up on the sofa. He's still sleeping thank God, blissfully unaware of the drama unfolding.

"I have to go back to the hospital and pick up a letter," I tell Mum, suddenly desperate to leave the house. Frantically I search through all the crap in my handbag for the car keys. "Kenan needs to go to another hospital in Valencia – today."

Mum doesn't move. She's in shock, but I know she'll get on with it as soon as I've gone. My actions on auto-pilot, I grab mum's cigarettes and my sunglasses, run out the front door and drive like a lunatic back to the hospital, chain smoking out of the window. With my other hand I rummage in my bag again, find my mobile and ring my best friend, Floria in England. I can't call Lev yet because he's still

30

flying. The thought of him being in the air makes me, unusually nervous.

"Floria, shit, Floria, it's Kenan, the doctor says he has leukaemia!" I blurt. I don't remember what else I say, but Floria is refusing to believe the news.

"They must be wrong, Gina, the blood tests must be wrong!" She's trying to reassure me and I grab on to that hope.

"Yes! Maybe they are," I say, "there is a chance isn't there? That they're wrong?"

I stay on the phone, one hand on the wheel, glad to have an automatic as I weave past the occasional lorry that hogs the road leading to the hospital. I hang up only when I reach it.

Normally, parking outside Acuario hospital is a right pain and we have to go to a car park opposite, but today I don't give it a second thought. I pull to a stop outside the smart entrance and leave the car on a yellow line. I push open the gleaming black door and head straight down to Anne's office, grab the letter and leave. Did I even see Anne? I can't remember. Bugger, I meant to ask her if the tests might be wrong, but somehow I'm back behind the wheel without even realising it. A voice in my head is telling me to get Kenan to Valencia as soon as possible, so I drive like a maniac again back home.

On the way, I ring another friend Paula, who lives near us in Javea. I tell her what's happened and ask if her father-in-law, Gerald can drive us to Valencia. He can, and will meet us at our house.

Mum has all three kids ready to go and is waiting when I arrive home. Kenan is awake now and Mum has obviously told him that he needs to go into hospital, because my poor baby looks frightened; it's a look I will see too much of in the coming months.

He's asked Mum why she's packed so many pyjamas in his bag and how long he's going to be in hospital for, but that is a question none of us can answer right now.

I sit down next to him on the sofa, hug him and desperately try to reassure him that everything is going to be OK, although in truth I am as scared as he is. Checking my watch I tell Kenan I have to ring Daddy, who should have landed by now at Stansted Airport in England. I move to the window and stare outside seeing nothing. I ring Lev. My heart is pounding, and I worry if the words I am saying are, in fact, correct. I sense his shock. God only knows how Lev must feel, miles away from us all, but he pauses only a second at the other end of the phone before saying he'll meet us at *La Fe* hospital in Valencia as soon as he can get back.

Minutes later, Paula's father-in-law, Gerald arrives. For Kenan's sake, we all try to behave normally as we leave the house and get into the car. It's impossible of course. We don't even know how to get to Valencia, Spain's third largest city. None of us speak Spanish very well and my child is desperately ill, so staying normal isn't really happening.

We leave Javea and as we join the motorway to Valencia, I silently urge Gerald to go faster and get us there sooner, even though he is already hitting the speed limit.

We arrive in Valencia an hour later with no problems, but the maze of one-way systems means we can't find the hospital. I'm growing more and more anxious because my only concern is getting Kenan seen by another doctor. However Valencia, fast developing into one of the most vibrant cities in Europe, is hectic and the roads are completely mad. We get caught up in the huge multi-lane roundabouts and are beeped at by drivers, hell-bent on moving around as fast as they can – London doesn't compare. Poor Gerald is fried, but after repeated stops to ask taxi drivers where the hospital is, ironically, it is Kenan who spots the *La Fe* Hospital sign, amongst a mass of other buildings. As the car comes to a stop, I hear myself whisper, "No."

We're here and it has been both the longest and shortest journey of my life. I step out of the car, oblivious to the sounds of the city around us, and stare at the huge structure in front of me – a typical 1970s square block, studded with hundreds of regular square windows. They appear to be staring right back at me. I notice, after my whirlwind tour of Valencia, that the building fits in well with its surroundings, sat as it is in the forgotten part of town that has neither the charm of the old, nor the impact of the new. Not that I know a lot about this yet. I see a bus garage and a shopping centre, but not much else. As it turns out, these are the only two things we will need anyway.

Three divided sections lie within the sand-coloured walls of the hospital: General, Maternity and our destination, Infantil. My eyes follow the steep steps up to the entrance doors and then it hits me – what the hell are we doing here? At that point, before we go any further, I take a moment to gather my thoughts, turn and put my arm around Kenan.

"Shall we go home, Darling, back to England? We can get you better there. We can catch a plane today and be back by tonight."

Kenan immediately shakes his head and says, "No, I like it in Spain."

His reply rocks me because, in my mind, I'd assumed he'd just say yes and we'd leave. But he wants to stay. Every bone in my body strains to grab him and get the hell out of there and go back, because I just don't know if I can cope here, with the language, the culture difference, this mad city. But I don't have the presence of mind to sift through my options right now, so I allow myself to be swept along by events, too scared to do anything else.

Gerald helps us with the children and the bags before leaving to fight the chaos back to Javea again. I thank him and then me, Mum and Kenan, walk slowly up the steep steps to Infantil, carrying Angelo and Louis. Moving through the doors, my legs are like jelly, my mouth dry and my heart is pushing against my throat, beating loudly enough for me to hear it. I can't speak at the *Ingreso*[4], so instead I silently pass the letter Anne has given me over to a no-nonsense looking lady on the other side. She asks me some questions. I don't know how to answer them but something inside me knows what she needs and I give her Kenan's name, date of birth, 9th May, 1996, and our home address. Within minutes, all hell breaks loose. A nurse comes out of nowhere and signals us towards a set of lifts, which we obediently enter, crowding closely around Louis' pram.

---

[4] *reception*

34

On the second floor, the nurse leads us straight to a set of double doors with chairs lined up outside and tells Mum to wait there with Angelo and Louis. I look up and see the sign ONCOLOGY, fixed on the wall above us. My head feels like it's going to explode.

A lot of Lev's work in England involves laying floors in hospitals and as I do the paperwork, I have typed many, many times on estimates and invoices, *Oncology Ward*, but they have always just been words; they've never meant anything. Now the words are personal, they mean something.

I'm aware that the nurse is waiting for Kenan and me to go through those doors, into a world that has crash-landed on our lives and one I don't want to enter. But we follow her, sheep-like, into the ward beyond, and while I walk, I gaze in through the windows at young, sick children. A tiny baby, no more than six months old, is lying in a bed crying, but strangely I feel detached of any emotion towards it. It's like walking around a school and seeing kids but not really noticing them.

The nurse shows us into a small room and helps Kenan into bed, setting up more blood tests and planning to get him some dinner. All the activity makes me feel out of control, not a feeling I'm used to, and I can tell that Kenan is petrified. To the nurses he looks like any other normal, eight-year old boy, but I am his mother and I know that Kenan is scared, although he is hiding it well.

I check my watch and am shocked to see it's already six o'clock in the evening. While the nurses sort out Kenan, a tall, thirty-something, male doctor comes in to see me – he wants a word. Funnily enough, I can't help but notice that he's quite good-looking. What a strange thing to notice at a time like this. He speaks English too; fantastic. I do and I don't want to hear what he has to say, but I'm grateful that someone is going to explain what the hell is happening to Kenan.

"I'll be back in a minute, Darling," I tell Kenan, and go with the good-looking doctor into a bland, functional office on the ward and listen while he explains exactly what having leukaemia means, and what treatment it entails. I listen in silence; at least I think I'm listening. I know I'm not taking everything in, just the bits that have Kenan's name in.

He needs to undergo an intensive course of chemotherapy, which will start almost immediately to give him the best chance of beating the leukaemia. I start to experience a feeling of watching myself in a film. This isn't happening; this doctor isn't even real, so I sit trance-like and nod until the film is finished. He says a consultant will be able to tell us more tomorrow after they've done further tests.

I go silently back to Kenan, who has, to my amazement, eaten all his dinner, even though it's paella. Kenan hates paella. He's always been a very fussy eater, ever since he was a baby. He simply doesn't get on with food, well not with the food I want to him to eat. When he was younger, desperate for him to eat, I used to give him a milkshake and chicken nuggets which, like a lot of children, he loved, so that's what he ate much of the time. My constant efforts to get him to eat properly were usually met with 'Yuck' and 'I don't like that.' Kenan, basically, enjoys eating junk, not paella and it felt odd to see him wolf down a whole plateful of the stuff. Why couldn't he do that at home?

It's been a while since I've seen Mum, so I tell Kenan I'll be back soon and go out into the corridor where she is still holding vigil with Angelo and Louis. She looks knackered, which doesn't surprise me. It's hard taking care of a four month old and an active three-year old in a hospital.

"Hi." I say, sitting down on the chair next to her. "I've seen the doctor, not that I remember much of what he said. Kenan has to have chemotherapy but they're going to run some more tests first."

I can tell most of what I'm saying is going straight over her head, because she starts to busy herself with chasing Angelo, who's running off down the hushed hallway again. When she comes back, I tell her that tomorrow, they're going to move Kenan to the Isolation unit and that he'll be given chemotherapy pretty much immediately.

"He needs a special tube called a Hickman line to be put in under anaesthetic first though," I tell her, surprising myself that I've taken that much in, "so they can feed the chemotherapy and other medicine in through it."

My words sound foreign, like they belong to someone else. Mum stares at me and mumbles something about something, so I leave them again and go and sit with Kenan.

"What's happening, Mummy?" Kenan asks me. What do I say now? I decide that fudged honesty is best for the moment, because I barely know myself.

"The doctors think you have something called leukaemia, which is why you've been feeling so bad.

but it's all going to be OK. Daddy is coming home to see you, he should be here soon. The doctors will come and explain it all to you, OK?" He nods, but I see that he's still scared.

"Look," I try to reassure him, "you have to stay in hospital for a while, but after that you'll be well again."

I don't know what I'm talking about, but it makes us both feel a bit better. A nurse comes in and rabbits away in Spanish and I manage to get the gist of what she's saying, which is that she's going to take Mum and the kids down to a special, family waiting area, in reception, where they'll be more comfortable.

"I'll be back as soon as I can," I tell Kenan because I want to go with them and check they're OK. We go back down in the lift to a room with big, comfy chairs. The nurse brings Mum some blankets and some yogurts, drinks and biscuits for the kids. It's fine but my poor mum is done in, both mentally and physically. Angelo has 'lost' her twice on visits to the canteen because he thinks running around the huge island that divides up the eating area from the self-service area is hysterically funny – especially with poor Mum chasing him with Louis in the pram – and she's had enough. Thankfully Angelo appears to have run out of steam, as well.

Mum only had me, so she's always been amazed by the mayhem more than one kid brings. I can't help her though because I need to get back to Kenan, but I promise to pop down every half-hour or so to see her. To be honest I feel totally useless in both places – I can't do anything to help Kenan or

Mum, so I distract myself by counting the minutes until Lev arrives back from England.

It's ten-thirty at night when Lev finally arrives. He joins me in Kenan's room, exhausted of course. In less than twelve hours he has left Spain, landed in England and returned to Alicante Airport to pick up his car. He has then driven home to Javea, because I had asked him to feed the dog (trying to pretend everything is normal) and raced up to Valencia, where he hailed a cab to follow to *La Fe*.

I am so pleased to see him, as is Kenan – he's thrilled Daddy's back. We stay with Kenan for a while before I tell him I need to talk to Daddy outside. As I begin to tell him what I know the handsome doctor spots us. He has the test results. In my head, I telepathically plead with him; beg him, to tell us that the paediatrician in Beniarbeig has got it all wrong, that the new tests have shown it's all a silly mistake. But as I meet his eyes, he only confirms what we are dreading. Kenan definitely has leukaemia. Acute myeloid leukaemia, or AML as I come to understand is how it's referred to.

While we are trying to take in this devastating absolute truth, the doctor drops two more bombshells. Kenan will eventually need a transplant, and that he has only a fifty-fifty chance of survival. This isn't something I expect to hear. Life or death never came into it.

The floor sways from underneath me as my legs go weak and I collapse on to Lev. He holds me up and makes me listen to the doctor, who explains the hard, harsh facts of what Kenan is about to go through. He can't tell us how long Kenan will be in hospital for, or what the outcome will be. My head is racing with practicalities of all things. How are we going to cope? How are we going to look after Angelo and our new baby? How are we going to be here for Kenan every day? We can't have the little ones at the hospital with us – it's not a place for them to be hanging out. Besides, the doctors won't even let them near Kenan. What do we do?

I must be babbling because the doctor tries to tell me that it is crucial, for everyone involved, that we don't try to plan ahead too much.

"Don't think," he tells us, "take it day by day." But his well-meaning words only fuel my growing panic.

The doctor is done for now, so he leaves, telling us that a consultant will talk more with us tomorrow. Lev and me return to Kenan's room hand in hand, to find him looking surprisingly cheerful. I think in a way he's pleased to know that there is something wrong with him and that the doctors are going to make him better.

Without warning, I feel a yearning to get my mum and the boys out of this hospital and into a hotel. Thinking of the other two helps me calm down because I can do something for them. They need a bed for the night, not just a chair in a waiting area, and I can do that. Lev wants to see the boys too and Kenan is happy enough for now, so we leave him resting, collect Mum and the kids and walk together, in silence, over the road to the nearest hotel.

By now, it is midnight and Angelo and Louis are asleep. The hotel we enter is like any hotel; a room, a shower and a place to sleep. Once they're settled, Lev and me say bye to my mum and head silently back to the hospital. There, Kenan is falling asleep too, so we sit with him for a while and then Lev tells me to go and try and get some sleep in the hotel.

"I'll stay with Kenan tonight," he says. "There's only room for one of us in here anyway. I'll ring you if anything happens."

I'm grateful, because I don't think I can take anymore today. I leave and during the short walk to the hotel I try to think of how I am ever going to deal with this.

I hear Mum before I see her. She's pacing the floor in the corridor, yelling down the phone at Dad who is still in England. She can't understand why he isn't here, why he didn't come back with Lev. He has things to sort out apparently, but Mum is having none of it. I motion at her to quieten down because she's screaming at him.

"If you don't get back here by tomorrow night then don't bother coming back at all!"

To be fair to Dad, I don't think he can really take in how desperately ill Kenan is. He has looked forward to his trip for so long now and he's desperately homesick too; I think it's clouding his judgment. But Mum needs him here; we all do, so he promises to catch the first flight out in the morning. Wearily, I realise that, emotionally, we are all going to be tested until Kenan is well again.

I pray that night. "Please, turn the clock back twenty-four hours, to a time when leukaemia isn't a part of us, to a time when we are just a normal family and not trapped inside this horrible nightmare."

Lev

The minute after Gina called me with the news about Kenan I got onto the internet and rescheduled my return flight to that evening. I was shaking while I was doing it and I couldn't think straight. What was the matter with me? I had to be strong for Kenan, I thought. He needs me.

My dad and Tony took me back to Stansted and I smoked like a trooper all the way even though I hadn't had an oily for two years. We sat around a table in Starbucks with a coffee and my dad and Tony spent the time until my flight, trying to reassure me that Kenan was going to be OK. I sat there in silence. I knew they were talking bull but they were just trying to help.

The flight back to Alicante was busy, filled with the usual suspects, mainly Brits flying off to their 'promised land'. All running away from what they believed was the Karzy of Europe, namely the UK.

"Viva España!" I would always blurt out when something went wrong at home in Javea, which it often did thanks to the dodgy electrics and archaic system of using gas bottles to heat the house and water. Kenan would laugh his socks off and Gina would tell me to piss off back to England. Well come on! The gas would *always* run out on a Monday morning when I was about to get in the shower. In the winter, I'd be there, standing outside in just a towel, freezing my bollocks off as I changed over the gas bottles. Or the electric, front gate would get stuck half-way when I was in a rush trying to get the motor out. Or we'd have no water or electric when it rained heavy. The incompetence of Spain is how Kenan and me labelled it.

Deep down I love it though; the feel of the sun, the fun of the sea and the outdoor life, fishing with the boys and watching them ride their bikes through the orange groves. It's a great place for young kids.

Sunday was always beach day in the summer, or sometimes we'd barbeque around the beautiful coves of Granadella. They were good weekends, worth the travelling, as it meant I spent more quality time with my kids. The lifestyle is definitely better than in the UK. People thought I'd never make it work commuting.

"When are you coming back?" they'd say, the jealous sods. I have made it work though.

I have to commute because there's no money to be made in Javea. The only English with any money are, usually, either dodgy or property-boom estate agents, and there's the odd, successful builder too. The trouble is, Javea was once a place for retired, old gits who'd made their money. Not young families, of which there are now more and more. I'm sure a lot of people coming out here to live leave their brains behind at Dover. They make a few quid on their drums back in the UK and then piss it all up the wall.

Mind you, wine is cheaper than milk for bleeding sake! That's not how we were gonna do it, be in the sun and skint. No way!

All those things ran through my mind on the flight. I didn't speak to, or acknowledge, anyone; I just sat staring into nothing, thinking about Kenan.

When I'd sat down I'd looked up and saw that I was in seat number thirteen. I'm not superstitious but I couldn't help but think, shit!

I thought a lot about the funny things Kenan did, like stutter a lot – I always took the mick out of that one. Gina would tell me off but Kenan laughed. We had the same sense of humour and he knew how to laugh at himself.

I have no idea what time I got to the hospital in Valencia. It was late though. The eagle landed in Alicante at about half-past nine. I jumped into my Peugeot, 'Nigel Manselled' it round the A7 motorway and got back to Javea at half-past ten that night. I fed Kato, our dog, swapped the Peugeot for the ML and caned it to Valencia. I just wanted to see Kenan and I was like a robot. I'd never been there before but the way my mind was it didn't matter which city it was. I stopped a cabbie and in my best 'Spanglish' said, "Donde[5] *La Fe* hospital?"

I followed him right there. I parked and ran straight up the stairs of the hospital, found Gina and gave her a big cuddle. I then went into Kenan's room and sat with him while Gina and I waited for his test results. God knows what was going through the poor little sod's mind.

That was when I started feeling angry inside. I knew I had to keep it down and stay focused but it was so hard. We left him after a bit and that was when we met Gina's good-looking doctor, who told us that our son was now fighting for his life.

---

[5] *Donde - Where*

Chapter Four

Kenan grew up in the diverse and historic county of Essex, northeast of Greater London. In the early noughties, whilst we lived there, it was best known as the home of footballer's wives, 4 x 4 Range Rovers, Juicy Couture tracksuits and Burberry. If you couldn't afford it, you faked it.

The place thrived on ex-East Enders like Lev and me. Small-time gangsters and numerous car dealers turned 'Lord of the Manor' – or being Essex, I should say 'Lord of the mock-Tudor mansion'.

Lev and me own a flooring business and by the time we'd trodden the well-worn path from the East End to Essex, we were fortunate enough not to have to fake it anymore.

We hadn't always had money. My dad handed down the company to us when he decided (in a moment of madness, he later said) to retire, and whilst it was already successful, we realised that there was potential to make it bigger. It was a boom period in the economy and people wanted to spend, so Lev put in the hours and I waited an equal number of hours at home for him to come in, however as the bookkeeper I could see that the results were worth it.

Relatively quickly, we had our smart cars, lots of clothes, the bling Rolex watches and, as we moved further away from our roots down the Central Line into the leafy Essex countryside, increasingly lovely homes.

Although we both grew up submerged in the bustling street markets, noise and hustle of the East End of London, our childhoods were quite different. I was an only child and lived in a nice home that my parents owned. I attended the famous Sylvia Young Theatre School in London, until the day came when even my mum had to leave behind her dream of me becoming a prima ballerina. Lev came from the opposite side of the tracks. He grew up with his younger brother on a decent, but typical, council estate not too far away from our 'posh' house. His parents divorced when he was young and, to be honest, Lev could have gone either way in life. He realised, however, that a life of crime wasn't going to fulfil the one ambition he had – which was to make money.

We met in our early twenties, his 'uptown girl' he called me, and he began to learn the floor-laying ropes, working alongside my dad.

Our first home together was in Chingford and I remember it like most young couples remember their first home I suppose, with a sense of pride and a naughty smile. The prefabricated, two bedroom terrace arrived on a warm, sunny day on the back of a lorry, (as opposed to *off* the back of a lorry) and measured ten feet, six inches wide and twenty-one feet long.

Once the roof had been fixed in place we moved in and Lev painted it pink for me. Our two little window boxes – one at the front, one at the back – were my pride and joy. That house was our love nest and we enjoyed lots of late nights and lazy weekends. We moved out a year and a half later in need of a bigger house because by now we were married and I was pregnant with Kenan. It was the start of a fast climb up the housing ladder.

Our next house was a three bedroom, end of terrace in Buckhurst Hill, and I spent a lot of time there by myself, after my boss suddenly made me redundant from my job as a sales clerk in Walthamstow. I was six months pregnant when he called me in to the office and gave me the news, and with a belly growing as fast as mine was, finding other work wasn't an option. I suppose I could have made a fuss, but I'd intended to stop work anyway after the baby was born and, in shock, my immediate thought was at least I can enjoy putting my feet up for a few months.

I was bored within a week, so I filled my days decorating the nursery while Lev worked longer hours to give our little family the best start he could. That's what he said anyway!

Three months later Kenan was born and I slid into postnatal depression. Once I felt better again, Lev spent most weekends working, leaving me with plenty of hours to fill.

It was autumn and the weather was lousy, but now I'd finally fallen in love with Kenan, nothing was going to stop me proudly parading my gorgeous boy up and down Queens Road in Buckhurst Hill, shopping 'til I dropped with my mum and then hanging it all from his Mamas & Papas pram. Essex girls will know that Queen's Road is the land of designer dreams: Gucci, D&G, Prada, Moschino, you name it, it's there. I loved spoiling Kenan, simply because I could. Popping into Moschino and popping out again with a tiny pair of baby boots made me feel good, although naturally Kenan couldn't care less. But I wanted him to have everything.

I loved too, that people often stopped the pram to look at him because Kenan honestly was a beautiful baby, with the most gorgeous, long eyelashes. I usually dressed him in blue, as quite often he was mistaken for a girl. (I used to tell him all the time how beautiful he was, until he asked me to stop embarrassing him when he was about eight, and I grudgingly changed it to extremely handsome).

One day, when Kenan was about three years old, the headrest was stolen from our black BMW whilst it was parked up on the drive. Lev decided that Buckhurst Hill was turning into the crime capital of Essex and three months later, when he walked out to go to work and found his van missing, enough was enough. We were moving. Work was still going well, so we packed up and went on further down the county to Epping where we bought a four bedroom, two-bathroom, detached house in a quiet cul-de-sac. My mum said we were mad – 'The curtain's twitch in cul-de-sacs,' she told us – but I shrugged her comments aside but wished I'd listened when she turned out to be right.

From the beginning we just didn't fit in there. Our neighbours were snotty types who thought you could only own a Mercedes or a BMW if you wore a suit and worked in the City and Lev, of course, worked on his hands and knees as a lowly floor-layer.

Mostly, they ignored us and mostly we laughed and said, "Sod 'em."

But then I changed the colour of our house from magnolia to a lovely powder blue – well I thought it was lovely – and the Resident's Association had a real go at us. I nearly waved the white flag then. That's how petty the place was.

There was one good thing to come out of living in the cul-de-sac and that was our friendship with a couple called Angie and Gary, whom I mention now because Angie is an important part of this story later on.

They moved into a house almost identical to ours, shortly after us. Like us they already had one child, Harry, who was three, the same age as Kenan and Angie was pregnant with their second. I went over as they moved their stuff in, introduced myself and we, instantly, became really good mates.

When Kenan and Harry started school, Angie and me took turns to do the school run and, if we were having a bad day, we took refuge in each other's house to enjoy a good bitch and a moan, normally about our husbands or the other people in the cul-de-sac.

Angie had a little girl, Olivia, and I recall, with fondness, the two of us hanging out of her back door puffing away on our cigarettes, chatting and drinking coffee whilst Olivia crawled around happily inside.

It was on one such afternoon that Angie broke the news that Gary had been offered a job in Abu Dhabi which was too good to turn down. They were renting out their house and leaving as soon as they could. Angie was the only mate I had around there and I was gutted our friendship was being forced to end. However, they had one important event to fit in before they left. They were required to get married, because you're not allowed to live together in Abu Dhabi if you are an unmarried couple with children. They organised the wedding amazingly quickly, but this was Essex, and Angie pulled out all the stops to ensure her big day took place in true 'Essex style'.

It was February, but the weather was fine and she looked gorgeous on the day, and stepping into the horse-drawn carriage that pulled up outside her house (how the stuck-up neighbours loved that!) Angie, so totally down to earth, beautiful and bubbly, couldn't stop giggling at how posh she felt.

A few days after the wedding, Angie called round to ask my opinion about something.

"What do you think this is?" she asked, and lifted her arm to show me a lump. Neither of us considered that it was anything to worry about, but to be on the safe side I suggested she ought to see the doctor. Her doctor subsequently told her it was nothing sinister so, confident she was in good health, we said our sad goodbyes soon after and off went our only friends in the cul-de-sac to Abu Dhabi.

Living there wasn't the same without them, and although none of us knew it at the time, Angie and Gary's lives were never to be the same either.

Chapter Five

It's early when I wake the next morning, so I stand, eyes closed, under a cool shower, grateful for these minutes alone to gather my thoughts, while the kids are still sleeping. I'm surprised that I've slept at all, but yesterday clearly drained me more than I realised and whatever little sleep I've had has done me good – I don't feel swamped by the same black despair of yesterday. Today, I am determined to fight, fight for Kenan, every step of the goddamn way.

I remember that the Hickman line is being put in this morning, so I get my clothes on quickly, leave Mum and the kids asleep and head quickly to the hospital, running up the steep steps, eager to see Lev and Kenan. Kenan looks fine, but Lev is drawn and knackered. We sit in Kenan's bare, square room, doing little more than smile at the succession of nurses and doctors who come in and out in spite of the early hour. He's being prepped for his Hickman line and at some point during the morning Kenan is taken away from us and goes to theatre.

While we wait, a doctor comes to explain that the line will be connected to the main artery in

Kenan's heart to provide an entry point for the chemotherapy and other drugs that will need to be fed into his little body. It sounds horrible, brutal, but it means Kenan won't have to be endlessly poked and pricked about every time the doctors need to give him intravenous medication.

A nurse comes to see us and says that Kenan will be going to an Isolation ward when he comes out. From now on, no more than one person at a time will be allowed to sit with him and anyone going in or out has to scrub up and change clothes first.

A while later Mum arrives from the hotel, loaded down with the boys. She's managed to find a park within the hospital grounds and Angelo has at least had a runaround in the sunshine, so I meet her for a coffee and a ciggie (I'm still smoking) to try and sort out how best to organise the boys. She says that she and Dad will look after Angelo and Louis, but in my heart I know it'll be too much for them. It's not that they're old – they're only in their early sixties; but it is exhausting looking after a three year old and a baby full-time.

As it turns out, the doctor who told us the day before not to plan too much in advance was right. My friends, most of whom I haven't known long, have been ringing and texting, offering to help out with the kids, so Mum and me decide that Angelo will go to nursery full-time and that she and Dad will have Louis. Friends will look after him for a few hours each day to give them a break.

As we're ironing out the details, Dad calls Mum's mobile to say he has arrived at Valencia Airport. He is on his way to the hospital. Mum's tired expression lifts, for a second, on hearing that Dad is back, before it crumbles again with exhaustion.

We sit waiting, on the warm, oddly comfortable steps outside the hospital, until Dad arrives. The reality finally hits him when he sees us. His face falls and I spot the tears spring into his eyes as he, at last, realises that this awful thing isn't happening to someone else, but to his grandson and to our family. But I can't let him cry.

"Please don't, Dad," I plead. "Don't cry. We have to all stay strong for Kenan's sake. No tears."

He pulls himself together and goes straight to see Lev. Mum is shattered and needs to get back to Javea, so soon after Dad comes back they leave for home in our car with Angelo and Louis, who are tired and fractious as well. My heart breaks seeing them leave.

"Mummy will be home soon," I tell them, kissing each of their soft cheeks, although I have no idea when I will be. The boys will have to come back to Valencia in any case, because they need to have blood tests along with Lev and me to see if any of us are suitable donors for Kenan. I'm really torn about Louis going through with it because if he's a match, he'll become the youngest ever bone marrow donor. We'll have to cross that dilemma if it comes to it.

For now though they need to go home, so I wave one part of my life goodbye and turn back towards the hospital, to the other.

Kenan is out of surgery. The insertion of the Hickman line has gone well, but we're not allowed into his new room yet. We can only watch him through the large, glass wall that runs around the ward in a U-shape, outside the Isolation rooms. It's killing me seeing Kenan sleep alone. I want to be with him, to hold his hand. There is an intercom we can speak through but that's of no use to us right now.

The doctors come and tell us that they'll be monitoring and testing Kenan for *x, y* and *z* for the rest of the day and first thing tomorrow they will start the chemotherapy. My God, the speed at which everything is happening is scary. But, with nothing more we can do here we eventually leave our sleeping boy and swap the confines of the hospital for those of the hotel.

Early, the next morning, Wednesday 6th April, just two fleeting days after Kenan's shock diagnosis, Lev and me walk nervously, hand in hand, up the hospital steps for the start of our little boy's chemotherapy. I am both dreading it and excited to get it going, desperate for it to begin and desperate for it to end. After all, this is going to cure him, right?

By focussing on the chemotherapy I feel strangely calmed, but Lev is in turmoil. He's had a particularly rough night and can't face speaking to anyone this morning. Even his mobile, his usual lifeline for work, is turned off, so because friends can't get hold of him my phone rings constantly. I welcome the connection with the real world and gladly leave it on until we step out of the lift on the second floor.

For at least the millionth time, I wonder what the hell we are doing here. How has this happened to us? Kenan was running about like a normal, healthy, young boy just a couple of weeks ago, yet now he is a leukaemia patient, in an unfamiliar hospital. I now fully understand the meaning of the phrase, 'having the rug pulled from under you.'

As we enter the Isolation unit, I catch sight of Kenan sitting up in bed waiting for us and I smile, relieved that he looks cheerful enough following his operation, yesterday. I notice the room is scrupulously clean (the nurses laugh when I ask about the risk of MRSA, which has been regularly hitting the headlines in the UK) and I'm shown how to scrub up and put on my mask before going in. In Isolation, it's strictly one person at a time, so Lev waits outside watching through the large window. I'm not sure what Kenan makes of my get-up, but if he thinks I look a right idiot in my mask, floppy trousers and shapeless jacket, he is sweet enough not to say so.

"Hi, Darling," I say from behind my mask, and walk over to give him a cuddle. My stomach is clenching, but Kenan looks relaxed despite the presence of the Hickman line, which I can now see poking through his chest underneath his pyjamas.

"Hi, Mummy," he replies, like it's an ordinary day. It isn't of course; in a few minutes he's going to start chemotherapy. Yesterday afternoon we met the consultant assigned to Kenan, Dr. Carlos Garcia – (he's asked us to call him Carlos from now on) who, we were pleased to find out, had worked for three years at the Royal Marsden hospital in Surrey. It's reassuring to have some sort of link with home. He speaks fluent English, which is a great relief to us as our Spanish is embarrassingly hopeless. He's warned us that this first course is going to be intensive and aggressive, the aim being to destroy the cancer cells quickly, thereby putting the leukaemia into remission.

Carlos seems young for such a responsible job, early thirties perhaps, but over the following weeks we come to appreciate how lucky Kenan is to have him as his main doctor. At only five feet four he isn't much taller than some of his patients, but they clearly adore him and Kenan has taken to him instantly. He loves the fact that Carlos treats him like a grown-up as he has always been good with people older than him, although there are things of course, that Carlos has told only me and Lev, mostly technical stuff that might affect Kenan later on in life.

He's told us too that if everything goes well, Kenan will be able to leave in about a month and be looked after at home. It seems a long time to me. He will need to come back at set intervals over the next few months for three more courses of chemo to mop up any rogue cells left roaming around. The way Carlos explained it, didn't make it sound too bad at all.

Sitting, waiting with Kenan for the chemotherapy to start is a weird feeling though. It's not something I've ever been up close to and, to be honest, I have no idea what to expect. I don't know what it is or how it's administered, and it's extremely disturbing that something I've only ever seen on the television is about to be given to my son.

A nurse walks into the room carrying a bottle containing a clear liquid which looks like nothing more than water. Is that it? I'm surprised, because I've been expecting this amazing *cure* to be more … well just more somehow. But this is it, a bottle of clear liquid that the nurse efficiently hooks up to the machine next to Kenan's bed and then connects the tube to his Hickman line.

The drip immediately begins to draw the liquid slowly through the tube into Kenan and I sit expecting all sorts of reactions from him. Nothing happens. Nothing at all, although half of me believes that he is going to start throwing up or that his hair will fall out on the bed – my imagination is in overdrive!

Thankfully, he seems to be in no discomfort at all, so I relax a little and we play cards, chat and watch DVDs whilst the bottle gradually empties its contents. It takes ages. It's funny because I know what's happening is enormous, but it doesn't *feel* like it is; it just feels all a bit surreal. I keep glancing at the bottle as the clock ticks by, and asking Kenan constantly "Are you OK?"

Kenan is fine, perfectly well in fact, he insists. I think he wants to tell me to shut up! Maybe this whole chemo business isn't going to be so bad after all. Another half-hour passes before Kenan says he needs a wee, so the nurse comes in with a urine bottle and hands it to me along with a pair of protective gloves. I look at her puzzled.

"It's all right," I tell her, shaking my head. "I don't need the gloves."

The last thing I want is for Kenan to think I want to wear them. But she insists, telling me they will protect my hands in case I spill any.

"What if I do?" I ask. In broken English the nurse explains that Kenan's wee on my hands will be like acid and may burn my skin. Silenced by her words, I do as she asks and pull the gloves on. By the time I put the wee in a jug and leave it by the door, as requested, I realise that this isn't going to be easy at all, that it isn't something that is going to pass by without pain, and that it is about as serious as it gets.

I meet Lev's eyes through the glass – he already knows.

Carlos wasn't kidding when he said the initial course of chemo was going to be intensive. Just as I think it's all finished, the nurse takes away the first, now empty, bottle and connects another and when that is finished, another one. Me and Lev alternate sessions, sitting with Kenan for the next four days, while he patiently goes through having the same number of bags pumped into him each time.

Thankfully, he's not having any of the dreaded side-effects associated with cancer patients; in fact the only thing he's suffering from is boredom. Is it possible that he won't have any side-effects, I wonder?

Thanks to Carlos, who is so positive, reassuring and friendly, we've all coped better with the first week than I imagined. So well in fact, Lev has decided to return to work for a few days, mainly because Kenan has been nagging him to, non-stop. Being only eight years old (and a chip off the old block as far as money is concerned) Kenan has got himself into a bit of a state that we might not be able to buy all the things he likes, if Lev doesn't work. I don't mind Lev going because Kenan is happy enough and with the chemo over, we're now just waiting for him to get strong enough to come home.

So Lev leaves and I feel, unexpectedly, alone, although I'd never dare admit it to anyone. It's tougher being here without Lev than I'd imagined.

The nurses are brilliant, I have no complaints, but I do feel very isolated due to my lack of Spanish. If I was in England it would be different because I'd be able to chat with the nurses and ask what's going on. All I can say here is, "Es todo bien, es normal?[6]"

They always respond with the same reply. "Si, muy bien[7]" – which is good, of course it is, but I'd feel better if I could ask more. It's unbelievably frustrating.

During our few days here, I have got to know some of the other mums with children having similar treatment and they've invited me to have a cigarette with them now and then, but it is desperate trying to keep up with the conversation. I want to chat with them, to find out why their children are here. I want to take comfort in their words and feel reassured by the common ground we all share. Some of their children are losing their hair and being sick so I know the other mums understand my fears. But I can't keep it up for long – I'm exhausted just listening, so I stop meeting up with them.

Instead I've decided to go shopping, because being alone in a crowd feels more comforting somehow and my composure is much brighter when I go back to Kenan.

And he needs me now. He'd been doing so well, but the day after Lev leaves, the effects of the chemo suddenly kick in. How naive I was to think he might be spared. Kenan is being sick, often, and looks so frail. Already it's tearing my heart out. I'm shaken by how fast the weight is dropping from his small frame and I don't know what to do to help.

---

[6] *'Is everything OK, is it normal?'*
[7] *'Yes, very good'*

The one thing I can't do is break down in front of him, I have to hold it together, so when he's sick I tightly wrap him in my arms and try to reassure him that this is all 'normal' (for a person with cancer). That it is a good sign that the treatment is working, that he is going to be OK. I rub his back and each time he heaves into the pan I wish that it was me; wish I could take away his pain. But I can't, we just have to get through this.

He amazes me with the way he handles it and I have so much respect for him. There is no self-pity, just acceptance, but I wonder how much an eight-year-old can really take and understand?

I've slept in Kenan's room for the couple of nights since Lev left and he has been so ill. I go through the scrub in, scrub out routine several times a day. It's OK mostly during the day because I keep quite busy by looking after Kenan or talking to the doctors and, when he's sleeping, I pop over to the shopping centre next door for a spot of retail therapy. The nights are harder though. I try and sleep next to him on a 'pain in the arse', lie-back chair that keeps jerking upright. From there, I can quietly observe Kenan sleeping in his bed. He is beginning to look pale and thin, and the word 'why?' dances endlessly around in my head. Why my boy? Why my baby?

Eventually I sleep and although I never expect more than a few minutes escapism, for some reason I have slept peacefully without dreams and I awake feeling, somewhat, refreshed. I've toughened up now too after watching Kenan over the last few days and no longer fear seeing him go through the inevitable stages of his illness. I'm not scared he's not going to live, he is, and I have only optimism that the doctors here will cure him. I know he is strong and that I need to be strong for him, but I also know I can't do it on my own. The family has to help. So, picking up a pen one afternoon whilst Kenan sleeps, I write out a rota system that splits the time spent at the hospital with Kenan between me, Lev and Mum. The rota will free me up to spend a few days with Angelo and Louis and also give Lev time to go back to work without feeling guilty. I read it back:

ROTA

Me   Sunday through to Tuesday then change over with Mum
Mum   Tuesday through to Thursday
Lev   Friday until midday Sunday. (Lev to then spend Sunday afternoon with A and L in Javea)
Me   Meet Lev briefly Sunday at changeover
Lev   Fly back to England Monday morning.

Once done, having a rota makes perfect sense to me. I rush to show the nurses how Lev and my mum will stay with Kenan as well from now on, but their response isn't what I expect. My idea of leaving Kenan, even with family, is very 'un-Spanish', and I feel their disapproval. The mother should be the full-time carer. But I stick to my guns and tell the nurses that I'm going home for a couple of days to see my other kids. It's amazing how language barriers cease to exist in some situations; somehow we all understand each other perfectly.

As it happens, Kenan loves the idea of my mum and his daddy being here and you know what? I need to go; I need to get away from the distinct smell that only hospitals have, along with the sad faces and the volatile emotions that run through the place.

Being away from Louis and Angelo for two weeks has also left me with an unwavering desire to pull back some sort of normality for them. Perhaps I want to try and regain some control over my newly unpredictable life, I'm not sure. But the rota feels right to me for the sake of my family, so regardless of whatever the doctors and nurses think, I'm going.

We start it as soon as Lev comes back from England. I gather my stuff together, ready to leave on the bus back to Javea, but before I go, Lev pulls me aside and says he wants to do something. The change in Kenan, due to the effects of the chemo, has knocked Lev hard. Kenan has lost weight and his skin bears an unhealthy colour. Also Lev is upset to see Kenan's change of mood. He tells me that he can't bear to watch his silky, brown hair fall out as well. Already it is thinning, and Lev announces that he wants to shave it off.

He did it once before, when Kenan was four and we were going on holiday to Gran Canaria. I went mad back then but this time it is different, so I agree. Kenan isn't too sure when Lev suggests it but Lev makes a joke out of it and promises to shave his and Angelo's hair off too when he gets back to Javea, which Kenan likes the idea of.

One thing I hadn't counted on was that shaving off Kenan's hair would remind him of my friend, Angie, whom he saw suffering from cancer two years earlier. She lost her hair, but I'm amazed he remembers because he was only six years old.

"Do I have cancer, Mummy," he asks, "like Angie?" Shit, shit.

"No darling, you don't. You have leukaemia. It's different and you're going to be just fine."

After a moment's thought he says, "Okay then Daddy, you can do it."

So Lev does – he just shaves off his hair.

Lev

The last time I shaved Kenan's hair off he was four years old and we going on holiday to Gran Canaria. Gina did her nut then but it wasn't anywhere near the same situation as this time, of course. We were in a children's cancer ward for one and I felt bad about doing it, but I thought it would be better for him if he lost his hair all at once rather than watch it come out bit by bit. I just got on with it, making jokes all the time, as did Kenan, but afterwards I don't think he did feel any better, even though he said otherwise. That's Kenan though – always had his chin up, always keeping the rest of us going.

"Just think of Kenan," we'd say, when one of us started feeling sorry for ourselves. "How must he feel?"

When I got home I shaved Angelo and Louis' hair too – "All for one and one for all!" I told them – but I did it with more than a tinge of sadness.

Me and Kenan got quite used to it in the end and I used to call him Uncle Fester, until he told me he didn't like that and that he preferred the Prince of Siam! When he had to wear his mask, I'd shout "The boy behind the mask," in a haunting, scary voice, which he loved for a while until I'd milked it too much.

Then I called him 'The English Patient' but he didn't have a clue what I was going on about with that one.

We had a right laugh a lot of the time when I was there at the hospital with him, playing tricks on the nurses, hiding plastic ants and spiders under things or hanging a bat from the door and we would laugh as they walked into it. Luckily, they took it in good humour and it made Kenan happy. It all helped to pass the time.

Some of the nurses were real lookers too and I'd wind Kenan up by blowing them kisses behind their backs when they turned to tend to him – he hated it!

I used to say, "She fancies me that one". It was always the prettiest – and he'd threaten me with,

"You wait till I tell Mummy, she is gonna kill you."

She probably would as well!

Chapter Six

Do you remember my friend Angie from the cul-de-sac? Well, we kept in touch via email and phone for a while but, as these things do, our contact dwindled, before going quiet. I put it down to lack of time and everybody being busy, which was true enough in my case, but not in Angie's.

The real reason Angie's emails and phone calls had ended was because the lump she'd found, before leaving England, had grown bigger and unconvinced by the diagnosis she'd got back home, she had gone to see a doctor in Abu Dhabi. Tests revealed that Angie had cancer in the lymph glands.

When she contacted me again, Angie was already having chemo and she spent most of her days bedridden. She was suffering with awful headaches too. Her parents had moved over to take care of the children whilst she had her treatment, but she sounded so poorly when she contacted me, I felt deeply shocked and upset.

The following summer, after all her chemo was finished, Angie wanted to see a specialist in England, so she came to stay with us. Gone was all her lovely blonde hair and she wore a wig, which quickly became the butt of many jokes between her and Lev, who thought it made her look like Rod Stewart. But hairless or not, Angie was still the same old girl, full of life, always smiling and laughing.

She stayed for two weeks and we didn't waste a single day. We travelled on the tube to Covent Garden for a pampering at The Sanctuary, health spa. We shopped in London and indulged ourselves with meals out at restaurants in Epping. My friend Floria sometimes came with us and so too, did Paula.

Angie met with the specialist and although there were no guarantees, of course, that the cancer wouldn't return, on the whole it went well and Angie was really positive after her appointment. She returned to Abu Dhabi a lot more confident about her future.

One day, whilst checking my emails, I noticed one from Angie saying she was coming home for good. Gary's contract had ended and they were returning to the cul-de-sac. But by this time we didn't live there anymore. We'd moved out about a year before, after I'd grown restless without Angie to talk to. I had also given birth to our second son, Angelo by then, (I'd had an ectopic pregnancy in between) and Kenan was now six, so we wanted some extra space.

Kenan was growing into a sensitive, deep-thinking, young boy, with a quirky sense of humour and, just like his dad, he had a nose for earning a pound or two. He'd inherited, from my side, an obsession with clothes because he took a lot of pride in how he looked, even at that age. In fact Kenan was neat about everything, from the way he brushed his hair, to the way he organised his pencil case. He loved our new house, which was still in Epping but was a real step-up. The blurb at the estate agents read something like:

Spacious, detached five bedroom house, three bathrooms, two en-suite. Half-acre garden backing on to paddocks, private driveway, carport, double garage……

Even though business was good, this was a big move for us and we were terrified the day we signed the contracts. We kept asking ourselves if this was honestly, what we wanted, but we took the plunge and bought the house of our dreams.

I didn't give a second thought to the wave upon wave of electricity pylons which stretched like neighbours' washing lines across the fields at the bottom of our garden. Nor did the huge mobile phone mast that loomed above our house, cause me any concern. They were invisible to me. Had I known that Kenan was going to develop leukaemia, I might well have had second thoughts.

I later found out that four other children in the immediate area developed leukaemia as well and I can't help but wonder if these, seemingly harmless, structures had any bearing on that. The jury is still out on whether living close to pylons is harmful to people's health or not, but I do know for sure that childhood leukaemia is steadily rising and I can't just dismiss it away as coincidence. Thankfully, due to medical advances, more children are surviving it too. I approached a local paper with the fact that five children within a short distance of one another had developed leukaemia, but no one bothered to follow it up. I guess with no proof there's no story, although I hope, for all our sakes, that the truth will be revealed sooner rather than later, whichever way.

Naturally, none of this crossed our minds as we moved in, blissfully ignorant of any possible dangers to our health. We were totally carried away by the fact that we, two East End kids, could grow up affording to buy a house like this. Kenan and Angelo had their own playroom, their own bathroom and what could have been mistaken for a park, in the garden. Spoilt little buggers they were, bless them.

We had everything that we'd dreamt of – almost. Lev wanted one more item to make our home complete – a big dog. We already had a little Yorkshire terrier called Daisy, who had fitted very well into our other houses, but now we had a big garden Lev said we needed a big dog. Men and their size hang ups, eh!

So one morning, Lev took Kenan and they drove all the way to Wales to collect our new Japanese Akita puppy. He looked just like a brown and white bear cub. By the time he was five weeks old you could barely carry him he was so big – his paws were the size of an adult's hand. Fully grown he was going to weigh nine and a half stone. We named him Kato, a la The Pink Panther (one of Lev's and Kenan's favourite films), because it was the only Japanese name we knew!

We loved that house, especially throughout the summer months when we threw big barbecue parties for our friends and I couldn't wait for Angie to come and be a part of it.

But everything was different when she came back. What she hadn't told me in her email was that the cancer had returned and, this time, it was horribly aggressive. Her headaches were debilitating and she had recently lost the use of her left arm. Immediately on arriving back in England, she started more chemo. but the cancer continued to grow.

I used to overhear Kenan talking to Angie's son Harry about it, and they were as aware of what was happening as any six-year old can be. Her daughter Olivia was still too young to understand, but she knew her mummy wasn't well.

Everybody did their bit. I helped with the kids, got the shopping, sat and chatted with her, and Floria, who'd done a beauty course, tried to cheer her up by painting her nails and giving her facials. Even though Angie was getting worse with each day, she still bubbled and giggled. Her courage even made the neighbours in the cul-de-sac stop and talk to us and offer to help, but we didn't want it by then.

For a few months, Angie passed between home and hospital, but eventually she told her doctors she simply wanted to be at home with her family. There was nothing more anyone could do. The Macmillan nurses visited her regularly to support her through her last days and I'll never forget how much pain she was in; or how hard she fought.

Two days before she died I called round to her house with Kenan, who came to play with Angie's boy, Harry. I sensed a lot of tension in the air as I sat with her, holding her frail hand while she drifted in and out of consciousness. When she did wake, smiling as always, she looked at me and said, "Gina, tell the kids how happy I was and how much I love them."

I knew then it was almost over and it was gutting. I was so angry because she had so much love in her and was such a positive person. Kenan and Harry came into the bedroom and I was happy for them to see her. Within reason, neither Angie nor I believed in sheltering children from what is life, however tragic. Kenan came and stood next to me. Angie looked at him and smiled her wonderful smile again.

Her funeral was in the cemetery in Epping and after the service, Harry and Olivia both released a white dove from the boxes they were clutching, helped by their daddy, Gary. I will never forget her, or that moment.

I don't know if Angie dying had any influence on our decision to move to Spain. Maybe subconsciously it gave me a desire to grab life as it happens, but the reason we told ourselves we were going was because of Lev's work schedule.

We were living the true 'Essex' life and I admit I was right in the thick of it. We had the money, the house and the cars, but work was pretty full on, which meant me and the kids didn't see a lot of Lev. Kenan and Angelo woke up without Daddy at home and he didn't come back until they were just going to bed. This routine continued at the weekends as well. I know many families live like that, but long-term I didn't want it to be for us.

Crime still dogged us on occasion too, although unlike before, not in our own backyard. Lev's van was nicked again, this time in Tottenham while he was collecting materials for a job. A week later my dad spotted it in Walthamstow when picking up his mate, Robbie 'The Jock', who'd worked for him for years.

He couldn't believe it when he saw Lev's van parked close to Robbie's house. He rang Lev, who had been working late so he was still in bed. I heard from downstairs in the kitchen, "You're joking!"

The next thing I knew, Lev's flung on some clothes and disappeared out of the front door. The police had never held out much hope of finding it, so when Lev called them they simply said, "Take it away if it's yours," which is exactly what he did.

In one week he'd had his van stolen and then had stolen it back again. We've laughed for years now about that story.

But it wasn't the crime, or even the work that made us leave. Looking back now, I think we went for no other reason than we were yearning for something more from life. We half joked about moving to Spain, although I was less sure about it than Lev, until my mum and dad came round one afternoon and said that if we went, they'd come too. That swung it – we would go.

Why Spain? Well, we're not country types and moving further into the countryside would only have kept Lev away from home longer and Spain with its marinas, boats, restaurants and expat community seemed as good a place as any. The appeal of an outdoor life for the kids where they could play in relative safety was another good reason for the move, but, above all, we hoped the slower pace of life would help Lev switch off and unwind from work.

Retirement wasn't an option as we were both only in our early thirties, so we agreed that we'd keep the business going as it brought in a good income. Lev would stay and work, part of the week in the UK, then spend long, work-free weekends in Spain with us.

We'd previously spent a summer holiday in the small town of Javea on the Costa Blanca, midway between Alicante and Valencia, visiting my friend Paula and her husband Martin, and we'd liked it immediately. The weather was good, so were the beaches and the schools, and there were plenty of English people already living there, which we thought might help us settle in. Once the decision to go was made we put our 'dream' house on the market and Mum and Dad did the same.

They sold their three bedroom, mock-Tudor house in Woodford Green first, and left before we did, to find their new home in the sun. They popped back every now and then to help me pack up my house which was taking a lot longer to sell than we'd anticipated. The 'usual suspects' came around week after week. People who genuinely loved it but for one reason or another it wasn't quite right, people who stepped through the door because they had nothing better to do than nose around other people's homes on a Sunday morning and there were the 'Jack the Lad' types too, who'd arrive in their jazzed up BMWs with the obligatory, 'blonde bombshell' girlfriend. Lev and I knew right away these guys were full of it; they were still paying off their cars for bleedin' sake. But unfortunately the economy was starting to change and there wasn't as much money about, so with the house not selling, we, eventually, dropped the asking price in order to get our buyer.

The timing of the sale wasn't great either as by then I was heavily pregnant with our third child. It was another boy, we found out, which I wasn't happy about, because I'd been hoping for a girl. But the disappointment passed of course, and I was looking forward to his birth by the time we were ready to leave.

I was thirty-four weeks pregnant and had already made enquiries about having the baby in Spain. I'd found a private hospital called Acuario in a small village, Beniarbeig, and an English midwife as well, so I felt prepared.

We also bought a house I was happy with in Javea, after weeks of searching. The property market there was booming at the time, but so many of the houses I saw were unbelievably shabby and not worth the asking price. Finally, an agent took us to a view a newly-built, modern villa, spread over three floors, and I knew we'd found our home.

Although set high up on a hill, we were on an urbanisation so there were still plenty of neighbours around us, which for me was important, because the last thing I wanted was to be cut off from civilisation. The view from the villa was stunning; it had its own pool of course, along with an outside kitchen and eating area. Even though it wasn't quite the size of our old house in Epping, it felt right.

Kenan chose the bedroom he wanted and, at last, the day came when we were all set to leave our old life in England to start a new one. I flew over to Spain with Angelo, my mum and dad. Kenan and Lev drove over with the dogs: Kato, who was now his fighting weight of nine and a half stone, Daisy, who had a wired-up jaw after Kato had attacked her over a bone, and my parents' black Standard Poodle called Jessica. Luckily we had a left-hand drive Mercedes ML so there was plenty of room.

We left a couple of days before them and, as we were leaving, I remember thinking that I had never seen Kenan so excited. He was eight now and driving over with Lev was the adventure of a lifetime for him. They were catching *Le Shuttle* from Folkestone and then driving through France, down into Spain. I stood on our driveway on that crisp, October morning and kissed them both farewell. I knew in my heart that they were going to have a great time, but still I felt apprehensive. It was a long drive and my hormones were all over the place.

We were moving to Spain, saying goodbye to all that had become routine and familiar, and I couldn't wait for us all to be together again.

Lev

I remember the trip to Spain with Kenan so well. Kenan and me were setting out on this huge adventure together, for a better life in España. Gina was travelling with Angelo, the bump and the outlaws, Tony and Brenda, whilst me and Kenan had the three dogs with us, and we were driving over in our new Mercedes ML320. It had gangster-black paint, black leather, tinted windows and fat wheels: the Full Monty. It was a left hooker and I had saved a mint buying it in the UK. I think the dealers have got wise to that one now though. Kenan loved the car.

Gina had packed a pile of luggage the night before she left, so we were well loaded. You know what birds are like. I didn't think the dogs (Daisy, Jessica and Kato) were going to fit. God knows what was in the cases and I didn't have the bottle to argue with her – she was heavily pregnant.

Kenan was too excited to sleep so we decided to bed down together as Gina and the gang had already gone. We were both a bit anxious as I'd never driven to Spain before and Kenan kept asking how long it would take and would we have enough petrol and water for the dogs and what if we broke down and, and, and ...... ! In the end I told him to shut up and go to sleep, we had to get up early. That was Kenan though, 'Mr. Worry Guts'.

At six-thirty the next morning we kissed my mum goodbye and set off. It was an hour's drive to the Channel Tunnel, through drifting fog, and Kenan sat next to me eating his usual breakfast of yogurts, bananas and more yogurts. Talk about a build up of friendly bacteria. We arrived bang on seven-thirty, drove through and lined up to get on the train. Out of the woodwork popped two 'jobsworths', checking us out – we were driving a left hooker on English plates. Kenan started freaking out as if we had a few kilos of Colombian marching powder in the boot. He always did that when he saw anyone in a uniform that looked like a copper. They waved us over and I got out. By this time Kenan was hyperventilating. In the back of the car Daisy was yapping, Jessica was barking and Kato was snarling.

"Excuse me, sir; is this your vehicle and what is your reason for travelling?" Oh please, as if I'd want to kidnap that lot! They lifted the lid and checked the chassis numbers with their silly, little torches. I couldn't help thinking that they should be stopping the stuff coming in rather than pestering a heavily taxed Brit going out. Then the 'Normans' went round to the boot – that was funny. They opened it up and saw a very hot and bothered, fed up, nine and a half stone Japanese Akita, surrounded by suitcases, snarling at them. They bottled it then, bless 'em, let us go and we were on our way.

We drove onto the train, by which time Kenan had stopped having a 'paddy' and we were laughing about the two 'Normans' and how they'd bricked it when they came up against Crumble Dog. That was Kenan's name for Kato when we all played WWF on the floor. Kenan was Steve Austin, his favourite wrestler of course and the most famous at the time, Angelo was Mini Steve, Kato was Crumble Dog, I was The Undertaker and it was them against me. I was always the bad guy!

Kenan loved the train and I agreed that it was the best experience I'd had for a long time. We got out of the car and stretched our legs. Kenan wanted me to take some photos of him posing next to the car so he could text them to his friend Alana. He was such a poser at times, wonder who he took after? Must have been his mother!

Twenty minutes later we were off the train straight into 'Frogland'. We drove along the coast then down to Le Mans with Elvis booming. I introduced Kenan to Elvis' music and he loved it; my 'old man' introduced me and I told Kenan, that if he ever had a son, to play him Elvis, never let his music die. We had a five album compilation which would last us well. We sang our socks off, we knew all the words.

Just outside Le Mans we filled up the car, walked the dogs and gave them some water. It was such a buzz for Kenan and for me, father and son off on this adventure. We sat side by side, and I taught him how to read a map as he was going to be my co-driver. We shared a French stick before loading the hounds back into the motor, stocked up on Red Bulls and burned rubber!

By this time it was half-past five and I was getting a bit, not tired, but bored with driving. I really wanted to enjoy this trip with Kenan, savour the time we had, but I knew we had to press on to get to Gina and the others. If me and Kenan had had our way, it would have taken a week though.

He was the dog's bollocks at reading a map, a natural. It was his attention to detail that made him good, he didn't miss a hamlet let alone a town, turning the music down and blurting out the names as we passed them. He was like a human Tom Tom. We argued over a couple of junctions but he was always right. Honestly, I've had twenty year olds working for me who can't even suss out an A to Z, the donuts!

We hit Bordeaux about seven-thirty and I said to Kenan, "That's enough mate, fancy some French grub?"

"Wow, Daddy ….is it nice?" he asked, the fussy git.

"Just you wait." I told him, (couldn't wait to neck a glass of Chablis!) and we drove on until we found a 'pukka', little hotel just outside Bordeaux.

"Do you take dogs?" I enquired over an empty desk. A funny, little, French geezer popped his head up from behind the counter and said, "Of course, monsieur."

I smiled to myself thinking; wait until you see my lot! A travel-sick Yorkshire terrier, a pissed-off Standard Poodle and a car-lagged Japanese Akita.

Me and Kenan laughed whilst we walked back to the car to fetch the dogs. The French geezer reminded us of a character from one of The Pink Panther films, which we both loved so much I had bought Kenan the whole collection for his birthday. We caused a big stir going through the foyer. Kenan almost wet himself from laughing, it was like a stampede.

Our room was a small one on the furthest wing of the place and it was freezing. But beggars can't be choosers when you're 'Cru____ tour and we were having such a laugh. We h____ beds next to each other so we pushed them together to keep warm. We always cuddled like that. It's something I never had from my dad when I was a boy so I'm always kissing and cuddling mine. I used to say to Kenan, "I wonder when you're going to be too old for a cuddle on the couch?"

Anyway, Kenan said we needed to cuddle to keep warm as that's what they do in the Arctic to survive. He saw it on the Discovery channel, his favourite. Bleeding know-it-all.

I couldn't wait to show him some good French cuisine so, after we'd fed and watered the dogs, we went down for dinner. It was a typical French gaff, big, oak beams, brick arches and a roaring, inglenook fireplace. We got seated and I ordered my bottle of Chablis, Kenan his usual Diet Coke. For starters I had stuffed mushrooms. I tried to get 'Rain Man' to have some but no luck. He just wanted the French bread. Then we noticed homemade burger and fries on the menu, Kenan's favourite – thank God for that! He loved it and ate the lot. I had veal which was gorgeous, like eating butter. For dessert I had an Irish coffee and Kenan had ice cream. We sat by the fire, me with my second Irish coffee, Kenan with his cocoa. That night we slept like babies, even though there were three snoring hounds in the room, which all ended up on the beds with us by the morning. At least we were warm.

Next day, we were up with the larks. It was way too cold for a shower, so we topped and tailed quickly. The hounds were whining, they wanted to go out, apart from little Daisy who had been quite comfortable kipping on my pillow all night. Bless her. It was a brisk, winter's morning, Jack Frost was about and, as we walked the dogs, Kenan asked me where all the people were. He was right; it was a ghost town even though it was a Saturday morning. That's the trouble with living in London – you get used to hustle and bustle twenty-four seven, even as a child. We ate our breakfast which wasn't bad, but no one does it quite like the English.

Back in the ML and off we went along the Bay of Biscay. It was cold but there wasn't a cloud in the sky – beautiful. Elvis was still giving it some, Kenan was drawing and the dogs were sleeping. Next stop was Biarritz, where we filled up with petrol and walked the dogs. Kenan was mucking about filming me, which I didn't find funny as I had a killer hangover – must have been the Irish coffees.

He kept taking the piss saying, "You alright, Daddy? Got a headache, have we?"

I could see the funny side but I was too grumpy to laugh. We bought a load of crisps, chocolate, coke and Red Bulls and we were off again. I noticed that Daisy wasn't drinking her water though, which bothered me. Something was up.

The sun was still shining when we reached the border, at San Sebastian, at midday. We didn't even have to show our passports as there was no one there. Bit different to Blighty, eh? Kenan wanted to stop so we did. We played a few games at the truck stop, mainly shooting zombies and racing cars, as he was at that age when he was still into them. Mind you I've never grown out of them.

We ran out of food for the dogs but it was probably better to starve them as they were travelling. Daisy was getting worse; she wouldn't even get out of the car. Kenan was trying to force-feed her water and it sort of killed our fun a bit because we were both worried about her now. We needed to get to Javea as quickly as possible and get her to a vet. We were in the right motor to do it, so after a couple of burgers and fries; we stocked up on supplies and 'Nigel Mansselled' it to Madrid, through the mountains. There wasn't a living soul on the road so we just put the car on cruise control and sat back.

We hit Madrid at three o'clock in the afternoon. What a hole I thought, reminded me too much of London. Kenan was sleeping now so I had no Tom-Tom and, of course, I got lost. He woke up and said, "I knew you'd get lost if I fell asleep."

We had a big barney and both being as stubborn as each other, didn't speak until we stopped at a garage, on the road to Valencia. I kept thinking how rapidly he seemed to be growing up on this journey, or maybe I'd just never noticed it before. I mean, I had never spent so much time alone with him. Maybe that was it; we were just getting on each others nerves and we were both worried about Daisy.

We made it up on the way to Valencia which was four hours of long straight, boring roads. It was like Nevada. I let Kenan have a can of Red Bull as a peace offering and we ended up having a long chat about my life. He was asking me what I had done, so as he was my son and this was a rites of passage journey and all that, I told him everything, good and bad.

After reaching Valencia it was only another hour and a bit on down the road to Javea and we arrived at about eight-thirty in the evening. We pulled up at the outlaw's ranch. They all came out and Kenan and I looked at each other, sad our trip was all over.

Everyone was excited to see us though and we were knackered. At least there was a good 'Ruby' waiting for us at the end. As for Daisy, well old age got the better of her and sadly she died, six weeks after we arrived, from kidney failure. The trip was probably just too much.

Chapter Seven

We've received the results of the blood tests. None of us are suitable bone marrow donors for Kenan. Although I feel relief Louis isn't a match, I'm gutted that none of us are – I was sure one of us would be. Now Kenan must go on a donor list and we have to wait.

The doctors have suggested another option that they say he may benefit more from; something called an autologous transplant, which is effectively washing his own blood and putting it back into him. It's less invasive, but they can't make a final decision until after the chemotherapy has finished.

The rota system is holding up well and is running like clockwork. Me and Mum are using the bus service to get to and from Valencia, as it's much easier than negotiating the horrendous drive to the hospital. We've even worked out which seats to sit in so we can wave at each other, bus to bus, every Tuesday, when we change over shifts. It's a small, stupid thing but strangely important to both of us. Taking the bus also means I have some time to switch my mind away from life at home to life back at the hospital with Kenan and vice versa. In some ways I feel as if I'm getting the best of both worlds, having time with Angelo and Louis, but then getting a break from looking after two small ones and spending quality time with Kenan.

The bus leaves from a town called Denia, about half an hour's drive from Javea, so Dad drops me off and the moment I get on the bus I relax. It travels the scenic route through the small towns and villages to Valencia, so all in all takes about two hours, most of which I spend gazing out of the window.

I cry quietly, sometimes. It's easier letting my barrier down within the confines of the bus where no one knows me. But usually I just sit and eat my bocadillo, doing nothing, until the bus pulls into the station. By the time it arrives, mentally I am ready to be with Kenan again.

Kenan is used to our routine too, so much so that he knows what time each of us is due to arrive and he hounds me with text messages asking where I am.

Lev and me are like ships that pass in the night though, so we meet for a quick lunch first, before he has to head back to see the other kids in Javea. I yearn to talk seriously to Lev about Kenan but communication has become difficult between us, even though Kenan is doing well. Lev is growing more and more optimistic about the future and so it's just not working at the moment.

I leave my lunch with Lev feeling empty inside. It's been almost three weeks now since Kenan was admitted and walking towards the Oncology unit, I think that at least it is Sunday, which, apart from the necessary tests and medication, is pretty chilled. Kenan is still very frail, but says he's starting to feel a little better, and we slip easily into our normal, Sunday routine. First we play games, chat a while and then watch a DVD. His room is much more cheerful now it has his personal bits and bobs in and the day passes uneventfully.

Come Monday it is back to business as usual for Kenan. At six in the morning the nurse wakes him up and performs routine blood tests. Kenan is used to this by now so he falls straight back to sleep again, but I'm restless and at about eight o'clock I get up, unable to spend a moment longer on the lie-back chair that won't lie back. Finding a cubicle, I have a quick strip-down wash and as I like a cigarette first thing, I grab a coffee from the vending machine, go outside and sit on the steps. Lighting up, I call Mum to check on the other two boys and I have a quick chat with Lev before he leaves for England.

Kenan has woken up again by the time I go back upstairs. He's been washed by the nurses and he's wearing fresh pyjamas, which frustrates me. I want to help, but it is all done in bed because of the multitude of IV drips he's connected to. The poor kid even has to go to the loo in bed – he hates that.

The doctors arrive later, accompanied by under-study medics, and although I can't understand much of what they say, I know more or less what they're getting at. We don't see Carlos every day, he's usually only about if there are any problems or if he needs to give us some information.

After the doctors' rounds, a teacher arrives to give Kenan his Spanish lesson. The hospital has organised this, which is wonderful. I take the chance to steal a break and leave the hospital for a wander around the local shopping centre.

I'm happy that Kenan is being made to keep his studies up, because it gives him something else to focus on other than being ill. I'm not so happy that he has developed an issue with food again. I've noticed that he picks at breakfast time and at lunch, waiting for teatime when he gets a hot chocolate and a couple of packets of biscuits.

By the time I get back from shopping he's sleeping again, so I watch him until the nurses come and wake him up for dinner. He refuses to touch it and today I get cross with him. He needs to eat … can't he realise that? I don't understand why it is always such a battle to get him to eat more. As usual, I give up in the end and, infuriated, go and have my dinner. Sitting alone at the table, I stare at my plate of salad, suddenly not in the mood to eat either. I push it away, and go to have another ciggie instead. I forget about being cross with Kenan. How can I be? So I go back and both of us get comfy with a DVD and relax.

Before going to sleep, Kenan leaves a wee sample for the nurses so it can be checked. Everything is methodically tested. I need another ciggie, so after making sure Kenan is cosy and tucked up in bed, I buy a hot chocolate from the vending machine and head outside for a final chat with Mum, before calling Lev to fill him in on the day.

Kenan can't sleep until I am back and as it's late we both go straight to bed. But I can't get settled on the completely crap, lie-back chair and we both end up crying with laughter. Try as I might, it won't stay flat. Each time I lie down, the end pops up again. At last, I work out that if I manoeuvre another chair underneath the end of it, it'll keep it down long enough for me to lie down at the top end. Easier said than done when you're only five feet, two inches! But a few exhausting minutes later, I've done it and we are finally both tucked up in our respective hospital beds. The laugh has done us good.

"Night night, Kenan, I love you," I say quietly.

"Night night, Mummy, I love you too."
That's more or less how the days are now – routine and without anything too distressing to deal with. I'm sure that it won't be long before I can take Kenan home, and with that thought I drift off to sleep.

Lev

I couldn't help but learn a hell of a lot about leukaemia after Kenan went into hospital. A cancer of the blood forming cells, leukaemia is the biggest of all childhood cancers. According to the Leukaemia Charity, numbers have increased in the past forty-odd years, but thankfully the survival rate has risen significantly in that time too.

Still, no one has figured out why it happens. I read that anything from environmental causes to genetic diseases could be to blame. In the last few years the boffins have discovered that certain changes in DNA can trigger bone marrow stem cells to turn into leukaemia, but what they have known for a long time, is that there are several different types of leukaemia, and however you dress it up, it's often a killer.

To determine the extent of Kenan's strain of leukaemia, (AML) the first thing they had to do was, what they call in the trade, a sternal puncture. This is when a needle, the size of one normally used for knitting, is plunged into the sternum, the bone on the front of the chest, which is the easiest place to extract bone marrow from. It's then analysed to see if cells are maturing or not. The cells that don't mature are called blast cells and they clog up the bone marrow.

The sternal puncture is a nasty procedure. On the day Kenan had it done, I was asked to help hold down his legs while two nurses held his arms. I can remember how loud he screamed, even now. I felt such anger I just wanted to pull the nurses off him and take him out of there, take him home where it wasn't happening. Afterwards, he was out of his box as the drugs wore off, laughing and talking. Wished I had some too.

Later, we watched a DVD while he had his dinner. But I couldn't get the sternal puncture out of my mind, and after seeing something like that, Gina wonders why I can't shake off the worry I feel for Kenan's future. It was bloody traumatic and made me lose my faith in God.

"Why are you doing this to him?" I said to myself over and over again.

I wish I had a pound for every time I asked it.

Chapter Eight

If a memory can be called treasured from the time I spent with Kenan in Valencia, it was when my oldest and most cherished friend Floria came over to visit.

She'd had her flight booked to come and see us all in our new home in Javea ages before Kenan had been taken ill and she called to ask if I still wanted her to visit. It suddenly hit me how much I needed her to come, and believe me usually I don't need anyone. I am simply not that type of person, but I really wanted her here.

Floria and I go back years. She is a dark, Greek beauty, slim yet voluptuous (think Nigella!), bubbly and friendly. It's no exaggeration when I say that everybody who meets her likes her.

I remember how, when we were young, walking down Walthamstow market, the stall holders' jaws would drop. There was Floria with her hourglass figure, big boobs and long, thick, dark hair and me, the little, skinny one, following behind. She's never really known the affect she has on men though because she's not vain or false in any way. She was my 'best lady' at my wedding and was there when Kenan was born. Although we didn't christen any of the children, we always refer to her as Kenan's godmother or Aunty Floria.

If Floria had a flaw, it was her choice of man, because she continually went out with the wrong guys. Many a night she turned up at our house to pour out her latest tale of romantic woe, as Lev opened a therapeutic bottle of wine. But she has now found Antonio, the man of her dreams, who she was seeing when she came to Valencia. Coincidently, Antonio's parents are Spanish and he speaks the language fluently, which meant he later came in quite useful as a translator.

Anyway, I didn't quite realise how much I needed Floria with me until she called, but I did. She gave me a special lift and support I didn't know I was so desperate for.

When she arrived at Valencia Airport, she took a cab to meet me at *La Fe* hospital. The hospital provided an apartment nearby that the families of children at the hospital could use, about a fifteen minute walk away, so as Kenan was sleeping at the time, I took her there first. Officially, we had one room as it was shared by other parents who needed a place to stay, but luckily for us we were the only ones using it.

The place was basic but OK, with a living room, a balcony, a small kitchen, bathroom and three bedrooms. It was clean at least, but it felt sad and lonely, just like the people forced to use it. If I'm honest it made me feel quite scared being there.

Floria and me took turns staying with Kenan the week she was there. First Floria was with him for two hours, then I was, then his teacher came, which allowed us to grab some lunch together and have a heart to heart chat. Kenan loved his Aunty Floria and between us he was well occupied. At the end of the day I'd tell him we weren't staying, but we didn't leave until about ten o'clock and were back by eight in the morning. I think he was glad when we left because by then he was always totally knackered.

On our way back to the apartment we usually stopped for a drink in one of the bustling Spanish bars. One night while walking back through the jostling crowds after our drink, some kids let off some bangers – nothing strange about that in Spain – and we nearly jumped out of our skins! Running off, screaming and laughing down the road, we were like two carefree teenagers again, our worries about Kenan forgotten for a tiny moment.

It was a very special time for me and I enjoyed it whilst hating it at the same time. I poured my heart out to Floria as we lay in the gloomy bedroom in our two single beds. We did this for four nights, until it was time to change shifts again with Lev.

I kissed Kenan goodbye and Floria hugged and kissed him as much as one could with a mask on their face.

Sometimes Kenan asked, "Mummy, can you take off your mask so I can see your face?"

And so I did, but always from the other side of the glass window.

I'd forgotten that Floria had never seen our house in Javea and that she'd never met Louis. Angelo had come running up to me, calling 'Mummy, Mummy,' as soon as we got home, and I'd hugged him and then given everyone gifts. Floria had loads of presents too, as always.

I took Floria down to the Arenal, the sandy beach in Javea and showed her around, but it wasn't the best time for her to experience the bars and ice cream parlours. Still, she only had a couple of days left before she went home so we tried to make the most of it.

When the time came for her to leave, every part of me wanted Floria to stay. She was my security and I was scared of what the next week held, back at the hospital, without her. She'd picked me up when I'd crashed down and I already felt lost without her. But her life was in England and her job in London so she had no choice but to go.

Many of our other friends were wonderful too and rallied round us, offering what support they could. As word spread back in England about Kenan, the phone started to ring off the hook. Lev's friend, Peter rang at least four times a week to speak to Kenan. Sometimes Kenan would say he was busy and to call back! That always pleased Peter though, because he knew it meant Kenan was having a good day.

One afternoon I arrived at the hospital to find that our old friends, Mitch and Kelly, had dropped everything at home and flown over. I was stunned. Lev and me are godparents to their second child, Grace (Lev loved the idea of being a 'Godfather') and we used to live the high life with them in Essex, attending events like the Rhys Daniels Trust ball at the Hilton Hotel in London. It helped balance our social consciences as we were all so caught up on the 'more is better' hamster wheel at the time.

Rhys Daniels' parents lived in Epping and we enjoyed helping to raise money for children with

Batten disease. For us, I admit, it was really no more than a great night out, mixing with celebs like Chris Tarrant, Amanda Holden and Ray Winstone. Now I realise how difficult and painful it must have been for Rhys' parents, Barry and Carmen. They were saddled with the nightmare that two, of their three children had died from Batten disease, while everyone around them enjoyed themselves. Believe me, there is nothing worse.

Some friends found Kenan's illness difficult to take of course, but whenever anyone had tears in their eyes I always said, "No crying, he will be OK. I'm not going to cry because it's not over."

But I did cry, although, as is my way, nearly always in private.

Chapter Nine

Kenan has been in hospital for three weeks now and despite his thin appearance and smooth, shiny head, seems to be doing really well.

"I'm bored," he moans continuously, which I take as a good sign. Unable to move around freely, he's growing more and more frustrated by the confines of his room, but short of saying he can come home, I can't think of anything to make the hours he spends in bed any easier.

He's received loads of presents from friends and family both here in Spain and England, but he's a kid and unfortunately they're not keeping his attention for long. He's even received a phone call from a T.V celebrity! Jamie Rickers, who presents the children's T.V programme *Toonattik*, rang him after my friend in England contacted him. Jamie even said 'Hello' to him on the programme. Kenan couldn't watch it, but he was so excited anyway. I'm at a loss what to do for him, until one morning, Kenan inadvertently gives me an idea.

"Why can't I see Angelo?" he asks. That's it! I'll bring the boys in to see him. They're both free from coughs and colds and I know just seeing his brothers, even from behind the glass window, will cheer Kenan up. There's one small problem. Children under twelve aren't allowed in Kenan's area.

What the hell, I'll smuggle them in! I can't see what harm it'll do, so I hatch a plan. My mum's life-long friend, Penny, is over from England helping out for the week so the timing is perfect. Penny loves the kids and she's always fussing over how dark and big eyed Louis is and how blonde and angelic Angelo looks (he's far from angelic of course!) Immediately I call Mum and ask her to bring the boys up on the bus with her, Dad and Penny.

Worried, she says, "But I thought they weren't allowed in, Gina."

"Look, I'll clear it this end. Kenan's bored out of his mind and I know it'll cheer him up. See you later."

I can't believe how excited I am, waiting for them to arrive. I keep checking my phone for messages because they're taking longer than usual, but I've not accounted for the rush hour. The bus is packed and by the time they step off, they are all absolutely knackered, hot and sweaty despite the air con, having stood practically the whole way. Trying to feed Louis, who's just starting the messy business of solids, and keeping Angelo amused with endless snacks, has left them a bit frazzled to say the least.

I'm wearing my whiter than white velour tracksuit to meet them and Mum takes one look at me and remarks to Penny, "Look at her! She looks as if she's on holiday and we look like a couple of old crones!"

It's only then that I notice that they are indeed covered in the kind of mess only kids can wipe all over you. I have to grin though. God I'm pleased to see them.

"Come 'ere," I say, hugging them all. It feels ages since we've all been together. "Let's go then," I urge, settling Louis into his pram and practically marching them towards the hospital. "It's going to take a bit of a cloak and dagger approach," I mutter over my shoulder have to be careful not to be seen going up to the

"I thought you'd sorted it out, Gina!" Mum exclaims, her footsteps slowing down behind me.

"I have, I've worked out how we can get in without been seen. It's only the woman on the front desk we have to worry about. His nurses are cool about it – promise." Well, that's a little lie, but I'm sure the nurses won't mind.

The large double lifts on the ground floor have doors on both sides, so we walk in the hospital entrance and head straight towards the side which are out of view of the 'Gestapo Chief' at the desk. We stand outside the consulting rooms as if waiting to go in and I press the button on the lifts. Timing is everything now. The moment the doors open we cram in quickly and I press the button for the second floor. We've done it without being seen – *phew!*

The nurses, far from being annoyed, are thrilled to see us with the kids. They start making a huge fuss of them, especially Louis, who is being passed around for endless hugs and kisses – thank goodness the Spanish love children.

The layout of the Isolation rooms form a U-shaped unit, and with the 'Visitor's Gallery' around them there's plenty of room for us all to see Kenan through the ever-clean glass. He sees us coming and his face instantly breaks into a grin when he catches sight of Louis and Angelo – it's the first real smile I've seen in three weeks.

We can speak to him too through the intercom and Mum, Penny and Dad each takes a turn. But Angelo is very quiet. He's too young to understand why Kenan can't come out of his room or why he can't go in to see him. Although I know it's stupid of me, I feel really disappointed that Angelo isn't jabbering down the phone to his big brother. Anyway, the important thing is that Kenan is happy and seeing his brothers has lifted his spirits no end.

We stay for about twenty minutes before I sense that it's time to get the kids out of there. Angelo is running around the corridor, his arms out wide, pretending to be an aeroplane, which, I guess, sadly means they have to go.

"See you soon," Kenan says, waving weakly to everyone, happier now than he's been in a long while.

"I'll be back in a minute," I tell him through the intercom. I help Mum, Dad and Penny smuggle the boys out again, grabbing a quick coffee with them then kissing Angelo and Louis goodbye, before leaving them to tackle the bus back to Javea. I miss them already as I head back upstairs to Kenan. I know that the rules are there for a good reason, but sometimes you have to do what *feels* right in life and the few minutes they were here were worth it. I've enjoyed it almost as much as Kenan to be honest.

Kenan's tired after all the excitement and soon falls asleep, so with time on my hands I go shopping again. It's becoming a bad habit, going shopping while Kenan is asleep – I've got so much stuff I'll never use, it's shameful. The thing is, it's a real pick-me-up. The very fact that I can leave his bedside and shop means he's doing OK, that he's getting better and stronger which means it'll soon all be over.

I head further afield than the shopping centre today, for a bit of window shopping at one of Spain's most famous department stores, *El Corte Ingles*, which is a bit like Selfridges or John Lewis. But for whatever reason, my recreational pastime is having the opposite effect – I feel really low. Perhaps it's because the kids and my mum and dad have been here; I'd forgotten how good it feels to have my boys all together.

I walk past the beautiful bags and clothes, but I don't see them. Usually they warrant at least a wishful sigh or two, a stroke, a flick through to see if they have my size, but today is one of those days when it all seems too unfair. Why is this happening to Kenan? He isn't yet nine years old, he's just a child. He should be running around with the sunshine on his back, playing and learning with his new friends at school. But he's lying in a hospital bed, bored out of his mind with tubes coming out of his bony chest and his hair shaved off. It isn't right!

I am being watched by the shop staff. God, I must look really dodgy, then I realise that I'm crying. Crying as I pray, hope and wish that they may *still* have it wrong and we can be allowed home with a bottle of antibiotics. I need to leave and get back to Kenan. Being on my own at this moment is just bad, bad, bad.

I practically run to the hospital, slowed only by the tearful blur in front of my eyes, but he's still sleeping when I get back, so instead of putting on my mask and going in, I return downstairs for a ciggie, sit on the now familiar steps, gradually calm down and get myself under control. Then I go back. I change my clothes, put on my mask and go in to his room. There's a pack of cards sitting on the table next to Kenan's bed. Friends have sent Kenan all sorts of presents; DVDs, Nintendo DS games, art books, board games. And yet, this simple pack of cards is one of his favourites. He's sure as hell becoming a mean poker player since being in bed almost 24/7, thanks to Lev. I pick up the cards and shuffle them, smiling as I think how Kenan will want to play me for money when he wakes up. He's a chip off the old block that one.

"Hi, Mummy," he says then, snapping me back to the moment. And so we play cards – he wins – we watch a DVD and settle into our routine.

It's been a little more than three weeks now since we arrived at *La Fe*, and the doctors are talking about letting Kenan come home. Although it feels like an eternity to us, he's amazed the doctors, apparently, with the speed he's recovering from the chemo. This is great news, but secretly it makes me nervous because I know he won't be coming home fit and healthy, just well enough to not be in hospital. He'll still be fighting leukaemia. I'm ready for that, but I'm not confident I am capable of looking after him medically. Maybe I can find a nurse to help me. I'll have to worry about that later though, because for

Kenan the greatest obstacle at the moment remains boredom – he's even missing school, or to be precise, he's worried about how much school he is missing – so typical of Kenan.

"Mummy," he says, one afternoon. "All my friends at school will forget me and when I go back they won't play with me anymore."

"Don't be silly, Darling, of course they will," I reply lightly, but privately I think what if he's right? It *is* going to be hard to make the transition back into a school he's barely started at.

He has made one good friend, Vinesh, who is quite similar to him; low-key and quiet. Kenan can run around with the best of them and loves playing tennis, but he's not really into 'typical' boys stuff and Vinesh is just the same. Maybe I should ask him to visit? Before I can arrange anything, Paula rings me to ask if she can visit with her daughter Emily, who's at the same school as Kenan and has known him all his life. Great! I tell the nurses this time, and they give the all clear as long as they stay behind the glass window.

When Emily turns up the next day, my eyes fill with tears, because it's like Santa's arrived. She's brought with her a load of pictures and cards from his class. All the kids have made something for Kenan and they've taken a group photo, wishing him better. The tears sting at my eyes as Emily holds up each card for Kenan to see, through the glass.

Kenan can't physically handle anything because of the risk of infection, but the smile on his face tells me how happy he is that he hasn't been forgotten after all; that his friends are thinking of him. Emily's visit has perked him up no end.

A few days later, I get all weepy again. From out of the blue, Kenan's Spanish school teacher, Ramon, turns up to see him. It's a surprise to us both because he hardly knows Kenan personally. I can't believe Ramon has taken the time to bother to come and see Kenan on his day off. Kenan keeps looking at me a bit awkwardly from his side of the glass, because he's not sure what to say to this very kind and considerate man, who just so happens to be his teacher.

Ramon only stays talking to him via the intercom for ten minutes or so but it means everything to me. That's one of the great things about living in Spain – the compassion people have for children and I find myself thanking them wholeheartedly for that.

Chapter Ten

Of all the many challenges we faced during Kenan's illness, leaving him in hospital and going home to Javea for the first time was one of the most nerve-wracking. I was worried how people were going to react to me. Would they pity me? Avoid me? Or would they criticise me for not staying with Kenan? I didn't know, but I knew I couldn't bear it if people felt sorry for me. I needed everyone to be strong, so I could be too. Besides, I was genuinely optimistic about Kenan's future and had no doubts that he was going to recover completely.

Although his body was weak, his spirit had started to come back soon after the side effects from his chemotherapy began to subside, and it was because of that spirit I could come home. Surprisingly, one question that I was asked a lot was why we hadn't gone back to England and I realised that many people still consider Spain to be almost third world when it comes to medical care. But we couldn't have been happier with the hospital or the expertise of the doctors. We would have flown straight home, in spite of Kenan wanting to stay, if

I'd thought for a single moment that he wasn't getting the best medical attention.

We knew too that *La Fe* had one of the top Oncology units in Europe and worked closely with respected cancer research hospitals in the USA, which gave us confidence too. Carlos was brilliant, so patient and gentle. So, far from being nervous about staying in Spain, I was reassured. Besides what were we to do? We had had to make a split second decision and I'm sure to this day, that we made the right one.

Saying all that, going back to Javea and facing people was, as I say, strangely intimidating. Even meeting my own children was difficult. I collected the boys from Mum and Dad's house and I couldn't believe how much I was missing out, on Louis' life in particular. Louis had grown very fretful in the time I had been away. Being ferried around from place to place to give Mum and Dad a rest had not done him much good, bless him – he was only a few months old after all.

Angelo seemed really cool about my comings and goings, accepting my cuddles and presents, but Louis grew increasingly upset. When I went to pick him up, that first time back in Javea, he just looked at me, then at my mum and then back at me again. He was genuinely confused as to who his mummy was and, truthfully, I didn't know my baby anymore. They change so fast at that age. I didn't want to have to deal with Louis just then, so I begged my mum to come home with me. Already his routine had changed and deep down I was scared that I would get it wrong. My mum gently, but firmly, refused.

"He is your child," she said, and hard though it was, I knew she was right. I had to do it; I had to bond with him again if only for a few days at a time.

Angelo was just glad to be back in his own bed again. It amazes me how children can adapt to the surroundings they're in and how they simply get on with it. For a few days I would be with them then I'd leave again. By then Daddy would be back for a few days but he then would go, back to England, and they'd be back at my mum and dad's house again. It didn't seem to affect them, but who knows? Kids always seem so incredibly resilient, whether well or unwell.

Louis became very clingy for a while but then Kenan was as a baby, too. We solved the problem of his 'pass the parcel' lifestyle thanks to Joyce, who owned the nursery Angelo was at. She offered to take Louis in full-time, and although normally I wouldn't choose to send my kid to a nursery at four months old, it turned out to be the security he needed.

Joyce refused to accept any payment for it either which astonished me, because at the time we barely knew her or her husband Philip – it was a *genuine* act of kindness. As the parents of four young children themselves, I guess they understood we were desperate for help and during those weeks that Kenan lay in hospital, I certainly learned who my true friends really were.

Even so, by the third week of Kenan's stay in *La Fe*, the strain of trying to juggle my life between Kenan there and Louis and Angelo at home started to get me down. I felt like I was being pulled in all directions. After the boys' visit to the hospital I realised just how much I was missing our family being together. In such a short space of time, every aspect of our lives had changed and my emotions slipped dangerously close to the edge.

Neither me nor Lev was doing too well. While we put on a strong show on the outside, inside we both swung like kids on a swing – up and down and up again. It took just a tiny pull to bring us down.

I know now that all couples, when thrown into a major crisis just have to get on and deal with it, but I learned that we all do it in different ways. Some couples bond together and become a stronger unit, some isolate each other and go it alone and others just tear each other apart. For us, it was a bit of all of those things. We coped, but while I needed Lev to be a unit, he preferred, instead, to go it alone. His unrelenting scouring of the internet to collect as much information as possible about leukaemia only angered me.

At that stage I couldn't deal with the scores of facts he accumulated. I was living day to day, dealing with the situation head on rather than educating myself about the long-term effects or possible outcomes. Lev tried to tell me but I wasn't interested and so a rift formed between us. It wasn't helped by the fact that we didn't see much of each other. Yes, we spoke plenty on the telephone, but the only time we actually spent together was when we changed over shifts on a Sunday. For a quick hour or so, we'd sit and chat at the canteen across the road from the hospital. Hygiene rules meant food had to be eaten away from patients (their food was prepared on-site) which suited us as it meant escaping from the hospital for a short time.

Talk never came easily – especially about Kenan. We were so sensitive of each other's fragility that we danced around it, unwilling to risk bringing the other down. Yes we were comfortable in each other's company, but our conversations were stilted and muddled. I'd ask, "What's happening in England?" wanting to hear what our friends over there thought about Kenan, but hearing only about work instead. We couldn't talk about the reality of what was happening. Occasionally Lev tried to tell me that he'd been working on a children's Oncology ward, but I switched off the moment he started to speak about the survival statistics he'd picked up from the doctors there.

In turn, he didn't want to hear any of the deeper fears I had, whenever I attempted to discuss them with him. I desperately wanted to spend more time with Lev too, but he said that when he wasn't in England or at the hospital, he needed to spend his time with Angelo and Louis – not with me. That was tough to take, but that's the way it was – he just didn't seem to need or want time with me. It was his way of coping.

He stopped drinking alcohol and put himself on a strict diet too. He lost loads of weight which I think was his way of holding on to a fragment of control over what was happening in his life. At that time, Lev felt like a walking time-bomb, ready to explode at the slightest thing and therefore if staying away from me helped, then I had to accept that.

I've taken a long-winded route to admitting that, in truth, we simply infuriated each other. He annoyed me by not discussing my feelings and that, in turn, exacerbated his anger towards me because I was so needy. But I wasn't about to beg for his attention so, instead, I pulled away from him. I hid how I ached to tell him how alone I felt on my days at the hospital; how the attractions of one of Spain's most vibrant cities meant nothing (for some reason people thought it was 'better' all this was happening in Valencia) and of my guilt at being separated from the other kids.

I wanted to tell him how I spent nearly every waking hour going over and over in my head the run up to Kenan's diagnosis. Of how I'd doubted whether Kenan *really* felt that poorly and of the times I thought he was only seeking attention. I felt so guilty it made me question myself as a mother. But I couldn't tell Lev. He wasn't ready to listen.

Our stand off lasted for about six weeks, and I know this because this is how long it was before we made love again. The thought of any enjoyment was impossible because it was engulfed with guilt. How could we enjoy ourselves when Kenan was going through all that pain and fear?

But me and Lev were drifting and we both knew that to get our family unit in order and make us strong again, we had to get our relationship back on track, for *all* our kids' sakes. From that moment on we promised to at least try and pull together and to discuss every eventuality. Naturally we had, and will forever have, our ups and downs, as ours has always been a fiery relationship. But we worked hard at holding our family together and that's what kept us going.

Lev

It was a very confusing time for all of us, which was why I needed to get information. I just wanted Kenan better and needed to find out what was happening and why. I used to try and explain to Kenan how leukaemia worked and what it was, during our long talks at the hospital. He used to say, "What have I got? What is leukaemia? What is AML?"

After a very deep breath I'd say, "Right, your bone marrow's not working properly. Bone marrow is where cells are made."

"What are cells, Daddy?" Err ...... "What is bone marrow, Daddy?" Err .... After taking, yet another, very deep breath I'd say, "Right mate, bone marrow is that spongy, brown stuff in the middle of the bones that Kato likes to lick and suck out. This bone marrow makes stem cells. Stem cells are baby cells and when they grow up they turn into red blood cells, which carry oxygen around your body, kind of like fuel pipes in a car. White blood cells are the body's 'bouncers', and stop the troublemakers getting in and causing problems like infection. Platelets are the other cells and they are like the engineers; they go and fix your cuts and help your bruises to heal."

"So what happens when you get leukaemia, Daddy?"

Right, OK, I can do this, another deep breath. "Your bone marrow clogs up with these baby cells which are called blast cells. The body keeps producing them. So your bone marrow gets all clogged up and that's why they never grow up into red cells, white cells or platelets. They stay baby cells and keep queuing up and blocking the rest. That's why you get out of breath, because the red cells aint got no fuel. That's why you get ill a lot 'cos you got no white blood cells to keep the trouble out. That's why you bruise easily and get a lot of nose bleeds and your lips bleed, 'cos you got no engineers to fix you when you cut or bump yourself."

It was hard; sometimes I couldn't believe I was talking to my son. It didn't seem real, like I was on the outside looking in.

"Why me, Daddy?" That one used to screw me right up.

All I could muster was, "What about the other children on the ward? Why them, mate? But don't worry." I'd tell him, "You're gonna be OK, I promise."

What else could I say? Who knows what was going through Kenan's head. I used to try and imagine, fathom it out so I could say the right words to help him cope. But he was so strong, stronger than us lot of sad cases around him. So caring and thoughtful and, always, with that great sense of humour he had. I admired him, he was *my* hero.

Sure I was strong on the outside, and I had to show that at all times, especially to Kenan. But everyday I woke, I wished it was me and not him.

Chapter Eleven

Lev's parents have a long history of rubbing each other up the wrong way, which meant that whenever they came over to visit Kenan, they had to come separately, so as not to upset him. Lev's dad, Mehmet, arrived first from England to see him with his then girlfriend, Hulia. I must admit they did cheer the place up a bit.

Both being Turkish-Cypriot meant almost from the moment they unpacked I lost control of my kitchen. It was transformed into a magical, bubbling, Turkish tavern; a place where beans on toast was not allowed to sully the table.

Mehmet and Hulia blended into Javea perfectly. Every morning they'd set off to the market in the old town where they slipped easily in to the deep-rooted Mediterranean custom of men doing one thing, women another. Thus Mehmet sat with his brandy and coffee, whilst Hulia explored the market, picking out the night's dinner from the colourful selection of fresh vegetables and meats available.

Once home again, there was no let up for poor Hulia, who sat like a throwback to the past on our naya, painstakingly peeling and chopping vegetables into a huge pot at her feet. Mehmet kept up his part of the tradition, chilling out with another glass of brandy, coffee at hand, playing the guitar.

I soon realised that however one-sided this set up appeared to those of us pretending to share the domestic load, Hulia loved doing it. She felt proud as dinner bubbled away all day, with its delicious smells wafting through the house. I was nothing like Hulia, a quick, functional cook to her slow, loving one. Food usually came ready-made for me in packs, so nothing ever bubbled all day in my kitchen and her meals were great to come home to, after being at the hospital for a few days.

We enjoyed nightly lectures from Mehmet on respect for the Ottoman Empire and after we'd had our fill of food and stories, we'd leave the dinner table and head for the TV. Not wanting to sound ungrateful, I did though, at times, hanker for some good old English grub. Eating *paella* and meatballs from the canteen in Valencia, followed by green beans, artichokes and lamb stew when I arrived home left me craving bangers and mash more than once!

But we all grew really fond of Hulia and I'd have loved her to have been 'the one' that Mehmet finally settled down with, but he remains a true, loveable rogue, a Turkish 'Delboy' if you like, propping up his job as a mechanic with a spot of wheeling and dealing, still searching for that special woman.

We eventually said farewell to Lev's dad and Hulia and then Lev's mum, Maureen, with whom I have always had my differences, came over. She'd wanted to come earlier but a friend of hers had glandular fever and Maureen was paranoid she might have caught it. Her doctor had advised her to wait six weeks, after which she'd be safe to travel.

Obviously it was paramount that Kenan didn't come into contact with anyone that may have any kind of infection, and it was typical of Maureen to make sure she was healthy. She's the most allergic and paranoid person I've ever met. A simple paracetamol can bring her out in hives. She studies every food label, checks every sell-by date and, meticulously, inspects the side-effects on every medicine leaflet. Paranoia, in fact, doesn't even come close.

So, as you can imagine, Maureen took no chances when she came to see Kenan. She even wore her mask flying over with Lev and on the bus to Valencia. Lev was as embarrassed as hell and refused to sit next to her. I'm sure she did it just to annoy him.

Kenan was always thrilled to see his nanny though. Maureen had always indulged him and she was totally wrapped around his little finger.

If Kenan said, 'Jump, Nanny', her reply would be, 'How high, Kenan?'

When we lived in England, Kenan on occasion spent the night at Maureen's house, giving me and Lev a night off, and within twenty-four hours he'd turned into a child possessed. It always took a few days to get him into his old routine of 'Please' and 'Thank you,' instead of 'I want,' 'Now,' and 'No!'

It was up to Maureen if she allowed that kind of behaviour in her house but I certainly didn't, and I didn't want other people thinking that my child was a rude, impolite, little boy. Kenan has never been that.

Maureen quickly learnt the 'ropes' at the hospital and she fast became engrossed in life there. True to form she dedicated herself to learning the ins and outs of every drug that Kenan was taking and gave us her opinion on each of them – like it would make a difference. I tried to explain to her that we weren't dealing with a headache here; this was cancer, but she carried on anyway

With Maureen around however, it took the pressure off me a little, and so when Paula offered me a night out at a friend's birthday barbeque I accepted. I could do with a little fun, I thought. It was a new, slightly unnerving experience, being the mother of a sick child. People treated me differently when I was around, in Javea, even though they didn't really mean to. I guess they just didn't know what to say. At first I had been worried that people pitied me, but I soon realised that I had become 'the mother of that boy, who has leukaemia'. So a night at a party felt like a good way of showing people I was still me. To this day I wish I had never gone.

It was a big garden party for Sandie who was turning forty. She and her husband, Danny, have lived in Javea for years and there were loads of people invited. Lev didn't come home that weekend so I went with Paula and her husband, Martin while Maureen looked after the kids. I almost didn't make it, as, with perfect timing, Louis was struck down with sickness and diarrhoea, but Maureen talked me into going.

I was having a lovely evening, enjoying a few drinks, in the warmth of the setting sun – when a woman I'd never met before, suddenly appeared with her husband in front of me. She explained that she

112

had wanted to meet me and that they were the 'supposed' friends of a woman who had, tragically, lost her five-year-old daughter in a car accident a month previously.

She then said to me, a soft sympathetic smile appearing at her lips, "I was saying to my friend that it's much better the way her daughter died, than to watch a young child die from an illness." Excuse me?

Now, normally I would have floored her, but I was too gobsmacked to speak and the last thing I wanted was to make a spectacle of myself. Before she could say anymore, Paula came to my rescue and led me away, after which, all I wanted was to go home.

Mostly, people offered me only sympathy during Kenan's illness, but there were some, like her, who I will never understand. I'm sure she must have been too thick to realise the impact of her words – no one can be that cruel can they? – But they did affect me and they stayed with me as the date to Kenan being allowed out of hospital grew closer.

When Maureen left, Lev's dad came out again, like a tag team they were. When they did finally come out together it was a disaster, but more on that later.

Chapter Twelve

Today is 9th May, a very special day because, true to his word a few days ago, Carlos gave us the wonderful news that Kenan can come home. By some strange stroke of luck, it is also his ninth birthday – which makes it a double celebration, although we're not throwing birthday party of course.

Last year, for Kenan's eighth birthday, we hired a huge, Hummer-style limo and drove Kenan and his mates around Essex, stopping off to treat them all to dinner at TGI Friday's. Showing off at kid's birthdays was big round our way and it was so OTT, so typically Essex …. How I wish we were doing it again.

Lev and me are waiting outside our house for the ambulance which is due to arrive any minute. It's a lovely, spring day and that adds to my good mood. Although I'm excited, I can't help but feel nervous too, because the onus is on us now to take care of him.

I see the ambulance turn into our street and climb the hill and I just know that Kenan will be

114

revelling in the drama of arriving home by ambulance; much cooler than by car!

I want to fling open the doors right away, but me and Lev wait patiently instead for the doors to be opened and for Kenan to be gently helped out, before we finally are able to hold him and lead him into the house.

After being virtually bedbound for four weeks, my hands swamp his frail and skinny arms, but at least he's here, I tell myself. Kenan coming home makes life feel more normal again, or what passes for normal these days, and now he's back I am more determined than ever to get him well quickly and get on with our lives. Yes, he needs to go back to the hospital approximately every six weeks for more chemo sessions, and there's the final step – the transplant – which they have scheduled for August, but I never think outside the box that says that Kenan will get completely better. It's how I keep going.

Lev on the other hand still has his doubts, which bugs me.

Kenan's granddad, Mehmet, and his girlfriend, Hulia have come over from England and Hulia has cooked up a birthday feast to welcome Kenan home. The delicious aromas waft through the air as we go indoors. Like Mehmet, Hulia is Turkish, so it's been simmering away all day on the cooker, although I know for sure Kenan will turn his nose up at it. I'm looking forward to it, because I never have the time or the inclination to cook anything I have to wait all day for.

My mum and dad are round as well so we've a small, family gathering, which is enough, I think.

I've already promised Kenan that we'll throw a big party for his tenth birthday to make up for it.

I hope Kenan likes Hulia. Lev and me think she is perfect for Mehmet, but he's a bit of a player, Lev's dad – a woman in every port – so we'll see. Kenan may have some influence though, you never know.

As I thought, he doesn't touch Hulia's wonderful birthday banquet (I'm sure he wouldn't have even if he was well, he's such a fussy eater,) however Hulia understands. He manages to open his birthday presents, but it's not long before he needs a nap. It's lovely tucking him into his own bed again. While he's sleeping we all get stuck in, and the hours Hulia has spent cooking have been well worth it … it's all delicious.

Later, I happily say goodbye to Mum and Dad and settle the boys in front of the television. Lev, Mehmet and Hulia go to chill out on the naya as I wait for Carin, the nurse I've employed, to help me look after Kenan.

As the doorbell rings, so begins our new regime. I've hired Carin because I just can't take the chance of messing something up. I can manage the mountain of medication he has to take, on time and in the right order, but I'm too anxious to deal with the tubes in his chest that connect to the Hickman line.

Because Kenan still needs at least three more sessions of chemo before the transplant, the tubes have to be flushed out and kept meticulously clean. Already I think of Carin as my guardian angel – someone I can turn to, while Kenan is at home, to give me advice and support, because it's crucial that Kenan doesn't pick up any infections.

The chemo has already lowered, and will continue to lower, his immunity, so we need to be very careful with Angelo and Louis around. They pick up all sorts at nursery so Carin's medical backup to me is vital and money well spent. Our medical insurance will pick up some of the cost, but we still have to pay out a fair bit.

The insurance people have been right twats actually, and have caused us a great deal of worry because, when Kenan was taken into hospital, they told us we should have called them *before* he was admitted! Yeah right, like I even thought about it. Then, they told us we weren't covered because we hadn't been with them for a minimum of six months (five months two weeks). Luckily I'd paid for a year up front by mistake, and told them, during a furious row, that as they'd taken my money, they had to pay up and, eventually, they agreed.

However, Lev was collared a couple of weeks ago at the hospital by the woman at the *Ingreso* (reception). She told him that the money, held in reserve for Kenan's treatment, was nearly all gone.

Thankfully, with the help of 'Danny the Pool Man', who speaks fluent Spanish, we have managed to complete all the necessary paperwork, enabling us to get funding through the National Health Service, as we still pay our taxes in the UK. This allows Kenan to have the same room and continue with the same doctors.

Carin has already visited Kenan in the hospital to see how the nurses do things because procedures can differ slightly from one place to another. The hospital has provided us with everything we need: the saline and heparin, an anticoagulant to flush the tubes, gloves, drugs, sterile green sheets for the bed, syringes – everything.

There's another plus to Carin being here – it gives me the time to keep up with my chores, manic cleaning mostly – and I can also spend time with Angelo and Louis.

We all settle quickly into our new routines. Every morning, I get up at six o'clock and bleach the house from top to bottom to keep the risk of infection down. Then the hospital rings to check on Kenan and every six weeks we take Kenan back to the hospital for his chemo, as instructed. Kenan isn't well yet, but he's doing fine and, as the days pass, we grow more relaxed. Throughout the summer there are highs and lows of course, drama and calm, but everything is going to plan and Carin is the godsend I knew she would be.

Kenan loves her and can't wait for her visits. His favourite time is when she helps him shower. His tubes can't be submerged in water, so Carin comes every three days to shower him. I'd been worried he might be too embarrassed to let Carin do it, but he laps up the attention! We always have to coax him out, because he likes to wait until the room is like a sauna first. Then he lies on a sterile bed-sheet while Carin 'flushes' his tubes, to keep them clean and to stop them from getting blocked.

Kenan is brilliant I have to say, because he hardly ever complains. Instead he uses the time to indulge his favourite habit of asking a hundred and one questions, constantly quizzing Carin about what she is doing and why, and so he's rapidly building up a knowledge of drugs and measurements and knows exactly what, where and when something is needed – and why of course.

Taking Kenan's temperature at several points throughout each day is crucial because if it was to go up it may mean an infection is on the way. I always check it with Carin and I rely on her to tell me if we need to inform the hospital. Occasionally, it has gone up pretty high, throwing everyone into a blind panic. We have a plan in place, of course, which requires all hands on deck. I call Mum and Dad who then fly round to our house. Mum looks after the kids whilst me and Dad take Kenan to Valencia. It's a pretty slick operation, even if I do say so myself.

Except the time when, in the rush, Mum slipped over in the doorway which was wet because I'd been mopping the floor. I honestly can't stop cleaning the house. She really hurt her ankle and it was obvious she was in a lot of pain, but there was no way we could wait with her. Kenan's temperature was rising all the time, so we left poor Mum on all fours and me and Dad went to the hospital with Kenan, sleeping in the back.

I ring Paula, on the way, to ask her to go round and help poor Mum. The doctor says it'll be months before she will be able to walk properly on it again. When I think about it, it's uncanny how the incident rate of calamitous happenings has risen tenfold in our house, ever since Kenan has been ill.

Sometimes Kenan's rise in temperature is nothing more than a blip and he comes home again, having been taken straight back into the Isolation unit and put on antibiotics, as a precaution in case he's picked up an infection. His blood cultures are taken to find out why his temperature has gone up, and if the results show that he is fighting something, he has to stay in until he's clear. With perfect timing, Lev seems to nearly always be away in England when these dramas happen and comes back, usually, when Kenan is home again.

Despite these episodes, throughout June and July, Kenan's health improves a lot, but the effects of the chemo means he isn't looking too good. We barely give his appearance a second thought these days, but I'm reminded of how much he's changed when my friend's husband, Andy, pops over with a gift for Kenan.

Andy used to work at the BBC, in the sports department and he has a signed photo and letter for Kenan from Gary Lineker, whose eldest son had battled with leukaemia as a baby.

"Hey look," cry Kenan and his friend Eli, who is over to play with him, "It's the man from the crisps' advert!"

How funny! They are so young and they have no idea he's a famous footballer.

This is the first time Andy has seen Kenan since he was diagnosed and he's shocked and upset. He asks me for a cigarette even though he doesn't smoke anymore.

"Don't tell my wife," he orders, lighting it up and drawing it in.

Lev's mum, Maureen, later comes out to stay with us for a couple of weeks and most days Kenan is strong enough to go for an early stroll with her along the beachfront. The chemo is slowly destroying the pigment in his skin however, so he has to stay well

120

covered and out of the sun. Sometimes I go with them, but he enjoys having Nanny to himself; he adores her, which I'm not too fussed about as mine and Maureen's relationship can be choppy at times, if I'm honest. Still, there is no room for personal grievances to get in the way (well not in front of Kenan anyway) as everyone's focus is on getting Kenan well again.

As the summer reaches its height and we complete the chemo, we receive some fantastic news. Kenan's leukaemia is in remission – I knew he would be fine!

The next stage will be the transplant. The doctors tell us Kenan must now go on a 'build up' diet consisting of protein, protein and more protein. So we start a routine of eggs for breakfast, fish for lunch and steak for dinner. By the time the poor boy has finished breakfast it's time for lunch! Daily, we struggle to get him to eat it all, it's exhausting, but when the time of the transplant arrives he's put on plenty of weight, he's strong and full of life and in the best health possible to cope with what lies ahead.

At the beginning of August, we take Kenan back in to hospital. The doctors have decided that he may do better with an autologous transplant, rather than a bone marrow transplant, which means he's going to have his own stem cells frozen and then put back into him, where they will create new, normal blood cells.

I'm so excited, because this is the final hurdle now. Trust Lev to remind me that we've been given no assurances that the transplant will work, or that the leukaemia won't come back. But why shouldn't everything be alright? I trust the doctors and, statistically, I think the odds are in his favour. I can't remember the figures Lev told me.

Although it feels like a lifetime, incredibly, it's been only four months since Kenan was diagnosed, and in just a few more weeks he'll be well on the road to being a healthy kid again.

The mechanics of what is about to happen have been explained to me and Lev, but again we haven't any real understanding. It's a two-part process. Part one is to take his own stem cells out, washing and freezing them, and then part two is putting the cells back into him, a couple of weeks later. That's it. I think the idea is that new cells will start doing the job of making new blood cells.

As always, Dad has dropped me and Kenan off at the hospital. Work has prevented Lev from coming, so the two of us go together for the first part of the transplant.

The nurses prepare Kenan in a side ward and we then head down to the blood bank – the *Sangre de Banco*. I'm so nervous I chatter all the way there. I soon stop when we enter the small room situated, rather depressingly I think, in the basement of the general hospital. There are so many staff bustling around I start to worry that all the commotion may frighten Kenan, but he looks so matter-of-fact about everything. His calmness relaxes me a bit and helps to bring my rising heart-rate down slightly. 'It is so nearly over,' I tell myself, like a mantra.

The first things I notice as we enter the room, where this first phase is to take place, are four strange looking machines lined up alongside one another. They remind me of old 1960s recording devices. On the walls are posters of Javea, of all places! They show the beach with its palm trees and the cafes that are dotted around the port area and the Arenal beach. How odd and out of context they look. If they're meant to cheer the place up a bit, personally, I don't think it works.

"Look, Mum." Kenan pipes up, "The Arenal beach!" and for a few minutes the posters do, in fact, turn out to be a very good distraction. While we chat about the posters, a nurse connects Kenan up to one of the machines before flicking a switch. I can only describe the whole process as, mesmerizingly, bizarre. His blood begins to pump slowly out of one tube, is kind of spun around in the old 'recording device' and then goes back in, down the other tube, now 'empty' of his own stem cells.

I have no idea how, but the machine has managed to separate the cells from his blood during the spin: All very high-tech. It isn't painful, but Kenan needs to stay still for, roughly, two hours while the process takes place.

I am totally absorbed in this feat of technology when, suddenly, the lights go out, part-way through a spin cycle. Before I can open my mouth, a generator cuts in and it strikes me there's been a power cut. I'm speechless – we've got used to the 'leccy' going out, living in the rural backwater of Javea, but here in a city hospital? Thank God for the generator. Now what?

The lights are flickering again! I can't believe it – this time the antique looking machine has actually given up. The nurses are onto it quickly though, calmly unhooking Kenan and attaching him to another one that, thankfully, is still working. I wonder to myself, how often this kind of thing happens – and more astonishingly, how is it allowed to happen? My nerves are on edge more than ever, as we wait for it to finish but, eventually, he's done – and without any more power cuts.

The total number of blood cells required has now been harvested and taken to be frozen in a huge freezer outside the Isolation unit. The temperature in the freezer displays minus thirty-eight degrees.

Kenan has spent two boring weeks in hospital, following the first part of his blood transplant, but part two, the final phase, starts today! The stem cells are being put back into Kenan's bloodstream and then, at long last, we'll almost be home and dry.

Once again, I am actually excited and in a rush to get to the hospital for the procedure to begin. This part is just like having a blood transfusion, which he's used to by now, so today holds no fear for Kenan or me.

He's hooked up and the defrosted cells are put back into his blood, thanks to the marvels of technology again.

"The cells will know what to do next," Carlos assures me, as obviously I must look completely baffled by the whole thing. With that information, I sit, waiting and watching, all the time imagining the cells starting to do their magic – and before I realise, it's all over. The transplant is complete. Kenan needs to remain in for a while to make sure everything goes smoothly with the reintroduction of the cells to his body, but I have absolute confidence that it will go well. What a day!

I return home on a high and start making plans for things we can all do – but a couple of days later, all the plans and the elation come crashing down. Carlos has called and told us that Kenan's body is fighting against accepting the cells and, although he's fine, he has gone downhill slightly. He wants him to have one last intense dose of chemotherapy to make absolutely sure any cancer cells have gone. We're not home and dry after all. I'm devastated, but what option do we have?

Once again they waste no time and the doctors start the chemotherapy immediately, but this time Kenan reacts badly. The next few weeks are pure hell. Kenan suffers horribly and I can't believe how quickly all the weight he's put on, during our strict 'get strong and fat' regime, falls off him – it's gutting.

The sickness is worse than ever and he's getting stomach cramps, which he's never had before – sometimes they completely immobilise him. He isn't having bad headaches thankfully, which is one of my greatest fears as I'll never forget the agony Angie suffered with her headaches, shortly before she died.

All the doctors can do at the moment, is to monitor Kenan's stomach pains 24/7. It's a very worrying time right now.

For four, long, weeks Kenan is plugged into all sorts of drips and monitors and we travel back and forth to the hospital, worrying and waiting, praying that he will turn the corner, and at last he starts to show small signs of improvement. He's bad tempered and fed up in the isolation room. Only being able to walk slowly around his bed now and again, frustrates him, but it is all he can manage. He's desperate to get home and I feel so anxious for him, but with each day that passes the doctors seem happier with his progress.

Just as I just begin to feel confident again that he's going to be OK, Kenan reacts to a drug he is given and I'm forced to call a nurse as he starts hallucinating, singing and swearing his head off. It's kind of funny, but I'm nervous. Amazingly, I'm told it is a good sign; Kenan's body is actually fighting the drug. It's a happy day!

He improves rapidly from that moment on, each day growing healthier and stronger and then finally, finally, finally, after what has been a horrendous, unbelievable six months, the doctors bring us the news we have been waiting and praying for. The stem cell replacement has worked and the leukaemia has gone.

Kenan has won!

Chapter Thirteen

Kenan is recovering unbelievably fast now, just like a healthy child in fact, and I'm so happy and positive for the future that I can't stop clucking around like an old mother-hen. It's so wonderful to wake up every morning and have my three boys making a noise and sitting together around the breakfast table again. Simple things like that matter more to me now.

We're still making regular visits to the hospital of course and although on occasion Kenan requires blood or platelet transfusions to keep his blood count up, it's all stuff he's used to now and he's totally cool about it. His Hickman line fell out as well, which threw me into a blind panic and meant the usual dash to the hospital, so they've now put it into his leg, but that's the worst thing that has happened.

I make use of the time when he's hooked up at the hospital, browsing round the shopping centre across the road, enjoying my shopping at last, whilst the nurses do what they have to do. Life isn't completely back to normal yet, but Kenan is growing stronger each day and becoming more like his old self, which is fantastic.

Another piece of good news is that our close friends Peter and Annabelle are getting married here in Javea in a few weeks and now Kenan is home they've asked if he will be a pageboy. It's a *big* ask because he's barely out of hospital and still not permitted to mix openly with people, but me and Lev think it's important for his self-esteem to do it. He'll love the attention and, as Lev is to be Pete's best man, it'll be a real *father and son* celebration.

Although Lev is chuffed as anything to be best man, at the same time he's feeling nervous and I suspect Kenan being around may help in a lot of ways. He's a funny and confident guy Lev, but strangely, now Kenan's OK, he's started to struggle with everything that's happened and he is definitely feeling edgy about his speech.

He's lost weight again, although, typically, he's hidden it well. I only noticed when he tried on some trousers for the wedding the other week.

I think he's having panic attacks as well because he totally freaked out, trying stuff on and practically ran out of the changing room. I know it's stress, after all the trauma we've all experienced over the last few months. But better out than in, as my grandma always used to say. I wish he'd talk to me about it, but I know Lev well enough to know he'll cope in his own way. He'd hate for me to make a fuss, so I'm going to let him be – unless he wants to talk.

The day of the wedding, 2nd October, starts with the sun shimmering and the temperature gloriously hot for the time of year. The location, in the gardens of the Parador Hotel, set on the peninsular right at the edge of the sea, is about as romantic as romantic gets.

Pete and Annabelle actually got hitched in England a couple of weeks ago, thereby avoiding the reams of paperwork required to get married here in Spain, but they consider today as their wedding day. Most of the guests don't know, in fact, that they're already married. When I see Annabelle for the first time, she looks the perfect bride, all beautiful and glowing and I can see she's enjoying every moment. Pete, on the other hand, looks handsome in his smart, cream suit, but he has the fear of God stamped all over his face. Lev was the same on our wedding day. He looked like he'd rather face a firing squad or enlist in the Foreign Legion, than get married. Another example, if one was needed, of how men and women are so different.

Kenan stands out with his bald head shining in the sun, but he still looks so handsome as he walks down the aisle with the other pageboy and two bridesmaids. I clock several of the guests' shocked faces, but I can't blame them, most of them don't know he's had cancer. I feel only absolute pride in my boy today; here he is, after having been through hell, getting on with life again.

Although in recovery, Kenan must try to avoid catching anything, so must still wear a mask inside crowded places. This means he is not able to join everyone in the banquet hall for the meal after the wedding vows. So, instead, me and Kenan eat together in Pete and Annabelle's hotel suite.

We can't miss Lev's speech though, so when we've finished eating he puts on his mask and we head downstairs.

Lev's speech goes down a storm, thank goodness, but the most amazing moment of the night, my moment, comes when Kenan goes and stands up, side by side with his daddy and speaks a few words of his own, for which he gets lots of 'Oohs' and 'Ahhs' followed by the biggest applause of the night.

What a fantastic day!

October is turning into a busy month for Kenan. He's now been asked if he'll take part in a fashion show in aid of Cancer Research at the Marriott Hotel in Denia. Paula's daughter, Emily, and Eli (on whom Kenan has developed a crush) are doing it, but I'm concerned Kenan isn't strong enough yet. He wants to do it so much though (I've forgotten what a born show off he is), so we're going to see how it goes. He'll have to pull out if he gets too tired.

Mum and me take him to the rehearsals and it's hard to look at him without crying because he's doing 'normal' things! Normal things like changing clothes by himself and walking by himself, for the first time in ages with healthy children, and he seems really happy.

He copes with the week of rehearsals and to my relief when the big night arrives; he's still feeling OK, although a bit sheepish about it now! Deep down I know he is going to love everyone watching him though.

We arrive early, while the place is almost empty, and settle him away from the other models in the changing room. He has his mask on. It impresses me no end how he's never fazed by wearing it, or by the fact that he stands out from the other kids because he's bald. He's more embarrassed by the kiss I give him, before leaving the changing room for my front row seat.

Talk about being the *proud* mum!

Lev, his mum and my mum are here too and, as the lights dim and the music starts, we get our cameras ready. The compère introduces the show and the first set of young models walk down the catwalk wearing clothes from the local shops in and around Javea.

Flagged on both sides by Emily and Eli, Kenan then walks out looking handsome and very well dressed. His smile as bright as the lights shining down on his bare head and I fight back the tears. That's my Kenan, my son, the fighter who's battled leukaemia, endured chemotherapy and been through a transplant all within six months. Look at him now! What a star.

I hear someone crying to my left and, turning, I notice an elderly lady pointing to Kenan, and I just can't help myself from leaning over and telling her, "That's my son."

The show is a triumph and I know that people will talk about it in Javea, for ages. Afterwards, the local paper appears backstage and takes a picture of Kenan and the other models, which I duly purchase later, in duplicate, and send to my friends in England.

For days afterwards, people stop me randomly in the street to ask how Kenan is; I don't even know many of them. Kenan is famous and happy to be so!

It's turning out to be a hectic 'coming out' month for Kenan, because now Lev wants to take him to a Halloween party.

The Spanish usually honour the more serious *All Saint's Day* on 1st November: the day to mourn and remember their dead loved ones. However, more and more Spanish traditions have joined ours and vice versa, so a few ghoulish Halloween parties have been planned.

In England, Lev and Kenan would be dressing up and going out trick or treating, but that doesn't really happen here so we're all going to a party instead at a restaurant called Tusk, along the beachfront.

Lev has been racking his brains all day what to dress Kenan up as and, at last, he has it. Bleedin' obvious really with his bald head and all – Uncle Fester!

Kenan loves the idea, so Lev paints his face grey and darkens the faint rings beneath his eyes, puts him in an oversized jumper zipped up to his neck, dark trousers and a pair of big, clumpy shoes.

"Wow, I look great!" Kenan says, looking in the mirror, and I smile at Kenan's ability to laugh at himself. Angelo and Louis aren't so co-operative with Lev's efforts to dress them up, but still, we attract plenty of attention as we walk along the Arenal. Several times, people stop us and ask where Kenan got his bald wig from, unaware that it's Kenan's own head. We aren't letting on though because tonight he fits in and everyone is staring at him for the right reasons, not because he's a kid who's had cancer. Tonight he's the kid with the fantastic costume and Kenan revels in it.

Again, people talk about it for ages afterwards commenting on how good he looked. That night, 31st October, 2005 is a huge turning point in our lives – Kenan has pulled through; our whole family has pulled through and, we realise, the laughter is back.

Lev

Gina was well happy in October 2005, but although I was made up that Kenan was in remission, for some reason I was in a bad way. I'd lost loads of weight, was having panic attacks and I found it difficult to make decisions. My chest tightened at the slightest pressure put on me, but I tried hard to keep it together for Kenan's sake as I didn't want him or anyone else to know.

I was thrilled when Pete asked me to be his best man at his wedding to Annabelle. Peter was, and still is, the best mate a bloke can have and we've been thick as thieves, ever since we met in a flooring supplier in Tottenham.

Peter was close to Kenan too, ringing him almost every day that he was in hospital, and Kenan took advantage of Peter's good nature every chance he got; the little scamp, but that's how Peter liked it.

I love Peter like a brother, so naturally I was gonna stitch him right up at his wedding. I didn't do too badly, but my confidence was lower than it usually is and I was well nervous before I made the speech. Thankfully, Kenan stood next to me and having him there helped me roll with the speech:

"The Cheshunt Chav marries the Chichester Chick …. Annabelle Bond's bit of rough – Peter Melton……What a good name she's going to have now … should have been Melton-Bond, sounds like a posh chocolate bar …"

And on and on I went and while most people seemed to like it, Kenan thought I was great, which meant the most.

It was a beautiful day, in a stunning location overlooking the Mediterranean Sea. I can remember thinking, 'Too beautiful.'

Although Kenan was getting better, I was still tormented with the fact that had developed leukaemia at all – still couldn't stop myself from asking the million dollar question, "Why Kenan?"

Chapter Fourteen

It is remarkable how quickly life slipped back to normal when Kenan's leukaemia went into remission. Well, our version of normal. Granted, I had to take along a load of pills and potions for him whenever we went out, but heaving around a bag crammed full of antibiotics, morphine and steroids soon became the norm.

At the weekends, we avoided the crowds of the Arenal because of the infection risk, and went instead to the *chiringuitos* – temporary, wooden, small, beach bars that spring up every summer along the edge of the sea. They served great burgers and most importantly, as Lev remarked, a great beer.

We always enjoyed going there. It was lovely watching both Kenan and Angelo climb over the rock pools, trying to catch crabs in their buckets, laughing and giggling, enjoying the freedom, while Louis tried to keep up crawling behind.

The summer drew to an end and school was looming. I felt apprehensive as Angelo was starting 'big' school full-time, but on his first day he just casually kissed me goodbye and lined up in the playground with his classmates, even though he couldn't yet speak a word to them in Spanish. That was Angelo all over ... no crying, no tantrum even though he was only three years old.

Louis was not far off his first birthday, and although he wasn't walking yet, my God did he manage to get about. I constantly found him climbing up everything and he crawled everywhere, right behind his brothers.

Most of all, life was normal because Kenan was home. There had been times when me and Lev thought we wouldn't make it, but we were still together, although, inevitably, we had both been changed through our experiences. We still rowed like hell and threw insults at each other (which I hasten to add was normal), but Lev had become unnervingly pessimistic about life, whereas I was more optimistic and we had endless discussions from either side of the fence about Kenan's future.

I hated how Lev always looked at the negative, quoting endless statistics and the success rates for children in Kenan's position; those who had leukaemia in remission. I didn't give a toss about statistics and still lived day by day and, I daresay, he hated the way I buried my head in the sand.

In an effort to bridge the gap, one morning I suggested going away, just the two of us, for an overnight break in Benidorm where we could enjoy some 'us' time. Mum and Dad agreed to look after the kids and all week I looked forward to going.

A few days beforehand, I noticed Louis looked a bit off colour and I hoped he wasn't getting one of his endless colds, as the slightest infection could still send Kenan's temperature soaring. If only it had been a cold.

That day when I picked him up from nursery, there was note on the window, informing us that there had been an outbreak of chicken pox and, you've guessed it, that's exactly what Louis got. In fact most of Javea's little ones caught it that winter. Unfortunately, chicken pox was one of the infections the hospital had told me could be fatal to Kenan, because, although he was in remission, his natural immunity was still low. When I called to let them know, I was told to bring him back into hospital immediately. So once again it was up to Valencia, where Kenan was put on strong antibiotics to help his body build up a good resistance.

Poor Louis was quite poorly with it, but Kenan, thankfully, was fine and he was able to be at home around his brother. Mine and Lev's weekend went out the window, but part of me wasn't that surprised, given the way life had been recently.

Not to be beaten, we tried to get away again a couple of months later. Lev booked a hotel in the old part of Benidorm, nestled romantically amid the cobbled streets (and most importantly near the shops so I could spend loads of money!) We planned to see a show at Benidorm Palace and then have a slap-up meal. Perfect. I couldn't wait.

Lev was due to arrive home on the Thursday night as usual, before we set off on Friday and I was excited and felt really happy as I stood, for ages, in front of my clothes trying to decide what outfits to take. After concluding I'd have to buy a completely new wardrobe while we were there, my phone rang.

It was my dad telling me to put the news on. My heart sank – what now?

Bloody terrorists were thought to be planning to bomb the planes. Of all the weekends! All flights were cancelled in and out of any airport. I rang Lev. He was already at Stansted trying to get a flight home but of course there were none and the earliest he could make it back was Sunday. Why us? I was gutted our plans had been knocked back for a second time.

Upset, I called the hotel to cancel the reservation, only to be told it was too late to get our money back. Life just wasn't fair. Worn out with emotion I, tearfully, offered the booking to my mum and dad as a present, but they felt too bad for me and Lev, to take up the offer. So on top of everything else, five-hundred euros went down the drain that weekend.

Lev decided to make the most of his time in England and took on extra work, and he didn't make it back until the following weekend, by which time I was more pissed-off than I'd been for ages. I needed a night out, so Lev babysat and I went out with my girlfriends, Anne and Kim instead.

We'd all met when we had first moved to Javea at the local mother and toddler group. Both of them were a great help throughout Kenan's illness, taking care of Angelo and Louis and by just being around to talk. We reckoned we deserved a night on the tiles. Out came the little, black dresses and, along with our other friend, Marie, off we went, all 'glammed' up for something to eat. We stopped first for cocktails … a big mistake. Sod the food, the cocktail menu was much more fun!

We had such a laugh chatting about the things girls chat about when we're together – men, sex and clothes. The whole bar knew our preferences by the end of the evening, we were so loud! I needed it though: needed to let my hair down.

I staggered up the drive, swaying side to side, wishing I hadn't had that last Kir Royale cocktail. God I was going to have the hangover from hell tomorrow. I got in at two in the morning to find Lev sprawled on the sofa, out cold. All three kids lay around him fast asleep. The lazy bugger hadn't even bothered to put them to bed.

Empty pizza boxes were strewn across the floor. The dog had tried to eat the scraps *and* the boxes so bits of cardboard were everywhere. Where to start? I took off my 'killer' heels first and carried Louis upstairs to bed. Then, with a concentrated effort as my balance wasn't great, Angelo. There was no way I could lift Kenan so I woke him and steered him to bed. I left Lev where he was and went upstairs, happy that I'd had a great night out and, happier still, that Lev was downstairs on the sofa, leaving me to sleep without any unwanted distractions!

As Christmas approached, I couldn't believe a year had passed since last year's unexpected snowfall, which along with Louis' birth had made our first Christmas in Javea so special. Louis turned one on 18th December, but I felt as though I had completely missed his first year of life. I just didn't have the same early memories of poor Louis as I did for Kenan and Angelo.

I was determined to make up for it by ensuring Christmas that year was the best ever for all the kids. Kenan and Angelo really looked forward to Santa coming with his bag stuffed full of presents, and I spoilt Louis rotten to compensate for not being there for him.

Lev's mum, Maureen alternated Christmas between Lev and his brother and it was Lev's turn, so she came over from England to stay with us. Lev's dad, Mehmet also wanted to spend the season with us, but given there's more goodwill inside Frosty the Snowman than between them, we had no choice, but to say no – Maureen had asked first.

I decorated the house just as I liked it – understated and modern – and then Lev came home from England. Out came the bright, flashing lights and all the other tacky stuff that we've accumulated over the years, and as usual we ended up living in the equivalent of Santa's Grotto. The kids loved it of course.

Christmas Eve brought out the hyper excitement in the boys, so naturally they found it hard to sleep. We laid out the mince pie, carrot and milk by their beds and, after a few hours of 'Father Christmas won't come if you're awake,' they eventually fell asleep. Lev later dipped his shoes in flour and made footprints all the way up the stairs, from the fireplace to each bed, before we finally turned in.

Christmas 2005 kicked off early with an energetic Kenan and Angelo bounding into our bedroom. Louis, thank God, was too young to know what was happening, so remained fast asleep. Not that Kenan and Angelo waited for him to get up. By seven o'clock the first pile from the mountain of presents we'd indulged in, had been opened and I'd drunk about ten cups of sweet tea.

When I was growing up, my mum used to put a few presents by my bed and I could open only those in the morning. I had to wait until after dinner in the evening to open the rest, along with my mum and dad. We'd each do one at a time, watching, in between, what the other got. Lev joined this ritual when he married me, but always hid a present so that he had one left when we'd opened all ours. Why do men never grow up? I can't imagine most kids today doing it that way, but at least Christmas Day wasn't over by seven o'clock in the morning!

We'd decided to have Christmas lunch at the Marriott hotel in Denia, rather than cook at home, so later we got on our glad rags and set off, the boys all in shirts and matching Father Christmas ties. From the moment we walked past the big, understated and tastefully decorated Christmas tree which stood proud in the hotel foyer, (and looked just how I always wanted mine to, only never did thanks to Lev), I relaxed into the day.

Our dinner – a buffet of salads, hams, seafood and an endless selection of vegetables – was delicious, as were the unlimited chocolates and pastries that followed. The kids had their faces painted by entertainers and afterwards they watched a film while the 'grown-ups' spent some time together.

We knew loads of people as it was mostly English expats, and even with the temperature being an unseasonal 60 degrees outside, the day was perfect. I dragged Lev away from the bar at about eight o'clock before he got too drunk, to go home.

We still had to open *our* presents and I was knackered, but the magic of Christmas had rubbed off on me and even though Kenan and Angelo disagreed about almost everything as Maureen helped them get ready for bed, I listened with quiet happiness.

Nothing much had changed within the Gatoli-King clan, I realised. We were still the same crazy and chaotic family we'd always been – on the surface at least.

In March 2006, the doctors gave us more good news. Kenan could finally have his Hickman line removed, which meant no more nurse, no more tubes poking out of his leg and no more wearing special pants which concealed and held them in place. The first thing Kenan said he wanted, was to have a hot bubble-bath and then to dive into the pool. Freedom was just two days away and he couldn't wait.

My dad took us to the hospital and, cheerfully, we bypassed the intensive care unit, before settling into a small booth on a regular children's ward. It had three beds and, of course, a pesky, black stopover chair.

The first day we were there I stayed with Kenan, and settled him in with a DVD before heading off for a very important shopping trip. Well I didn't expect to be back in Valencia any time soon for a family day out! I had spent so long simply wandering around the shops unable to focus, that this time I was determined my retail therapy session would be thoroughly enjoyable – and expensive. So I shopped and went back to Kenan's room with loads of stuff for me, for Kenan and for Angelo and Louis. Mango, Zara, you name it, I had it.

That afternoon, Kenan had a straightforward operation to remove the tubes and he was thrilled. During the procedure I got chatting, in broken Spanish, to a couple of other mums on the ward and asked what their children were in for. Both said appendicitis.

When I told them that Kenan had had leukaemia and was having his tubes removed after eleven, long months they were aghast that I'd left him alone to go shopping. But by now, after almost a year of travelling up and down to the hospital, it was neither here nor there if I went shopping, it was just part of mine and Kenan's routine.

The next day, Mum swapped places with me and did exactly the same thing, but she bought tons more stuff than I did. The other mums on the ward clearly thought it all very shameful, and poor Mum couldn't understand why they were so off with her!

We collected Mum and Kenan the day after, all of us now looking forward to the coming summer, especially to watching Kenan play with his brothers and friends with nothing now to hold him back. We still had our hospital visits but by now they were monthly, so finally I felt I could relax and chill out.

An old friend, Caz, was coming over from England to celebrate her birthday which she shared with Paula, so we booked a pamper day and a big room, again at the Marriott Hotel in Denia, so we could enjoy a good, girly night out. Caz and I go way back and have been friends since we were five. We partied together, went out with boyfriends together, we even lived and worked together in Majorca. She was in the next room when, at the ripe old age of seventeen, I lost my virginity.

We were a couple of bitches most of the time if I'm honest and spent a large part of our youth down at Charlie Chan's nightclub in Walthamstow. You could say we were the original WAGS, flirting our way through clubs and conning a few drinks out of the men with money. Needless to say I was thrilled Caz was coming to Spain for her birthday.

First up was a meal on the Friday night after Paula had picked Caz up from the airport. Lev was on babysitting duty *all* weekend, which he was happy to do as he wasn't getting as much time as he liked alone with the kids, with all the commuting for work.

Caz was still a bubbly blonde with knockout curves and we all had a great night, catching up in a restaurant along the beachfront. The next day, after cleaning up after Lev (he never puts anything in the bin or the dishwasher) I started to get ready for my day of pampering and my night of uninterrupted sleep. But unbelievably, my plans were about to be knocked back again. It was getting to be an unpleasant habit by this time.

Caz called as I was packing my bag, screaming down the phone that Paula was having an epileptic fit. They had just been about to drop Paula's kids off at a friend's house when it happened. Paula had started the car, when, out of the blue, she had a seizure. Paula was totally out of control, foaming at the mouth and throwing herself onto the steering wheel. Her daughter, Emily stood frozen to the spot in shock whilst her son, Billy, tried to call out to her, but nothing helped. Poor Caz couldn't get hold of Paula's husband Martin, which is why she rang me.

Lev was out with Kenan and Angelo, so I called him and he went straight round.

The whole thing had lasted about 10 minutes. Louis was sleeping at home, so I got him up and, dressed in my old tracksuit, jumped into the car, zoomed round to my mum's to drop off Louis and sped round to Paula's.

By the time I arrived, Caz was leaning on a tree outside the house, shaking uncontrollably and was as white as a ghost. Lev had tried to get Paula out of the car but she was still in mental shutdown and didn't recognise him. Finally her husband, Martin arrived and managed to coax her out, into the house and into bed. Emily took Kenan and Angelo, leaving me and Lev to see Paula, who was slowly coming round. Obviously she was in no condition to go the Marriott.

Lev and Martin told me and Caz that they'd wait for the doctor and that we should still go, although we didn't really want to without Paula. We went in the end, but arrived so late we'd missed our massages and, as the hotel was fully booked that weekend, we weren't able to reschedule. We did get a complimentary glass of champagne (which went straight to our heads as we hadn't eaten lunch), and tried to relax in the spa but we couldn't stop thinking of Paula. Miserable, later that evening we ordered a burger from room service before snapping out of our malaise at about ten.

"Sod it," we said, and went out. We only managed one cocktail before went back to the hotel and ordered room service again – two hot chocolates! How the original WAGS had fallen. Knackered we slept like babies and had a delicious breakfast before going back home.

Incredibly the house had survived a night under Lev's supervision – he'd taken the kids out for dinner, they'd all slept in our bed and then he'd taken them out for breakfast.

Nice one Lev!

Chapter Fifteen

The months have passed through winter and spring and Kenan's health and appearance are improving every day. We're fortunate that we've had only the odd, minor setback to deal with, usually due to a cold or if he's been doing too much, but overall he's doing really well.

The Hickman line was taken out in March, eleven months he had it, in all, and although he still needs regular blood tests to check the leukaemia remains in remission, we're confident that the trials of the last year are now behind us.

Kenan's tenth birthday is approaching and, as promised, we're throwing him a huge party to make up for the one he missed last year, and also to say thank you to everyone that has helped and supported us through the most difficult time of our lives. We've hired a bouncy castle and Lev's dad, Mehmet, 'King of the BBQ' has agreed to do all the cooking, which is a great relief to me! No-one can beat Mehmet's Turkish flair behind the BBQ.

Kenan has invited all his friends and me and Lev have asked about another fifty, so we're

147

preparing for a houseful. I've roped everyone in to help out needless to say, the only hitch being that Lev's mum and dad have to be here together for the first time. We told them they're welcome to stay at the house, but that they'll have to share a room (with two separate beds) and, amazingly, they've agreed.

Lev is getting really wound up about them being together under the same roof, though – especially his roof! It's all very amusing, of course, to me, anticipating the fireworks. Me and Kenan are having a right laugh winding Lev up about it.

They arrive a few days before the party. The flight, according to Lev, was an embarrassing nightmare and I can see that he's not kidding. Maureen is stressed and bitchy, Mehmet, who doesn't like flying, is pissed and argumentative, and poor old Lev is well stressed, and pissed.

Apparently, Maureen spent the entire flight muttering asides at Mehmet under her breath whilst Mehmet, who's obviously had a few too many, didn't even try to conceal his animosity. God, what have we done asking them both to stay? The weather has been wet and grey for the last week too, which has affected everybody's mood. I'm getting a bad feeling about this.

I decide to try and defuse the atmosphere by asking Maureen if she wants to unpack her bags. Their room, on the lower ground floor, is laid out more like a small, self-contained flat, with its own bathroom and little kitchen, but as soon as Maureen clocks the two beds, she starts pleading with me to move Mehmet in with Kenan. As if by magic, Kenan appears, to rescue the situation.

"But, Nanny," he says, a cheeky glint springing into his eyes. "You and Granddad did used to be married. Why do you want Granddad to move?"

Well done Kenan, I think, hit where it hurts! It's easier for Maureen to reluctantly agree to share with Mehmet than to explain to Kenan that she and Granddad can no longer stand each other. I'm delighted that they're sharing because a silly part of me hopes we may help rekindle something – even a friendship would be good. But as the weekend beckons, it's clear that there isn't a chance in hell of that happening. They've barely said a word to each other. On the up side, the weather has changed – hooray!

Come party day the sun is shining and everyone, even Mehmet and Maureen, are pulling together to make it a triumph. In the morning, I get into my stride and issue everyone with jobs:

Maureen is to look after the kids

Mehmet is in charge of the BBQ

Lev is to help out his dad, bouncy castle, music, drinks

And I'll get all the stuff out we need, lay the tables, make salads and other side dishes.

We're a good team. Mehmet quickly gets into full swing and I watch him as he prepares the meats for the BBQ and organises the outdoor fridge with everything stacked neatly at hand. Lev gets on with the music, effing and blinding, while he tries to get the speakers fixed where he wants them. Maureen is wonderful keeping the kids entertained and I run around making sure everything is in place.

Before I know it the guests are arriving. I watch as Kenan leaps about like crazy as his friends come in. I know I have a huge smile pasted on my face as he looks just like them now. His hair has grown back, although thick and curly this time, not fine and straight like before, and I watch him jump into the pool, even though the water is freezing after all the rain. He has as much energy as all his mates, and I know for sure that he is, at last, completely well again.

Our guests are enjoying themselves; Mehmet's burgers are a hit, as are the hotdogs and kebabs. He's in full-on party mode, is Mehmet, thanks to Lev who's keeping him well oiled with gin. Talk about a smooth operator; singing and schmoozing, (with other men's wives) whilst cooking and generally entertaining everyone!

Lev is running around acting as 'general dog's body', doing whatever his dad asks him, which means I am free to enjoy myself!

Only Maureen isn't too happy. It's all the attention Mehmet is getting, judging by her barbed comments. It's hilarious!

"Are the burgers cooked properly?" she asks me at one point, then, "The barbeque does seem to be smoking a lot, Gina."

The kids are having a ball too. At one point I wrap Kenan up in a big towel to warm him after a long time in the pool and I notice that his tiny body is beginning to fill out again and see that the scars from the Hickman line are healing nicely. He looks at me and smiles – he is really enjoying his birthday. All the hard work has been worth it just to see the happiness in his eyes. It makes me want to hold him forever, but he has other things to do – he wants to play with his friends, not cuddle his mummy!

My mum then tries to have a dance with him, but his crush on Eli is growing and I think Grandma is cramping his style a little. As day turns to night, and the party moves inside, the kids eventually go to bed, but we grown-ups party on until dawn – what the hell, we deserve it. It crosses my mind that Mehmet might try and get amorous with Maureen, he's so pissed, but in the morning it only takes a nanosecond before I realise I've been hugely optimistic there. Maureen comes into the kitchen with a face like thunder while I am trying to clean up the debris, and announces that she's had to throw Mehmet out because he has seen her standing in only her bath towel and, as such, has invaded her privacy. Give me strength. Mehmet's version of events is that he needed some clean clothes from the room.

For the rest of the day they just glare at each other and hurl the odd insult. Thank God they are only here for the weekend, which, despite the 'Mehmet and Maureen Show', has been wonderful.

Something else wonderful is happening as well. Kenan can't stop talking about Eli. He even blushes when we mention her name. My baby is growing up, and it feels good.

Chapter Sixteen

After living in Javea for nearly two years, we decided to take a family trip back to England for a holiday, as by now England had become a 'holiday' destination and Spain was home.

Lev had, of course, been backwards and forwards regularly but, because of Kenan's illness, this was the first time we had gone together as a family. We stayed at Maureen's place in Chingford, all five of us squeezing into her three-bedroom, ex-council semi, which was cramped but cosy.

Maureen made us all very welcome and, as only nannies are allowed to, stocked her fridge full of English goodies the kids loved. The cupboards were groaning too, because (again like nannies always do,) there was food in abundance. Maureen also looked after the kids, which was great for me as I was able to pop out to the shops or for a coffee with my mates.

The weather was good, so we first treated the kids to a visit to a safari park we'd been to once before with Kenan. They loved the animals and the amusement rides and, as a family, we all revelled in a great day out. Kenan pointed out all the animals to his younger brothers, while Lev was like a 'Chinaman' clicking away on his camera.

A few days later we travelled to Wales to visit my nan, whom I hadn't seen in years. She was eighty-four years old and I figured I should go, in case she wasn't around much longer. It was the first time she'd met either Angelo or Louis, but Kenan remembered his Great-Nan and was looking forward to seeing her too.

We borrowed Lev's dad's car – an old N registration Mercedes – and after countless reminders not to 'burn the old girl' on the motorway, we set off. Louis slept most of the way, Angelo ate and Kenan played with his Nintendo. Always works well with kids – food and electronic toys.

I'd booked us into a quaint, 17th century hotel in Shrewsbury for the night, and we descended on this very quiet, elegant establishment late evening, much to the dismay of the other residents. But we were up and off again to finish the short journey to my nan's, after breakfast the next day.

Nan was standing, waiting for us outside her small, one bedroom chalet, which is housed inside a well looked after, warden-controlled, retirement development. The chalets were arranged around a cul-de-sac and Nan clearly wanted to show off her three handsome great-grandsons as we arrived. Like all good cul-de-sacs, the curtains were twitching and, as we got out of the car, the neighbours' doors opened too and before we knew it, we were being introduced to all my nan's friends.

Although ample for one old lady, the chalets were very small for a family of five, and after a *very* short tour around the house, the kids were asking what they could do next. A kid's playhouse wasn't far away, so we took Nan to lunch there and the boys tore around non-stop. I remember how proud I felt of Kenan as Nan kept on saying, "Don't they have a lot of energy?"

Nan only had my dad, and that was over sixty years ago, so I think it's fair to assume her recollection of children's energy levels had faded somewhat. I was so impressed by her though. At eighty-four she was still incredibly light on her feet and at only six and a half stone, quite the little lady. Thankfully, she was fit as a fiddle too.

Kenan came regularly to sit with her, asking questions all the time about the 'olden days' in his constant quest for knowledge. Angelo, our alpha male, kept trying to claim centre stage, demanding that Nan read his book over and over and Louis slept angelically. Nan loved it all. I don't know why, but I think of that day a lot. Perhaps it's because Nan's memories of Kenan will always be that of an energetic, polite and well-mannered boy, not a sick one.

When we arrived back at Maureen's that evening – and Mehmet had inspected the car – we relaxed and the kids played in the garden. Maureen had invited more of Lev's family to come over and we all spent a pleasant evening squeezed together in the living room passing old photos around and reminiscing about our own childhoods.

In all, there were two sons, three grandsons, two granddaughters, five nephews and one niece cluttering up the place with Maureen placed, proudly, in the middle. All the older ones fussed over the little ones and I watched on, happy to be there. As much as I don't really do the 'family' thing – being an only child – the memory is etched fondly in my mind.

Chapter Seventeen

September, and after the long hot summer, Angelo and Louis have started back at school and nursery. Kenan is starting back in a couple of weeks' time. He's moving up to the next class with his friends, despite missing most of last year, which is a huge relief. I'd been worried that the school might want to hold him back until he catches up.

Our kids won't be in school for long, though, because in about six weeks' time, we're all off for a 'once in a lifetime' holiday to Disney World in Florida! Kenan had wanted to go to Las Vegas, but I've managed to convince him we'll have much more fun visiting the theme parks at Disney World. We all need a proper break, somewhere to lose ourselves for a while, and we had promised Kenan we would go on an unforgettable holiday, once he was better.

We're pushing the boat out, going to America, but my great-uncle, Sid – God rest his soul – generously left me ten thousand pounds in his will earlier this year, with the proviso I spend most of it on the kids (or he'll come back and haunt me!)

I feel compelled to admit however, that we've already spent the money on a new kitchen. I'm not too keen on a 'visit' from Uncle Sid, though, so I told Lev we had to get the money together from somewhere.

I've booked Upper Economy tickets for us all with Virgin Atlantic, five nights in the Disney Animal Kingdom Hotel, with a balcony overlooking the grazing zebras, gazelles and giraffes, and then we're having a further five nights at the Dolphin Hotel which is right in the heart of all the fun. Even though it's pretty extravagant I feel driven to do it *right*. There is no way Uncle Sid is coming back to haunt me!

The kids are so excited about it that they are sending me potty, asking constantly how many days are left before we go – it's impossible to keep them off the subject. To distract them a little, I've given them a calendar so they can mark off the days until we leave. When Kenan starts back at school, I'm confident that our life is now completely back to normal. Every morning I have to contend with Kenan, Angelo and Louis, all driving me nuts and mucking around while I try to get them out of the door on time. It's wonderful!

Our recent run of good luck has just upped and left us however: fairly predictably really given that I've planned the holiday. Kenan started playing tennis again back in the spring; he even won a tournament in April, a year to the day he was diagnosed. But just a week after he started back at school, he went and slipped, whilst playing, hurting his arm pretty badly. He insisted it was alright, so the coach let him carry on, but that night his arm began to swell. By the morning, it was huge.

I took him to back to *Acuario* hospital and, after a quick glance, the doctor said Kenan needed an X-ray.

I paced up and down, muttering, "Typical. We're going on holiday to Disney World and Kenan breaks his arm!"

It's not quite as bad as that, fortunately. It's fractured and slightly splintered, so although his arm is in plaster, the doctor assures us it should be OK in time for our holiday. He may have to miss out on some of the faster rides, but as long as he's fit enough to go, we don't mind about that. Kenan, forever the actor, milked it of course, brandishing his cast around for everyone to see. All his mates have had to sign it. I was so relieved, it wasn't worse.

The boys are still, methodically, ticking off the days on the calendar until we leave – only two weeks left to go now. Lev came home yesterday, happy that the holiday is just around the corner and tonight he is cooking us a wonderful Mexican meal (and as usual using every utensil in the kitchen).

I've bathed Louis and put him into bed, so I can relax and enjoy my dinner. By the time we sit down at the table, Lev, like all good chefs, is merry, having had the wine flowing in the kitchen. My attention is taken up by Angelo, who is stirring the hot fajita mix of chicken and beef, so I barely notice Kenan stand up to get something from the kitchen.

Suddenly I hear an almighty crash. Now what? I push back my chair and run into the kitchen to find Kenan standing there with blood pouring down his face and a smashed bottle of Martini on the floor. I quickly realise it's the bottle Lev had put in the freezer, for me. It must have fallen out when Kenan had opened the door. What the hell was he doing in the freezer?

I can see that a shard of glass has bounced off the floor and sliced through his cheek, just under his left eye. Kenan is stunned; he hasn't realised yet what has happened. As his hand goes up to his face, where the flesh is gaping open, I scream, "No, Kenan, leave it!"

God, I've done it now. Kenan's hysterical, crying and screaming, "Mummy, I love you. I'm sorry, don't let me die, I'm going to die!" See what I mean? Forever the 'Drama Queen'.

Lev starts flapping around too and can't quite get a grip on the situation. I grab a tea towel and hold it firmly over Kenan's face to try and stop the bleeding. I notice then that his knee is also badly cut.

"Call my mum and dad, Lev, to come and look after Angelo and Louis. We need to get Kenan to the hospital."

Lev stares blankly at me. Grrrr men! He is in such a panic he can't remember their phone number. Snatching the phone, I quickly call them myself. No answer. Dad's mobile may be on, so I try that. No answer. My mum's mobile? No answer there, either. We'll all have to go to the hospital.

I instruct Lev to hold the towel on Kenan's face, and I get Angelo his coat and slippers on. I fetch a sleeping Louis from his cot, cover him with a blanket and fasten him into his car seat. Here we go again … back to *Acuario* hospital. We're seeing far too much of this place for my liking.

Lev's got it together at last though and has called ahead to inform the hospital we are coming, so they're expecting us, at least. He rushes in with Kenan, while I stay in the car with the other two, as they are both fast asleep.

We have had one bit of good luck … a plastic surgeon has waited for us and it's her careful stitching of Kenan's face that ensures there won't be a bad scar after it has healed.

My phone rings. It's Mum and Dad, who I've been ringing constantly – I was worried something might have happened to them, given the way things are going. However, they've just been out without their mobiles. I fill them in whilst pacing up and down outside the car, smoking a cigarette.

An hour or so later, Lev and Kenan come out and, all things considered, Kenan is fine. It could have been a lot worse. The surgeon has stitched his knee as well,

"Without an anaesthetic," Kenan points out, smiling proudly. "I just gritted my teeth and took it,"

What a sight he looks. My beautiful boy, with a row of stitches on his face, his knee covered in blood and a plaster cast on his arm. But he's so goddamned proud of himself I have to laugh – although deep down I am beginning to fret that we're not going to make it to America.

Once home and in bed, I promise myself that I'm not going to let Kenan out of my sight until we leave for Disney World.

With a week to go, we return to *Acuario* but this time to have Kenan's plaster cast removed. The doctor is happy with the results, although his arm looks terribly pale and skinny. We then wait for the plastic surgeon to examine Kenan's face. She's happy too with how it's healing, and after massaging olive oil into the scar to soften it and applying a skin coloured plaster to protect it from the sun, Kenan is good to go.

For the next three days, I try to wrap Kenan in cotton wool. It's hopeless of course, he just thinks I'm crazy and plays cat and mouse with me the whole time. The few days left feel endless, but eventually the day of departure arrives. We have made it; or rather Kenan has, and mercifully intact.

Phew!

Chapter Eighteen

The kids were so excited from the moment we left the house to set off for Disney World. They'd waited ages for this dream holiday, and there wasn't much me or Lev could say or do to calm them down.

The drive to the airport was full of chatter about what we were going to do and who was going to go on what ride first. By the time we got on the plane, me and Lev were worn out just listening to them, and this was only stage one of the journey! With no direct flight from either Valencia or Alicante, we had to fly to Heathrow first to catch a connecting flight to Florida. When we finally boarded the plane, the looks on the faces of our fellow 'Upper Economy' passengers, were a picture! It must have been their worst nightmare to find a ten year old, four year old and eighteen month old toddler, tucked into their midst.

But they need not of have worried. Kenan disowned us pretty much as soon as we boarded, leaving me and Lev to cart all the bags through the aisles, while he sat himself down, carefully arranging all the goodies from his free Virgin Atlantic rucksack.

By the time we joined him, Kenan was already sipping orange juice and checking out the film guide. Kenan watched films the whole flight, his headphones hardwired into his ears and I don't remember him speaking to us throughout the whole journey! Louis slept most of the way and Angelo ate his way through it, so all in all they all behaved very well.

Our holiday began with five nights at the vast Disney Animal Kingdom Hotel where we'd booked a family room overlooking the plains. The scale of everything there was just, 'Wow!'

It was surreal waking up each morning, looking down from our balcony onto the graceful gazelles and giraffes grazing from the tall trees. The hotel was completely immersed in its theme, from the massive thatched roof, wooden lodge that acted as the foyer, right through to the bedrooms. There were various theme parks to explore, and we figured if we filled up at breakfast and took fruit and buns with us, we could skip lunch and get round a park in a day.

But by the third day, Angelo and Louis were totally exhausted, so I took a day off to lounge around the ornate pools with them, while Lev and Kenan headed off for a day at Busch Gardens about an hour away, an African themed amusement park, which they both wanted to visit. It was as if my guardian angel was watching over me, because Louis fell asleep for a long afternoon nap and Angelo made a friend who he played with all afternoon. I totally relaxed with a Piña Colada and a ciggie or two, although some silly cow tried to have a go at me for smoking, even though I was in the designated area. By the time Lev and Kenan got back, early evening, I was well chilled. Lev was knackered, but Kenan was full of it and couldn't stop talking about his day.

When we moved on to the equally plush but even more posh, Dolphin hotel, we discovered our hotel balcony this time overlooked the boardwalk. The sights and smells below, I will never forget, but, it is the nights that I remember the most. When the lights came on, they brought to life all the restaurants and bars and their noise fused in satisfying harmony around us.

From our balcony we could see the impressive and intricate firework display that went off every night and must have cost thousands of dollars each time. Kenan and I loved to stand outside watching it, both of us mesmerised by the rhythmic blasts and the light shows that danced about in the dark sky.

Towards the end of our holiday, me and Kenan also realised our dream of swimming with the dolphins, and the reality was way better than we'd ever imagined. Lev watched, as we were introduced to our dolphin, Coral and as we stroked her nose, kissed her and got to know her a little, he took off with Angelo and Louis to the stands to watch us.

Swimming with Coral was one of the most amazing things I have ever done in all my life. She was effortlessly graceful and I held on tight to her fin, as she pulled me through the warm water until I was totally exhausted. Frankly, it was mind-blowing, and Kenan agreed too. The experience left both of us grinning like monkeys, speechless and I will treasure that moment for as long as I live, as it was one of the most special times me and Kenan ever shared alone together.

Afterwards, Lev surprised us with some pictures he'd taken. Somehow, even with Angelo and Louis in tow, he'd managed to scramble up the rocks surrounding the pool and had frantically taken lots of photos. Thank God Angelo and Louis were OK, because we now have the most fantastic pictures to remember it by.

Our two weeks in America passed far too quickly, as we were having such a wonderful time and it helped bond us all together again as a family, especially Lev and the kids. I even got the odd day to shop and I filled up the spare suitcases I'd taken with us. It truly was a holiday none of us will ever forget.

Flying home from Florida via Heathrow, we were able to make a quick stop at Lev's mum's, to freshen up before catching a flight to Valencia, from where we finally drove back to Javea. The journey took us eighteen hours but, nevertheless, we arrived home happy and relaxed. Little did I know that, in another eighteen hours, our life would change dramatically, again.

Lev

What a day, just me and Kenan, together at Busch Gardens, a day I often think about. Angelo and Louis were shattered after the visits we'd made to the theme parks, so me and Gina gave them a day off so they could just play around the pool at The Animal Kingdom Hotel – apt name for my lot!

The hotel was 'pukka' and every morning we'd sit outside on the balcony and watch the surreal sight of giraffes, wildebeests and other animals from the African plains eat their breakfast – and we were in the middle of Florida!

Anyway, after saying goodbye to Gina and the boys, me and Kenan walked the twenty minutes it took to get from our hotel room to the car park, and took off in the motor down the highway which led to Busch Gardens. It had always been a dream of mine to eat at a real American diner, so we stopped at one that looked the business for breakfast, along the way. I ordered the works – ham and grits (think that's their version of bubble and squeak) along with an endless amount of coffee, and although it was good it didn't beat an English brekkie, and generally, the place was a bit of a disappointment to tell the truth. 'Rain Man' ordered pancakes, but never ate them, as usual.

We then carried on to Busch Gardens, and luckily the place didn't let us down. What a park! The biggest roller coasters in the world awaited us – about six of them, all set in a picture-perfect safari park.

Kenan and me were very close that day and he kept cuddling me because he was so excited. At times I felt a bit uncomfortable, especially when people stared, but deep down I didn't really care what people thought. It's not my problem if some of the Yanks have a hang-up with showing their feelings. After all, we live in Spain where it's normal for strangers to greet one other with a kiss on each cheek!

On the first couple of rides, Kenan was 'bricking' it and kept dithering whether to go on or not, which made me lose my temper a bit. I told him he bloody better go on because I hadn't driven all that way for nothing. I should have kept my mouth

shut because he ended up dragging me on every ride
– twice! In the end they just weren't scary anymore.

We strolled around, chatting whilst we fed the
meerkats (Kenan's favourites). In fact, Kenan well
wore me out. For some reason, I was constantly
telling myself, 'Make the most of this day, Lev, it's
precious.' Perhaps it was because we didn't get to
spend much time together normally, or perhaps it was
because that was the day I noticed Kenan's lips
starting to chap and, although we didn't know it at
the time, it was probably the day he started getting ill
again.

We drove home exhausted and when we got to
the hotel, Gina was still lounging around the pool
with Angelo and Louis. She'd had a great day too –
she even managed to get into an argument with some
other guest, who'd told her off for smoking, even
though Gina was in a smoking area. Gina's response
when the Yank insisted she 'Stop polluting her
airspace' was to tell her to get rid of her enormous
gas-guzzling car and stop polluting hers!

That's my girl. Me and Kenan were in fits of
laughter.

We got along like mates on that holiday me
and Kenan, but him and Gina were a funny pair.
Always bickering, and they shared a bed too, which
made it even funnier for me to listen to. Angelo
wanted to sleep with me and Louis had his cot, so our
sleeping arrangements were made to suit.

It was the same at the Dolphin Hotel where
our room was huge. I suppose, like me, she might
have been worried about Kenan, even though we kept
it at the back of our minds. Gina has always been a
'better out than in' person, so maybe that's why she

quarrelled with Kenan. I just got drunk if I started to worry too much.

One night I made friends with a couple of Yanks in the bar, after leaving Gina watching TV with the kids. I agreed to a drinking contest but they had no idea they were dealing with a pro here. One of them was carried out! It was fun though and the blokes loved being entertained by the Cockney fella from London – they were a great audience! I've no idea how many drinks I was bought, but I do know I got lost on my way back to the room and fell asleep on a giant couch in the foyer, before being woken up by a security guard, who wanted to turf me out. I managed to convince him I'd forgotten which room I was in and he got me back to my bed, eventually.

Gina wasn't amused!

Chapter Nineteen

Kenan is beginning to worry me again. At times when we were in America, he was really tired after a day out, but we did do a lot of walking around in the heat. He's developed a cold now we're back, which I think he picked up on the plane, but it's another two weeks until his regular check up in Valencia and, not wanting to take any chances, I took him back to *Acuario* to see a doctor. He's been behaving peculiarly since getting back – just moping around with no enthusiasm for anything.

I was very nervous when the doctor examined him, but she confirmed that it was just a common cold. His glands are swollen and his throat is sore, so she's given him a course of antibiotics. But he's been on them for a few days now and I'm not convinced they're working that well. He doesn't seem to have improved much – his cold appears worse if anything and I know I sound like I'm overreacting, but it's almost like he's suffering from depression.

He's lost weight because he can't eat properly – his throat hurts too much to swallow. Maybe a trip

169

to McDonalds with some friends will cheer him up. Perhaps he'll have a milkshake at least.

Angelo and Louis are up for it, but for the first time I can remember, I have to persuade Kenan to come. He doesn't touch his milkshake, either; while we're there; he just sits quietly on a different table from everyone else, stirring his drink. Something is definitely wrong if he's not even interested in milkshakes.

"What do you think?" I ask my friends. "Do you think he's depressed?"

One or two of them try to talk to him, but he doesn't want to say much. None of them think it's anything serious, or maybe they don't want to say, in case it upsets me. I try to cheer Kenan up by offering him money to eat and God love him (and his love of money) he tries, but it's not going down easily. I leave the restaurant feeling thoroughly depressed myself.

His school work has started to tail off as well since we've been back and Kenan's teacher wants to see me. They are trying to push him but Kenan isn't keeping up. But you know what? His education is the last thing on my mind right now.

Nevertheless, on Monday morning I go in and using a translator, explain that as long as he is happy and alive I don't really give a toss about anything else. Not the best words I could use, but I am angry for some reason – in the back of my mind I feel that this may be serious again.

That night, I give the younger two a bath and while they are playing I ask Kenan a question I don't *really* want the answer to.

"Do you feel like you did last time, Darling?" dreading his response.

"No," he replies, turning away from me. But then I hear him mumble, "No, no, no. Please. No."

His words paralyse me. I can't remember putting the boys to bed after that, because I can't get Kenan's words out of my head.

Driving with Dad to Valencia, a few days later for Kenan's regular check up at *La Fe*, I try not to think that something might be wrong again. Like we always do, we sit and wait for the doctor, in our usual place by the window in the Day ward, until the doctor arrives and takes Kenan off for his blood tests.

"He's so quiet, isn't he, Dad?" I remark.

Dad nods, obviously troubled as well, but we don't dare let ourselves think it's anything other than a lingering cold – or a psychological problem.

Kenan returns after the test, his face drawn, and his thin shoulders slouched. Dad then goes for a coffee, while me and Kenan walk to another part of the hospital, where he needs a breath test, to check the amount of air in his lungs. He is never any good at this, but today he has hardly any puff at all. I can see he is struggling and that it's upsetting him.

"Come on, Kenan," I plead, "You can do it, Darling. Just take your time."

Before he blows again, the ward phone rings and the nurse pauses the breath test, to answer it. After she replaces the receiver, she turns and tells us we have to go down to the consultancy rooms to meet with Carlos, Kenan's doctor. Her face gives nothing away, but Kenan's face suddenly falls and unconsciously I start to shake. I ring Dad on the walk over and ask him to meet us there.

Slowly, we cross back through the hospital to Carlos' office and as soon as I see him, I know. Kenan knows too. Carlos looks serious as we sit down carefully into the soft seats across from his desk. He looks at me, then to Kenan and with a gentle voice, which is nonetheless straight to the point, says, "I'm so sorry Kenan. The leukaemia is back."

Instantly I grab Kenan's hand and squeeze it hard before I realise it is hurting him. His eyes fill with tears and I fight to muster all the control I have not to cry with him. I want to howl, want to bang the table, want to scream, "IT'S NOT FAIR!" But I am not going to let him see defeat in my face.

Instead, I say only, "We've done it before Kenan, we will do it again."

Tomorrow, Kenan will have to go back to his old, bare room on the Isolation ward, but for now he can come home and pack his bags. The dreaded Hickman line will be re-inserted for the chemotherapy and the whole awful process will start all over again. I send Kenan off to the canteen with my dad as I have to now call Lev. I have no idea how to tell him, and I am taken aback when he says that he is not surprised by the news.

He simply remarks, "I always knew it would come back one day." Did he? I didn't. Still, he's done in, I know he is.

I tell Lev to ask both his mum and dad to come over to help. Sod their petty quarrels. I need everyone this time and I am not taking no for an answer. I end the call and ring Paula to ask her if she will pick the kids up for me. I also ask her if she can find me a cleaner. Next, I call Floria for some moral support.

I don't cry – not yet – and after ending my call with Floria I head to the canteen to find Kenan and Dad. My poor baby is sitting quietly, hands in his lap, his face white with fear. My dad on the other hand is as red as a beetroot.

"Please, don't let the shock make anything happen to him too," I whisper to myself. I don't think I can take any more right now. Dad looks at me as I reach their table, "Kenan just said, 'What do I do, Granddad? I have leukaemia again.' What do we do, Gina?"

I don't know what we do. But I realise with a sinking heart that, without the benefit of ignorance, this time round we're all aware of what lies ahead. Kenan has that knowledge too, and the frightened look in his eyes is crushing.

On account of me demanding the whole family help out this time, whatever the consequences, Maureen has quickly organised her life back in England and has arrived in Spain within two weeks. She can stay for as long as we need her, for which I'm very grateful. Kenan loves her, and whatever our differences, she's a great support to have around, especially with the other two to look after.

Lev's dad, Mehmet can't make it until after Christmas, which in some ways is a good thing because it allows Maureen at least a month to settle in, before sharing a house with him again.

My mum and dad are here of course, so once more I put a rota system in place, and with the extra pair of hands around I am able to keep family life more stable. Word has started to spread around Javea that Kenan's leukaemia has returned and there are lots of offers of help coming in from friends too – this time I don't feel as if we have to do it alone. One bit of good news, is that my best friend of thirty-six years, in fact my whole life, has sold her house in England and is moving here to Javea. I'm thrilled she's coming.

Tracy lives in Lincolnshire with her husband Mike and their two children – Jack who is only two weeks younger than Kenan, and Tony, who is two weeks older than Angelo. Our grandmothers met at the school gates and the friendship has been passed down the generations. She's been trying to sell her house for ages to move here, but now the timing could not have been better. She needs to find a house here first, and she's called to say she's coming out at Christmas to look.

Because this is the second time Kenan has had leukaemia, it will be harder to cure and Carlos has told us he will need radiotherapy and a full bone marrow transplant to have any chance of beating it. We all know we're not a match, so he's been placed a donor list and who knows how long he'll have to wait. Time is crucial and I feel I'm really letting him down not being able to help him.

The chemotherapy has already started, intensively just like before, but unlike last time, he is suffering with the side effects straight away because his body is weaker from all the hell it went through the first time. This is how Carlos explains it to us.

"When you get a new car and it goes wrong, you put chemicals in it and it responds well. But as the car gets older and needs more chemicals, the response is slower." Basically, Kenan's young body has had so much medication pumped into it already that it is rebelling. He is prone to complications and is picking up colds very quickly as well, and every agonising day is becoming more of a worry.

Everything is worse this time around. And I mean, everything. Kenan has been in hospital for only two days but has developed a liver infection that is potentially very serious and I'm really concerned about how his treatment is going. Carlos has warned us that the infection could turn critical, although antibiotics are keeping it under control for the moment.

The truth of the situation at this stage is that we are now no longer dealing only with the leukaemia, but with a range of complications from its treatment – complications that threaten Kenan's life. Kenan isn't aware of this of course and it is my duty as his mum, to stay positive and not to doubt that he is going to get better. However, saying that, I'm struggling.

It hasn't helped that I've had to stay at the hospital full-time recently, because as a damp autumn has changed to a cold winter, flu is rife in Javea at the moment. Both Mum and Maureen are down with it. Maureen has bronchitis actually, so she isn't able to do much at all. I can't take the risk of catching anything, so I'm here for as long as they're ill.

I haven't seen Angelo and Louis for days. On top of that Lev was due back tonight but bad fog has affected all the flights from England. He's phoned to say he's starting a stint, from the film, 'Planes, Trains and Automobiles', and is hoping to fly back from Birmingham in the early hours of tomorrow morning – if he manages to catch the train to the airport in time. His dad should be dropping him off at the station about now. It's as if it's one set back after the other

Tracy and her family have made it over though, thankfully, to start house-hunting and are due to arrive here at hospital soon. I want to meet them outside, so I tell Kenan I'll be back with someone special, put on my coat and head for the steps, counting the minutes until they get here.

The feeling of relief when they arrive is immense. I hate to whine, but when I see them I realise how lonely I am here on my own again. Words can't describe how wonderful it is to see familiar faces that speak English! I need a cuddle, so me and Tracy stand outside the hospital and hug for ages but I'm conscious that poor Kenan is in need of his spirits lifting too. He's really low today, because he's been told that due to the liver problem, it's unlikely he'll be allowed home for Christmas.

I take Tracy, Mike and their kids up to Kenan's room and notice immediately from the blotches marking his pale face that my poor baby's been crying while I've been gone. I'm certain that seeing 'Aunty Tracy' will cheer him up and sure enough he perks up when he spots her. She's not allowed in the room, of course, but she manages to coax a smile from him from the other side of the glass, by pretending to fall down the stairs and pulling funny faces. I'm so glad to have good friends around me again.

Lev manages to get here the next day, and by the time he has arrived we're all in better spirits. Kenan's not having chemo at the moment because of the liver problem, so Lev and Mike scrub up and sit with him, staying for most of the day, playing poker and generally joking around.

When I leave later with Tracy, back to Javea to start house-hunting, the sky is winter dark, but I'm feeling happier than I have all week.

Christmas is just a couple of weeks away now, and the doctors have confirmed that Kenan will have to stay in hospital because of the problems with his liver. They're managing to control the infection, but apparently it is very unpredictable. With the chemo suspended he, at least, isn't having to deal with any side-effects, but I'm anxious that on the other hand it is slowing his treatment down.

He's monitored round-the-clock to check on the leukaemia and is being given a cocktail of different drugs everyday, but I'm as frustrated as hell right now.

There is no way I am allowing Christmas to be forgotten though. The whole family needs a bit of magic right now, so I have to start thinking about how we can bring Christmas to Kenan. Firstly, I need Tracy and Mike to move into our house so they can take care of the boys.

Mum and Maureen are still bedbound with flu unbelievably, which is beginning to piss me off because I need their help, but things are how they are so I'll just have to get on with it.

It's Louis' second birthday on the 18th December, but for the second year running I don't have the time to do anything for him. I feel dreadfully guilty, but thankfully he's too young to realise he's not having a party. Something has to give and my energy needs to be focused one hundred per cent on arranging the best Christmas I can for Kenan who is stuck, miserable, in a hospital bed.

In England it's so easy to get into the Christmas spirit with the crisp, cold air and dark afternoons, not to mention the endless commercials on the TV from October onwards. It's not quite that easy in Spain. The main celebration isn't until 6th January – *Los Reyes Magos*, or The Three Kings – the air isn't as chilly or the days so drawn in, but I'm throwing myself fully into the distraction of it none-the-less.

Kenan's more upset than I'd expected at not to being able to come home, but in a weird sort of way, me and Lev feel quite excited that we can at last do something to cheer him up. Over the next couple of weeks, I shop for presents and food, and by Christmas Eve I have everything Kenan has requested in his letter to Santa. He's ten now and although I suspect he doesn't believe totally in Father Christmas, he's still young enough not to want to leave it to chance either.

Lev has had an idea how to make it really special for him. He wants to get the presents into Kenan's room before he wakes up – which means breaking hospital rules. He says he's worked out a plan how to do it without getting into trouble – here we go again!

On Christmas morning, we wake at home very early and head for Valencia with Angelo sleeping in his car seat, and a big sack of presents stuffed into the boot of the car. Tracy and Mike are kindly looking after Louis and preparing Christmas dinner for the rest of the family while we are away. It's still dark and cold when we pull up outside the hospital, so I stay in the warm car with Angelo who's still asleep, while Lev puts his plan into action. Taking the sack of presents, he runs, two at a time, up the stairs looking like a crazy swag-man! He has to avoid the front desk – but once upstairs I know he'll be able to sweet-talk the nurse into putting the presents into Kenan's room.

He's been moved out of the Isolation ward as he's not having chemo, so I'm hoping they'll let us spend the day with him too. I'm half excited, half nervous that the 'Gestapo Chief' on the front desk may catch Lev, but ten minutes later he's back down, mission accomplished.

Kenan is still sleeping, but the nurse has said we can all go and wait for him to wake up. We park the car and creep quietly into the hospital. My tummy is fluttering with butterflies that are threatening to make me laugh. I feel about ten myself!

Outside Kenan's room, I look through the window, see my baby sleeping and so we sit down to wait. When daylight breaks through his room window, Kenan wakes up and the moment couldn't be more perfect. He stares at the sack Lev has placed inside his door, disbelief and joy all over his face. I nudge Lev to put on his mask.

"Come on." We walk together into his room with Angelo. "See," I say to Kenan, "Look what Santa delivered. I told you he'd come, didn't I!"

I'm not sure Kenan believes any of it, but he's playing along as much for Angelo as for himself. We spend Christmas morning happily together, sitting on hard chairs and the overnight bed, and although it isn't quite as it would be at home, all the planning and rushing around has been worth it a million times over. The nurses come and do what they have to do, and slowly Kenan gets through opening his presents, his delicate hands neatly taking off each piece of paper, his own mask firmly in place as Angelo keeps taking his off. At lunchtime, we leave Kenan to eat his Christmas meal, while we go across the road for burgers and chips instead of turkey and roast potatoes. In the afternoon, we settle down in Kenan's room to watch Angelo's favourite film at the moment, 'Pirates of the Caribbean' which Santa has been kind enough to bring. And in a bizarre way, it's one of the best Christmas Days I can remember.

A couple of days later, Kenan's friend, Eli comes to the hospital with the best present ever for him. Through a friend of a friend she's managed to get hold of a signed photo of Simon Cowell! On it he's written,

'Hi Kenan, get well soon, have a great Christmas, best wishes, Simon Cowell'

Wow! I'm as excited as Kenan. Me and Kenan are big into 'The X-Factor' right now, so it's given pride of place in his room where we can all see it. None of the staff know who he is because they're not really into 'X-Factor' here, so when one of the nurses asks Kenan if he's his uncle, Kenan plays up to it beautifully.

"Yes," he says, "he's my great-uncle, Simon who lives too far away to come and visit." Quick thinking Kenan and thanks for making his Christmas, Mr Cowell.

Chapter Twenty

Kenan went back into hospital in November 2006 and his granddad, Mehmet, arrived for the first time to see him shortly after Christmas. Mehmet's arrival boosted Kenan's spirits almost as much as the picture he'd received of Simon Cowell, which we were all grateful for, because recurring infections meant he'd been having an awful time of it in hospital.

My spirits however were being dragged down, and I could only blame myself. I had asked for all hands on deck and I know I told Lev to get both his parents over to Spain to help, but in hindsight, why the hell hadn't I seen disaster looming?

At least I was on the ball enough to know that Mehmet and Maureen wouldn't be able to share a room this time like they had at the party, so I'd given Mehmet a bedroom downstairs and Maureen one in another part of the house. I'd hoped they could be civil to each other for Kenan's sake and for the rest of us, but no, obviously we were expecting too much. They avoided one another like each was a bad smell, but at the same time tried constantly to score points

181

with the kids – it would have been comical if it wasn't so sad.

If Maureen made a cup of tea and Mehmet wanted something from the kitchen, they would step round one another steering clear of any body contact at all. I let it go because we already had quite enough to worry about. Or so I thought. Plenty more happened over the coming months to add to the stress load – particularly for Mehmet. It was as if we had a bad luck monkey on our backs.

Shortly after Mehmet arrived in Javea, he received a phone call to tell him that his former girlfriend, with whom he'd lived for years, in North Wales, had died. He and LLonis had split up a couple of years beforehand, and a short time afterwards she had been diagnosed with multiple sclerosis.

As her condition worsened, she had got back in touch in touch with Mehmet and asked him to take her to Switzerland to help her end her life. She said that living had become too painful. He promised her that after Kenan was back on the road to recovery he'd come and see her, and they'd discuss what to do.

Sadly she wasn't able to wait that long. As Mehmet left for Spain, LLonis ordered a taxi and drove to a nearby lake. She couldn't swim, and the walk into the deep water brought her the relief she sadly wanted. She had intended to take her own life, but Mehmet, naturally, was devastated. He was hurting badly, but aware he'd not long arrived and knowing we needed him here with Kenan, he made the heart-wrenching decision not to go back home for her funeral.

The bad luck monkey struck again a few weeks later, when Mehmet's life-long friend died

182

from cancer. A week after that, Mehmet had a vivid dream, in which his younger brother was screaming, but no matter how hard he tried, Mehmet couldn't get to him. Later that day, my sister-in-law rang and told Mehmet that his brother had died from a massive heart attack – the very same night as his dream.

This time I insisted he go back for the funeral. In two and half months Mehmet lost three people he cared deeply for. I prayed it wasn't an omen.

Kenan's condition was stable by the end of February, thankfully, and he was at home in-between his chemotherapy bouts. A donor had been found surprisingly quickly – a German man – and we kept joking that when it was all over Kenan would be able to speak fluent German. But right now we were hanging in there just waiting for him to get well enough to undergo the transplant.

The last thing any of us needed was conflict, but when Mehmet got back from England following his brother's funeral, tension levels in the Gatoli-King household grew unbearable. Mehmet had been under a lot of stress for the previous few months and he had very little patience with regards to Maureen. He wasn't interested in trying to build bridges and neither was she.

When I was around, all conversation, especially at mealtimes, became directed at me because the two of them refused point-blank to talk to one another. The pressure gauge was rising and with it the inevitability of a huge row.

It all kicked off one Sunday afternoon following lunch at a restaurant down on the beach.

When we stopped the car outside home, Mehmet immediately took Louis out of his car seat and carried him up the back way through our garden and waited on the naya outside, to be let in through the kitchen. The shutter was down so he couldn't see into the room. The rest of us collected all the stuff out of the car, before walking up the path and in the front door, not realising that Mehmet was outside the back. Incessant banging on the shutter quickly told us where he was so Lev went into the kitchen, let in his dad and Louis, and then all hell broke loose.

"You old cow, you saw me and heard me outside, why didn't you let me in?" he shouted at Maureen, unable to hold back any longer.

"I didn't see you," Maureen argued meekly. But Mehmet really needed to let it all out and called her every name under the sun, insisting that she'd just ignored him. Maureen stood her ground – and all this in front of the children.

To this day I don't know what the truth was, but I have had enough arguments with Maureen in my time to know that she's a master at playing the sweet and innocent. Enough was enough though. Usually it's me that loses my temper, but Lev had had it. The kids were upset, after all, their granddad had been shouting at their nanny, and he all but ordered the two of them to their rooms to calm down. We didn't need the added strain of Maureen and Mehmet showing themselves up, but on and on it went, nonetheless.

It was such a small thing really, but that was just the first of many petty rows that broke out and quite frankly, I grew increasingly sick and tired of it.

184

Chapter Twenty-one

Kenan is over his various infections, and is back home, fighting the leukaemia again. His chemotherapy has resumed, so the frequent trips to the hospital are a routine part of our lives again, but the rota system is back in place and we're managing.

It's common knowledge in our little town that Kenan's leukaemia has returned and people are being very kind, constantly asking what they can do to help. We're pretty much sorted on the day to day stuff, but there is one thing I've been thinking about doing for some time, that I hope everyone can join in with.

Unlike in the UK, Spain doesn't benefit from a lot of charity work and the hospitals are almost solely dependent on government funding. I'm hoping to get all the people who've asked if they can help involved, by raising some money for the hospital and Lev has come up with the good idea of a sponsored head shave. Kenan's hair is starting to thin again with the chemo, which is as gutting for Kenan as it is for us because his new curly head of hair is his crowning glory. He loves it. We're quietly hoping that a sponsored head shave will help soften the blow of losing it and make sporting a bald head again more fun.

A couple we know, Gary and Sandy own a small, friendly bar close to the beach and have said we can hold it there – it will be just perfect. I've printed off some flyers, contacted the newspapers and been in touch with the local radio station – Bay Radio. The station owners, Danny and Andy, are also friends of ours and me and Kenan have been on to plug the event – Kenan was a complete professional! His on-air request to local shop owners and listeners to donate prizes for the raffle has resulted in Sandy being deluged with gifts at the bar, which is great.

The first thing Kenan says when he wakes up on the big day is, "Mummy, what shall I wear? After all, I'm the guest of honour."

We spend ages finding an outfit he's happy with, so by the time he's dressed it's already time to go. We arrive at the bar and meet our scalpers for the day – Karen, Eli's mum, and her friend Paul. They've sharpened their clippers and have their scissors at the ready. Loads of people are already here, so after a grabbing a drink to calm my nerves, we start the head shaves.

Kenan and Lev are first and I have a lump in my throat as Karen and Paul get to work. I watch their hair fall to the ground, but feel strangely detached from it. Luckily they both look great when it's done.

Throughout the day, fifty or so people have their hair shaved off, including two very brave women, who finally agree to it after an increasing number of gin and tonics provide them with some

Dutch courage. They alone raise the fantastic sum of one thousand euros.

The local newspapers have arrived and taken pictures of Kenan, and he's loved being centre of it all. The day has been a huge success and, OK, we haven't cured Kenan's leukaemia or taken away the fact that he still has radiotherapy and a full donor transplant to get through, but we have managed to put it to one side for a few hours and have a bit of a giggle.

Kenan is on a high from the day, which has helped boost his will to fight, and we've raised nearly five thousand euros for *La Fe* hospital which is a spectacular result.

As for all the bald men, and the two women, walking around Javea, well thank God the weather is good this spring!

Lev

It was something positive to do I thought, good for Kenan and we had a good turnout, all the 'faces' of Javea were there, pissed as puddings the lot of them. I went first to get the ball rolling, but it was easy for me because I'd done it before when Kenan lost his hair the first time around. Kenan did it next, sitting beside me on one of the two chairs Gary and Sandy had set up on the front terrace area of the bar. Diamond couple they are (from Essex of course) – and they'd done a blinding job, laying out nibbles for everyone and organising a chocolate fountain for the kids.

The day got more interesting the more people drank, and Karen and Paul, who are West End trained, shaved away like a couple of sheep shearers! My dad looked pretty cool – like Mussolini, and Gina's dad, Tony, pulled off a mean *Telly Savalas*. Angelo, bless him, a chubby-heeked five-year-old looked like *Buster Bloodvessel*.

It's amazing how much some people were prepared to pay to see someone bald though – we got a grand alone for the raven locks of 'Gorgeous George'. He'd held out that far! And a pretty bird with long, dark hair did it too for a grand, along with her mate. Other guys were buying their way *out* of being shaved, knowing their wives would go mental. I made sure they coughed up and sent Kenan round with the pot to hassle everyone for a bit of dosh.

Kenan loved the day, eating his way through the chocolate fountain but, as always, he was thinking of the other sick kids.

"Daddy," he said. "This just isn't for me; it's for the other kids at the hospital as well."

I was real proud of him, because we had raised a 'shed' load too.

Chapter Twenty-two

At the end of February, Tracy and her family left England and moved to Javea. She was just the tonic I needed as Mehmet and Maureen were wearing me down. Also my mum, my rock and confidante the first time round, had started to yield under the strain and was showing the first signs of depression. I'd seen it before in her, three times in fact, but at this point it was the last thing I needed. In my experience, depression builds up for a long time, until it is kicked off by the most trivial of things, as it was for my mum.

The trigger for her depression, the straw that broke the camels back, was that she wanted to move house. She thought their three bedroom villa was too much for her to look after and she became consumed with selling it. Obviously it was more than that, but her obsession meant that she couldn't be there to help me. She was still happy to stay with Kenan in hospital – in fact she was able to cope better there she said, where she had some control – but she didn't feel well enough to help look after Angelo and Louis any more.

Whether or not she brought Dad down too or it was just our circumstances, I don't know, but he was as low as well, whining to mum about missing England. She in turn unloaded his whines on to me, but to be honest I just didn't have time for any of what I saw as, their self-indulgent nonsense. It felt as if my whole family was crumbling around me, so Tracy was my saviour, the life-long friend I could turn to, to help me out.

When she arrived she immediately took off my shoulders what she could. She looked after Angelo and Louis along with her own kids, and I was able to put my energy into looking after Kenan, overcoming his growing number of medical hurdles.

But it still didn't solve the fact that as a family we weren't doing very well at all. All of us were rowing with one another, especially Maureen and Mehmet, and when Lev's brother, 'Big Kenan', came out to see us, it only got worse. It was his first visit to our house – pitiful really, given that our Kenan had already come through leukaemia once – and I can only say it was pathetic watching Mehmet and Maureen try and outdo each other in front of their sons.

Mehmet got progressively more wound-up and started drinking more and, day on day, Maureen grew ever more fractious. She drove us all mad with her, 'What did I do?' routines, clearly intended to try and get Lev and 'Big Kenan' on her side instead of Mehmet's. It was exasperating. All of us are pretty hot-headed in our family – I blame the Mediterranean mix – but before long Tracy got herself caught up in the rows too.

One afternoon, she was seeing to the kids upstairs while I got dinner ready for everyone. The kids were running riot up there, except for Kenan (who was well enough to be at home) and Tracy's boy Jack, who were playing quietly on their Nintendo Gameboys. They were interrupted by Tracy who suddenly started arguing with Maureen, who'd followed her upstairs to help with the kids.

I don't know to this day what actually happened, but looking back, I think that might have been the start of Tracy trying to control everything and everyone around me. Coming down the stairs, she was screaming full-on at Maureen. At the bottom, Maureen 'dissed' her away with her hand and Tracy just went mad, lunging at her over the sofa. Once again, this was all in front of poor Kenan, who ran off in tears to his bedroom, leaving the rest of us standing there in utter amazement.

Even though neither of them would say what it was all about, I quickly defended Tracy knowing full well how Maureen can get to you. Part of me thought that Tracy had overstepped the mark with Maureen – she was in my house and shouldn't have gone off like she did – but, in truth, I couldn't be bothered with either of them. They could sort it out.

I went and sat with Kenan instead, who was crying in his bedroom. Maureen followed me in which infuriated me even more. I was just so sick of it all; the petty squabbles between Maureen and Mehmet, their points scoring over their sons, my parent's inability to see the bigger picture with their constant sulking and feeling sorry for themselves. At that moment I really thought *I* was going to crack. I had to do something to lessen the load and there was only thing I could do – Maureen had to go.

We told Maureen the next day that it was impossible to have her and Mehmet living under the same roof and that, as her relationship was now strained with Tracy, who was often around helping me out, it was better that she moved somewhere else.

We own a studio apartment in the beach area of town which was empty at the time, so she could stay there. Maureen cried and pulled at the heart strings but me and Lev stuck to our decision – for the sake of our sanity she had to go. Mehmet of course loved every minute of it. Maureen is steely though, and she refused to move into the flat. Behind our backs she called my mum with a sob story and my mum let her stay with them. It didn't last long given my mum's frame of mind. Once the spare bedroom was all messed up, Maureen was asked to move to the flat.

To be fair to Maureen, never once did she desert Kenan or shun from helping out with the boys. She did go back home for a break for a couple of weeks, but where the children were concerned she was always wonderful. She was here to do a job and that is what she did. It's so sad we couldn't all get along, but I could no longer live with the daily drama – it was literally draining me to my core.

Chapter Twenty-three

The part of Kenan's treatment that me and Lev have been dreading more than any other is the radiotherapy. He never needed it last time around, so this is new territory for us and, given the problems that Kenan has already had, we're anxious about it. Carlos has again done his best to explain to us how it will work, and all I can say is that it sounds invasive and gruelling.

His first session is in a month's time on 2nd April – our wedding anniversary. Our mission until then is to make sure that Kenan enjoys this month at home. His liver problem is still under control thankfully, although we've been informed it will never fully recover, and at the moment he is feeling as good as can be expected (which if I'm honest isn't great).

There's a bit of an atmosphere at home as the strain of extended family living beneath one roof is taking its toll. Maureen has gone home to England for a couple of weeks for a break and we all feel better for it. I include Maureen in that statement because all the bickering and finger-pointing has not been easy for her either. Of more concern to me though, is that it's been really hard for Kenan because he loves his nanny and hates seeing her upset during all the family rows that have been blighting his time at home.

Kenan's much more relaxed now she has gone back for a while. He's really keen to get out and about before he goes into hospital again, so when Lev suggested taking Kenan and some friends to *Terra Mitica* the other day, a theme ride park in Benidorm. I let them go, even though I was nervous Kenan wasn't up to it. After a night on the booze, Lev had to wolf down a big breakfast and a large coffee with a couple of painkillers to get there, but I found that quietly satisfying, given the stomach churning rides he had to go on.

Lev's brother, 'Big Kenan' went with them, along with Tracy's boy, Jack and Kenan's school friends, Emily and Eli, and at some point during the day Eli developed a crush on Kenan. Finally!

Kenan's been keen on Eli for ages! By the time they all got home, the girls were giggling and Kenan's face was blushing red every time Eli's name was mentioned. Young love is blooming for sure and Kenan appears healthier overnight, now Eli has walked into his heart.

Eli's mum and dad are friends of ours, Karen and Simon and they live in a beautiful part of Javea called Granadella, with Eli and her older sister, Alice. It's a bit off the beaten track but the views along the long, winding mountain road that takes you to their home are well worth the drive.

The pebble beach is surrounded by caves and it's a bit like living next to a pirate's cove. It is believed that Granadella beach was once a smuggler's den and there are people here who suspect it still is. I don't know, but I love the sense of drama it adds to the place.

Karen and Simon's house overlooks the bay and it's where we're spending today – Mother's Day. We're having a BBQ on the beach and everyone has chipped in with the food and the drink. Paula and Martin have come with Emily, Tracy with Jack and Polly, and our other friends Sharon and Ian are here with their daughter, Kirsty. It is one of those rare, perfect days when life feels complete. Even my mum and dad have popped down with their mates, Penny and Peter – although Mum is sitting in the car most of the time, as it's warmer than sitting on a rough blanket on the chilly stones.

It is a bit cold being only March, but the sky is bright and none of us really notice the nip in the air. The kids are having a great time running around freely between the beach and the house. I love watching them all – especially Kenan and Eli spending time together. But before we know it, the sun starts to go down and although none of us really want to call it a day and go home, we're all getting tired – especially Kenan. Reluctantly, we pack up and say goodbye to everyone.

Eli is hanging round our car for ages and she runs after us waving as we drive away. On the way home, Lev, always the master when it comes to hatching a plan, starts to work out a way to get Eli and Kenan together. To my surprise, Kenan is more than eager for Daddy to play cupid for him. So later on, they sit down and send Eli a text – would she like to come out with Kenan next week as part of a foursome? The other two being Emily and Jack, who don't really fancy each other but we're sure will go along anyway. A swift 'Yes!' beeps back on his phone. The whole thing is really cute for us, but Kenan is taking it very seriously and talks about it every opportunity all week.

We take him to down to the beach to meet Eli the following Saturday. She's waiting for him outside the pizzeria with Jack and Emily. Me and the other mums hang around like spare parts, before we're banished to a bar next door. As I walk off I hear a very confident Eli say to Kenan, "Come on," and when I turn I see him following obediently behind her. Ahh bless, it is so sweet.

Through the glass wall in the bar, we watch them have their meal and then they all play together on the beach until we call time and take them home.

The Saturday after that, Eli and Kenan want to meet up again, but this time we suggest the park. Treating them to lunch every week is a bit too much of an expense at their age! Emily and Jack don't feel 'that way' about one another, so this time it's just Kenan and Eli, which suits them better anyway.

We've packed up a picnic, Lev has bought a champagne style bottle of kid's fizzy fruit-juice and this time we drop them off at the park down the road. Again we are sent away, which means we have to keep driving round and round the park so we can spy on them. Not easy as there are a lot of trees in this park! It makes me reflect how young love is just so perfect, whilst grown-up love is permanently testing.

They spend nearly every day together after that date, before Kenan goes back into hospital and he is so happy. The day before he has to leave, Lev takes them both down to the beach again even though it is raining and talks Kenan into giving Eli a kiss.

So, outside the burger bar, in the pouring rain Kenan kisses Eli for the first time – a little peck on her scarlet-red cheek. Lev tells me later that she skipped off saying "I'm so happy now."

I knew from that moment, Eli and Kenan were destined to be soulmates.

April 2007 and here we are. The day has come for us to go back to *La Fe*, although we have no idea how long for or what to expect. On one of our last few precious days at home together, me and Kenan headed to the hospital in Valencia for a meeting with Carlos so he could tell us more about the radiotherapy and what was to going to happen. Also, Kenan needed to be fitted with a special body mould, which is where he'll lie when the treatment starts.

I was more tense than usual when I left for Valencia with Mum and Kenan, and my nerves got worse the more we walked around searching for the *Radioterapia* department – and I thought I knew the hospital really well by now.

For some reason, I've just got a bad feeling about all this radiotherapy business. Mum was nervous too, but Kenan was a blank page. He sat quietly between us while we waited to see the doctor, and said nothing when he was handed a surgical gown to change into before we went through to get the mould fitted.

We had to pass through a huge, metal, vault door, at least a metre thick, into a larger room, and at that point I could finally tell that Kenan was scared – so was I, but I kept smiling at him while the doctor explained how they were going to fit him to a mould and that he was to lie down in the model already there.

The doctor stood behind a Perspex screen and, as far as I could tell, plotted dots and measurements into a computer, while another doctor stood next to Kenan altering the spongy material until it fitted his body exactly. This is where he is going to have to lie when the doctors give him his radiotherapy; basically, stripping his body of his own ill-fated cells to prepare it for the transplant.

In our meeting Carlos explained that Kenan will need two, forty-minute, sessions a day for three days, one in the morning and one in the afternoon. During each one he'll have to lie, perfectly still, for twenty minutes each side – it sounds as if he's going to be roasted in an oven or something. I guess he is in a way. Luckily he can listen to CDs if he wants to, to help pass the time.

Afterwards, he went for an MRI scan in another part of the hospital and, again, he sat quietly between me and my mum, saying nothing. He called Eli on his mobile phone and I was shocked by their conversation – steel doors and bed moulds are so far removed from the type of carefree chatter that two ten year olds should be having. It was hard listening to him, because he is missing out on so much at the moment but, even so, I smiled.

He'd seen Eli the day before when our two families had met down the beach for a farewell dinner. To my surprise he'd got very upset which is unlike Kenan. He's like me and doesn't want to cry in front of people, but he's scared this time, really scared.

Now, as I sit in his bedroom packing his bags, I can't help but hope that putting him through this is going to be worth it and that the donor transplant will this time be the cure we expect it to be.

What if it isn't? I check myself, and refuse to think any further down that road. It's my responsibility to be optimistic and reassure Kenan that it will all be OK.

My heart is heavy today however. I always find this part difficult, him leaving and me never knowing when he'll be home again but, as usual, I get on with the job, keeping my feelings to myself. It's my own fault, but no one really knows how hard it is for me, sorting through the myriad of DVDs, PSP games, Lego sets and various toys which help to keep Kenan amused during his stays. It takes me ages to pack, because each time he goes into the Isolation unit everything must be brand new, sprayed with an anti-bacterial spray and placed inside a wipe-clean case, just to be allowed in his room.

The family is really getting to me, as well, at the moment – my head is whirling with it all. For the first time since this all started, my mum and dad are in no frame of mind to help me out with the kids and Lev's dad, Mehmet, has returned home to England for a week, to sort some stuff out. So with Maureen gone too, I've had to ask Mike and Tracy to stay at our place so they can look after Angelo and Louis.

We've got to leave soon, so I make sure the other boys are both OK and that everything is as sorted as it can be, for Tracy. Me and Lev then kiss them all goodbye and set off with Kenan for the hospital.

We've been asked to come in at five o'clock in the evening, in preparation for his treatment the following day. We're leaving early so we can stop in Valencia for a 'last' supper treat at an American burger restaurant that Kenan likes. There's nothing wrong with his appetite at the moment, that's for sure. Kenan eats the all-American burger with fries, washed down with a thick milkshake and then he demolishes a gooey, chocolate dessert – I can't blame him, given that he has only the delights of hospital food to look forward to.

Lev has adopted his silly mood like he always does in front of Kenan, asking him if we should move to America when Kenan gets out and eat all-American burgers every day. Part of me knows that Lev's only *half* joking too, because he's mentioned the idea to me several times. A fresh start might be a good thing for us all.

Kenan loves the idea actually, until he remembers Eli and reminds Lev he has a girlfriend now and doesn't want to upset her by upping sticks and moving across the Atlantic.

It feels really weird, sitting here in this restaurant; the three of us laughing, joking and chatting like it's a normal day out. I feel so blessed to have this time together with Kenan, but in the pit of my stomach I somehow know we're enjoying only the calm, before the storm.

We leave the restaurant and arrive at *La Fe* in good time. Kenan is admitted and Lev leaves for the hospital flat that's provided for family, while I reacquaint myself with the black, lie-back (or not) chair in his Isolation room, the same one he always goes back to.

Sleep eventually comes to me, although at some point during the night, Lev, unable to sleep in the apartment, comes back to the hospital and settles in one of the big, squashy, overnight chairs in the lobby.

In the morning, he comes to say goodbye to Kenan before leaving for work in England again. For the first time ever, Kenan asks him to stay and, of course, Lev says he will. I can see why he needs Lev around, with his silly pranks and light-hearted ways to take the edge off how serious everything is. But there is no need for us both to be here, and if my baby wants Daddy with him, I will say goodbye instead and go back to Javea earlier than planned. I'll swap shifts with Lev when the radiotherapy is over, in a few days time.

Shortly after I arrive home, Lev calls me. Kenan has completed his first dose of radiotherapy and is doing fine. The nurse had collected Kenan and taken him to the *Radioterapia* department where he was duly placed into his moulded 'bed' and zapped. He was returned to his room an hour or so later. I feel a little relieved knowing that Kenan now has one round out of the way and is doing OK.

Later, after the next session, Lev calls again but with less reassuring news. Kenan isn't feeling well now and my chest begins to ache because I'm not there with him.

"Fuck me, Gina," Lev says, "Kenan said this fly somehow got into the room and was literally radiated out of the air. Mid-flight it just dropped to the floor – buzzzz thud!"

The image sends a chill through me. How brutal radiotherapy must be – how brutal it must be for Kenan having his body killed off in such a way.

As the radiotherapy continues, the more sick and weak Kenan feels. All Lev can do is keep telling him that it's nearly over; that his body is almost ready for the transplant and then he'll be on the mend again. By the end of the third and final day, when I go back to the hospital, I feel enormous relief that it is over because when I see Kenan, I'm not sure he could have taken another day – he is so very sick and low right now. What a shocking difference a few days have made.

I ask the doctor if he'll be able to cope with the transplant, which takes place tomorrow, because the radiotherapy has left him in unbearable pain. But no one has any concerns about him not being able to go through with it. Kenan's reaction is – normal. Yeah right.

After a few hours together, I say goodbye to Lev and promise to call him when he lands in England, and me and Kenan settle down, ready for the transplant the next day.

As it turns out I don't have anything to worry about regarding the actual procedure of the transplant. In contrast to the radiotherapy it's very straightforward – just like a blood transfusion or the chemo. The nurse attached a small bag of the donor's blood to Kenan's Hickman line and that was it. We sat and played cards and watched DVDs as it seeped into Kenan's body. It only took an hour or so before the bag was empty and then I left Kenan to rest.

I'm having a quick ciggie outside, before talking to Carlos again. I can't stop thinking how ironic it is that a complete stranger can have a closer blood match to Kenan than any of his own family and I'm thinking about that as I head back up the stairs to Carlos.

"What do we do now?" I ask him, straight up, because I'm past pussyfooting around.

"Gina, now we wait," he replies. "We wait and hope that the transplant is a success."

Lev

I'll never forget the bridge that links the Cancer ward to the Radiotherapy unit. I wheeled Kenan along it, dreading every step I took, because each one took us closer to that imposing, vault-like room. Like Gina, I just had a bad feeling about radiotherapy. Ok, it was going into the unknown again, but no one had mentioned radiotherapy first time around and it arrived as a real curve ball.

I remember feeling cold all over when Carlos told me that Kenan was going to need it, and that feeling didn't change when the radiotherapy started. When Kenan told me about the fly dropping to the ground, well, I knew my instincts were right and to this day, I think letting him go through with it was the wrong decision.

Maybe I'm looking for something to blame, but if we'd given him another stem cell transplant, maybe we'd at least have had another couple of years with him. I have so much guilt and regret about that.

When he was diagnosed the second time, I wanted to take him, there and then, to a specialist cancer centre in America, which I'd discovered, through my internet studies, was considered to be one of the best in the world. I wanted to let them have a crack because I desperately needed to feel certain that I was doing *everything* in my power to get him better, but I kept my mouth shut.

Sometimes I question that decision so much, it's suffocating – should I have done this or that? – Who knows?

Maybe Gina's right, maybe Kenan's future was in the hands of a Higher Power, whoever or whatever that is.

Chapter Twenty-four

When Kenan went back into hospital for the radiotherapy and transplant, I had no idea how mentally draining it would turn out to be. Despite my reservations about the radiotherapy, in my head I'd imagined him up and running around virtually straight away, but the radiotherapy took so much more out of him than even we'd anticipated. His distressing reaction to it made it feel as if the walls were finally closing in around me and I almost caved under the pressure – I didn't know what to do anymore.

My family was still unable to cope with anything and my response was to grow increasingly angry with everyone. Most of the contempt I felt was directed towards my mum and dad who, in my view, were being weak and ineffective. I thought they were being selfish, thinking only of themselves, while Kenan lay in hospital fighting, so bravely, for his future.

The only people who didn't piss me off for one reason or another were Mehmet and Lev. Don't get me wrong, Mehmet was far from perfect but with

Maureen out of the house, life at home at least was less explosive.

But Mum was an emotional mess and feeling sorry for herself and, I admit, I didn't handle her depression very well. Dad had found a female diversion to help him out, and it was getting so obvious that there was no doubt my mum's confidence was being knocked by that as well.

Her name was Patsy and despite being married, she hung around my mum and dad a lot of the time, pretending to be my mum's friend. One night she was so drunk, she couldn't drive home and my mum and dad let her stay the night at their house. Some friend Patsy turned out to be!

When Mum went to bed, Patsy and my dad stayed up drinking until the early hours of the morning. Mum realised when she woke up that dad hadn't come to bed all night and it caused a huge row between them. Dad blamed it on the drink and said he didn't know what he was doing, but later that day I was out with both of them and Mehmet, when Patsy came in and made a beeline for my dad. A smile stuck on one of her two faces, she called him her 'knight in shining armour' which made me feel sick.

I blamed Patsy totally for the unease between my parents – she was taking the piss out of us all – and, finally, as I watched Patsy continue pushing her luck, flirting with my dad, showering him with kisses I couldn't keep my mouth shut anymore.

She was acting as though my mum wasn't even there, and Mum, well aware by now that Patsy was predatory, carted Dad off home, no doubt to give him what for. Mehmet went to the bar for some more drinks then, probably secretly hoping to move in on

Patsy now Dad had gone, so that was my chance to tell her what was what. She was droning on about how nice my parents were, but I cut her piss-taking words short.

"You do realise that my mum and dad have had lots of affairs, don't you?" This was true. "And, you" I told her, "are just one more pawn in their game. That Patsy, is all you will ever be. They are still together and always will be, so back off." I drank my drink and left.

My anger wasn't only at Patsy of course; it was deeper than that, although she was a satisfying target. I was under so much strain but I couldn't give in to it, never ever, and I expected the same from those around me. I was obsessed about keeping going, keeping everything moving along for Kenan, for Angelo, for Louis, for Lev and for my own sanity. If I said jump, I wanted those closest to me to jump, not to be weak and fall down.

My dad wouldn't stay at the hospital with Kenan, Mehmet did, so that was a weakness; Mum was turning into a pathetic whiner, so that was a weakness; Maureen and Mehmet just wanted to score points off one another in front of Lev, so that was a weakness – weak, weak, weak the lot of them.

I'm sure that Patsy was no more than an innocent distraction for Dad, a way for him to escape the turmoil around us and that Mum's deepening depression was stemmed in unrelenting worry about Kenan. Mehmet and Maureen were just two people struggling to get along after being forced to live together, many, many years after a hostile divorce. My anger brewed bitterly, in a way it helped me to cope. Getting mad stopped them all getting a piece of me.

I daresay they all probably felt the same way about me and my unforgiving, bitchy mouth, but big, bad Gina needed to be strong because strength was all I had.

I didn't have the patience to deal with other people's problems. Not when my son's body had effectively been killed off by treatment for a cruel, unpredictable disease and then brought back to life again. Watching my child being reduced to nothing was absolutely destroying me and even though my parents and Lev's parents often said they wished it was them, it wasn't, was it?

It was *my Kenan*, my baby, my life.

Chapter Twenty-five

Kenan has immediately started going downhill – and fast. The transplant that we've poured our every ounce of hope into, isn't working.

'How can it not be working?' I scream silently at Carlos when he tells me. The transplant is meant to cure him of this bloody disease! I can barely look Carlos in the eye as he tells us that Kenan's body is rejecting the donor blood cells. It's something called *graft versus host*, where the newly transplanted cells attack the patient's own. Only identical twins carry the exact same tissue types, so while Kenan's donor is close, the match is not exact.

Carlos says that it's a common complication for donor patients and we're not to worry too much. I don't care that it happens to a lot of patients, I wasn't prepared for it to happen to Kenan and whilst Carlos doesn't seem overly worried, that doesn't make it any easier to witness. It's not just a case of it 'not working,' Kenan's reaction to it 'not working' is horrific. His skin is showing us graphically what is going on inside his body.

Daily he's developing blisters all over him, inside his mouth and down into his gullet, which means he can't eat. His tongue has patches, similar to bite marks, all along the side of it which give him a lot of pain – he actually looks like a burns victim. And each hour I wait by his bedside he looks worse.

I'm not impressed by Carlos' reassurance that his skin will regenerate quickly – not quickly enough as far as I'm concerned. I'm so worried that I am bad-tempered with everyone at the moment, except Kenan of course, who is already agitated, uncomfortable and very down. It's not fair on him. It will be a week before we know if the donor cells have grafted or not – I'm not sure I can take much more.

On the rota system, Mum is due to sit with Kenan for the days leading up to the end of the week. I don't know whether to stay with Kenan or not, but to be honest, I desperately need to get away and do something else – even for a day. Tracy and Mike are at last moving into their new home in a town called Gata, about a thirty-minute drive from Javea, so I decide to help them and I leave Mum with Kenan for a while.

Unpacking boxes and cleaning proves quite therapeutic, and although I don't stop thinking about him, I manage not to focus solely on Kenan for a few hours. Then, unexpectedly, in the middle of all the chaos of unpacking, Mum phones me.

"Gina, the doctors don't want to wait anymore, they already know that the cells aren't grafting and Kenan's body hasn't accepted the donor."

I'm completely crushed. Shattered by the news, and devastated that I'm not there with him. Did they even warn us this *graft versus host* thing might happen? I can't remember. I'm livid, that's the only thing I do know for sure; bloody angry for Kenan and furious that I was allowed to leave the hospital when, clearly, there was a chance they might reach this decision all along.

Mum puts Carlos on the phone and he tries to explain what is happening and why they want to do something straightaway, but my head is in a fog. I am way beyond facts and statistics now. Cutting him off mid-sentence, I plead, "What if I take him to America right now, and get a second opinion?"

I know Kenan is losing the battle and I am desperate. Lev has already suggested going to the States and if it means we have to sell everything to make him better, we will.

"Gina." Carlos implores, in an attempt to calm me down. "Even in America, they will just start from the beginning all over again. I'm sorry, but Kenan's best chance is to do another transplant, using the same donor."

In my heart I know he is right. I know that even in America, the land of 'hope and opportunity', they can do nothing more for Kenan than what is being done already. I'm aware how closely *La Fe* liaises with specialist cancer units in the US (which is one of the reasons we stayed with it), and I know I have no choice but to respect Carlos' advice that the treatment there will be exactly the same as he's getting here in Spain. I relent and go home, unable to face the trip back to Valencia today.

The next morning I return early to the hospital, say goodbye to my poor mum who is tumbling further into depression as Kenan's illness drags on. He looks so poorly now. I try to slip away to talk with Carlos about out next move, but Kenan wants to hear for himself what Carlos has to say.

More than any of us, Kenan is fully aware that things aren't going as they should, so I let him listen. He has a right to know and he trusts Carlos – more than I do right now. In some ways it takes the onus off me in deciding how much I should tell Kenan.

Carlos' plan is to do another transplant, using the other half of the donor's cells, hoping that this time Kenan's body will accept them.

"What will happen if it doesn't?" Kenan asks him. His words make me physically recoil in shock, because it suddenly hits me how my baby is being forced to grow up. For the first time I realise that Kenan completely understands how grave the situation is and it is gutting how he is being robbed of his childhood. He's developed an old head on his shoulders for a child not yet eleven years old. Carlos takes his hand in his and softly says, "We will cross each bridge as it comes, Kenan. Besides, I'm fairly confident that this will work. Don't you worry – that is our job!" Kenan breathes in his every word, "You," Carlos adds, "just concentrate on getting better."

Kenan seems reassured by Carlos' words; however I'm not so trusting. For the first time since this whole horrid business began, I am no longer certain Kenan is going to make it, but while there is hope we have to keep fighting.

That afternoon, a nurse again hooks up the donor transplant cells and transfers them into Kenan. Once more, we can only wait.

I've *never* prayed so much in my life, and whether it was prayers or not, this time there is no kick-back from Kenan's body. A week later we are given the marvellous news we've prayed for. The cells have grafted which is marvellous, although we are still a long way from taking Kenan home. Although it has worked, every part of his body is in agony and his mouth and gullet are still burnt which means he can't eat yet. His eyes are red and sore and, I apologise for the graphic description, blood is oozing from every orifice – his vomit, his pee, when he goes to the loo. They can only give him ice to help numb the pain. It's no surprise that Kenan finally flips.

"Please God!" He cries out. "Why? Why are you doing this to me? Please, just let me die!"

Immediately, I grab his hands; I can't let him give up his fight, at any cost, I can't let him give up. I've been told God has a big chest so I beat it with all my might. "You know what Kenan? God's a c**t. You can do this without him, so come on and fight this with me!"

The nurses seem to understand exactly what I am saying even though I am speaking English. They look horrified, this being a stout, Catholic country and all, but you know what? I don't give a toss what any of them think.

It's not *their* child lying here, it's mine and I for one have no faith in God, or anyone else for that matter.

The days are crawling by, but Kenan is starting to make a little progress. Eli, his lovely girlfriend, has been ringing and texting him every day, which has helped keep his spirits up, although Kenan is too unwell at the moment to keep replying to her little love notes.

It's his birthday this week. On 9th May he'll be eleven and Eli wants to come and visit him. Sadly, I've told Karen, Eli's mum, that it may not be the best thing. I think it will be too upsetting for Eli to see Kenan like he is, and embarrassing for Kenan because he has no control over his body yet. I don't want Eli to see him like that.

On his birthday, he manages to open his presents (all sprayed clean with anti-bacterial spray of course). Usually, Kenan's not backward in coming forward telling us what he wants, but even though we told him he can have anything, and I mean *anything,* all he wants is the one thing we can't promise him, to get better and come home. It's so sad. Luckily, we've brought him something he loves though – an all-singing, all-dancing mobile phone with video call.

Mum's coming to take over my shift soon because I need to take Angelo, who has an abscess in his mouth, to the dentist. It gives me an idea. If I'm going back, I'm going to show Kenan his home. After the visit to the dentist, I call him on his new phone so that he can see his brothers on the video. It's the first time they've seen each other for weeks. It costs a fortune, but I don't care – it's a few minutes pleasure for Kenan.

The following day I show him the sea and the beach, and the next, his friends and, of course, Eli.

It's the perfect present and, hopefully, seeing his friends and family will help him to get better again and leave the hospital.

A few days later, after having a much-needed break, I head back up to Valencia, refreshed and full of optimism again, only to be greeted with more bad news. Although the cells have grafted, Kenan's liver problem has returned overnight and he is in excruciating pain again. It seems every day brings another problem to overcome.

He's constantly calling the nurses for more pain relief, but he's so stuffed full of drugs already they can't give him anything more. They're 'monitoring him'. Monitoring him! Listening to his screams for something, anything to take the pain away being refused makes me feel so utterly helpless and angry. I try my best to get something for him, but they won't budge, despite my protests. So, for three hours I sit and rub his back and try to calm him until, eventually, Kenan falls into a restless sleep. Seeing my baby in so much agony is like having a knife twisted slowly through me.

The rest of the family feel the same too. Lev's dad, Mehmet, told me at the end of one of his shifts that he thinks Kenan is losing his will to live, but I'm not prepared to listen to talk like that. We have to keep going! We have to keep believing that he will be alright.

I cling on hard to that belief and it takes a long time but my frustration and pain, at last, turn to euphoria as Kenan does indeed begin to improve. It's slow, but there is a small step forward in his general health every day and he is starting to grow a little stronger. One day Kenan wakes up, miraculously free of pain – just like that!

It's been two months from the date of the second transplant. I look at him through my tears, taking in the thinness of his body, his shiny, bald head but, at last, the life in his eyes.

Carlos tells us that Kenan can come home this week.

Lev

Kenan was on his last legs after the radiotherapy and the transplant, but when he was through the worst he still found the energy to let Daddy spoil him.

The doctors allowed him out a few days after he'd woken up without pain, for the first time in so many weeks, and he told me he would love a nice watch – a 'proper' man's watch – which I immediately agreed to because I love a nice 'kettle'.

We stood together in the *El Corte Ingles* department store in Valencia, staring at hundreds of them, ignoring the expressions from people trying hard not to stare at us. To be fair, Kenan did look like one of the walking dead (I'm sure he'd find that one funny!) and we were used to being gawped at by now, so it didn't spoil the pride I felt in buying Kenan his first 'pukka' watch. It was a special moment. He picked a lovely, little Swatch with a smart, brown, leather strap, but mixed in with the feeling of delight I had, was a feeling of trepidation. Given the hell Kenan had just endured, it was as if we both *knew* something was going to happen, but we didn't want to speak about it.

Normality was everything now. Me and Kenan knew each other so well, that I think we took an subconscious oath to let each moment be all that mattered.

He loved that watch, even though I think he only got to wear it once. I've got it now. I don't think I'll give it to either Angelo or Louis. Selfish I know, but I just want it for myself. I can't wear it, but I still feel the need to look at it sometimes.

Chapter Twenty-six

I drive up with Mehmet on 4th June to collect Kenan from the hospital, feeling full of hope once more for our future together as a family.

Maureen has been at Kenan's bedside, but still she and Mehmet give each other the cold shoulder as they continue their stand-off; refusing to get on, but today that's their problem – *nothing* is going to spoil this moment.

I hug Kenan, who's eager to leave; his bags are ready and packed. We just have to wait for the various doctors to come and give us our instructions on how to take care of him at home, before we can go. An hour or so later, laden down with pills and notes, we set off for Javea. I've been so excited about Kenan coming home, I've managed to put the word out to Bay Radio, and the presenter, Adam King, announces it on air for us. He plays, 'I'm Coming Out' by Diana Ross and Kenan basks in the attention.

I am intensely proud of him and marvel at how quickly the sparkle has come back into his eyes. Even so, there is something vaguely different about him – physically, of course, he has changed, but I

218

sense something more. It seems as if he's grown from a child into an adult over the last two months and it's a bit unnerving to be honest. I'm not quite sure how to treat him.

Arriving home, Angelo and Louis come tearing out of the house, so excited to see their big brother. They bounce around him like a couple of little 'Tiggers', so it saddens me when Kenan says that he just wants to go to his bedroom. I understand of course. He's tired and has little strength, even walking is an effort but, even so, I feel a bit deflated. Nothing is ever how we imagine in our dreams, is it?

As we walk to his bedroom, I watch him clock the scattered toys around the place with a look of panic in his eyes. Believe me, my house is never untidy but the children do play with their toys until putting them away before bed. Kenan seems a bit freaked by the disorder. The structured life he's had in hospital, with his medical routine, and toys and gadgets all given a proper place, has gone and I know instantly the carefree ways of Angelo and Louis are going to be a problem. Once again, it strikes me how much he has changed.

But he's home! That's what's important, even though I suspect we have a long, hard road ahead of us if we are going to succeed in getting Kenan back to the happy, confident boy he used to be. Everything is different now, of course it is.

Every day for the first week we make the long journey back to the hospital to get his liver checked. He still needs an antibiotic drip to keep the infection in check. We share the travelling between us all, although to be fair Mehmet, Lev and my dad are doing the lion's share.

A week later and Kenan has definitely improved but he is now becoming frustrated that he can't do physically what his head wants to do.

"I want to do everything, Mummy!" he keeps insisting and it doesn't help that the school holidays are just around the corner. The sun is shining and all the other children are splashing around in pools or playing at the beach.

"You will, Kenan," I tell him, "but it will take time. You must get better first."

Naturally, he wants to run before he can walk, because he's worried about missing out on things. Being home and 'sick' is only slightly better than being in hospital. So I'm struggling to keep him from falling into a dark place. He's stopped smiling now that the novelty of being home has worn off and he doesn't feel happy about anything.

Without his knowledge, I've sought advice from Carlos to see what we can do. He confirms that Kenan has depression but that we're not to worry too much. It's just as common in children as it is in adults given the right conditions. We'll have to wait for Kenan to adjust back into family life. Angelo's feeling it most, the poor thing. He keeps trying to play with Kenan like he used to, but Kenan, bless him, doesn't have the patience or the playfulness right now. It's like he's eleven going on fifty and it's upsetting to watch. When will the 'old' Kenan come back? I miss him, I want everything to get back as it was, yet I know I can't rush it. Still, perhaps meeting Eli again might help?

Shoving all thoughts of 'not running before walking' out of my head, I ring Karen and ask if she would bring Eli down to the beach. It's only been a couple of weeks since Kenan left hospital but I'll do anything to try and kick-start him back to life. I turn up with all the boys to find Karen and Eli waiting for us. Kenan's mouth is still covered with sores but his appetite is returning, so I bribe him with an ice cream. It's only when I see Eli's reaction do I stop and think, 'Have I done the right thing here?'

Eli can't contain her shock when she sees Kenan – how thin he is and frail he's become. I'd forgotten that the last time they'd been together he'd had hair and was over a stone heavier. I can see Eli is scared, but I'm desperate, so I pull her over to me, pleading with her to understand.

"Eli, he's still the same Kenan," I reassure her. "Please, just speak to him."

To her credit, Eli walks straight over and sits down with him. Within minutes I sigh in relief as they chat away like old times and order a huge slice of chocolate cake with ice cream to share. If anyone can bring him round again, it is going to be Eli.

A few days later, me and Tracy take Kenan and Jack shopping, something Kenan used to love doing. Maureen is looking after Angelo and Louis so I have the whole day free with Kenan. The boys head off around the shops together, leaving us mums to chat and, for the first time in ages, I have a warm feeling of contentment in my stomach. Kenan is still weak, but it is a breakthrough – he looks happy!

He is totally exhausted by the time we get home though and I hope we haven't overdone it. It's such a fine line we have to tread; I don't know what to do really.

Kenan's changed into his dressing gown and slippers to keep warm because he's so thin he feels the cold, even though we're approaching summertime. Lev is home and he makes the dinner, as we enjoy a family evening. Our life is coming back for sure.

Sunday we go for dinner with Tracy and Mike and all the children, and Kenan seems quite cheerful. He even manages to eat his dinner of salmon and new potatoes. He used to like fish so it's a pleasure to watch him enjoying his food again. He and Jack then mess about videoing each other with Kenan pretending to be interviewed. They're laughing and giggling and acting like, well, like eleven year olds. We're getting there, we really are.

The 'old' Kenan is returning and the future – dare I think it – is bright.

Although he's still quite weak, Kenan is at last having the odd day when he has bursts of energy. His old personality is coming back gradually and he's on form more often than not, which is great. Today, we're at one of the numerous hospital visits we still have to attend, but he's chatting away happily with the nurses. There's something going on however, because in the last few minutes, a sudden hive of activity has suddenly broken the usual calm on the ward. I wonder what's going on.

"What's up?" I ask Kenan, who for some reason has had an attack of ants in his pants.

"Look!" He waves me over to a window that overlooks the main road, and so I watch, none the wiser, as four, blacked-out Range Rovers park up outside *Infantil*. Out step several members of the Valencia football team, apparently – it's a bit like Arsenal or Manchester United players turning up at

Great Ormond Street Hospital. Blimey, there's a film crew here as well following the players and the huge entourage of burly blokes escorting the players in. I can't understand what all the fuss is about.

"What's with all the security?" I ask Kenan. "It's not as if they're going to be set upon by a bunch of sick kids are they."

The penny drops as a gaggle of giggly, flirty, female nurses appear out of the blue. Kenan is among the children on beds in the Day ward and, as the players come in, he is literally bouncing around with excitement. Each footballer stops at every single bed, signing autographs and having their picture taken before giving out goody bags – mostly memorabilia of the Valencia football team. I watch all of this in bemused fascination, because I have absolutely no idea who any of them are.

Some of the players, especially the younger ones, seem uneasy being around the children, most of whom are obviously ill with cancer. I feel a bit sorry for them, because they're clearly not sure if there's any protocol to follow. Kenan is revelling in the buzz, but I notice that some of the kids are just too exhausted to show any excitement.

The players stay for over an hour, but just after they walk out of the ward, Kenan tells me he wishes he'd got the autograph of one of the players he's seen on TV. Typical!

The players are all but out of the building, but after everything he's been through, what my son wants he sure as hell is going to get. I run as fast as I can, bundle my way through fans and the burly minders, (grateful for once that I'm only five feet two,) and thrust a piece of paper in front of said player, too exhausted to say anything. He signs it and I belt it back to Kenan, who is on such a high when I hand it over to him. At the same time, Carlos comes up to read Kenan's reports.

"That was great," I puff. "Cheered the kids up, anyway."

He looks at me and, despondently, shakes his head before telling me Kenan is doing very well. With that he walks away. It's not until later that I find out Carlos is fuming about the whole footballer thing. Highly paid players using his hospital for a bit of publicity didn't go down too well with him. The ward was supposed to be as sterile as possible and some of the children were just too sick to appreciate it.

In one way I agree. However, I witnessed for myself that the visit certainly brightened up a lot of the kids' day and Kenan, in particular, is thrilled with his autographs. I feel rather pleased with myself in fact for getting the one he wanted most!

We leave after getting the all-clear from Carlos and Kenan is in good spirits all the way home. The visit has given him such a boost that, as a treat, me and Lev decide we'll take him out on Friday night for a bite to eat, even though his mouth is still a bit sore. Karen, Simon, Eli, Paula, Martin and Emily are coming too and Maureen has agreed to look after Angelo and Louis for us.

Come Friday, I get quite carried away and dress up to the nines. At the restaurant, Kenan looks well and obviously enjoys the attention of Eli and Emily, who, as the night progresses, act more and more like his two personal nurses. I guess I must relax a little and let my usual guard down, because I certainly glug a few more drinks than I would normally. The company helps of course, but it's just that, well, it feels good to be out!

I stop counting how many Slippery Nipples, or whatever they're called, I have, but it must be too many because I can't remember much of the evening. I do remember Kenan stating the blindingly obvious,

"Mummy, I've never seen you drunk before." I am that pissed that when we get home, *Kenan* has to help *me* up the stairs, take off my shoes and practically put me to bed – bless him.

When I wake up the next morning, my head is thick and throbbing, thanks to the Slippery Nipples. I down a couple of paracetamols, muttering the proverbial, "Never again," before wondering if Kenan is awake yet.

I go and look in his room. The sight of Kenan struggling to walk sobers me up instantly.

"What's the matter, Darling?" I ask, my chest tightening.

"My knees hurt, that's all," he answers. "I'm OK."

"You probably did too much last night," I reassure him, kicking myself for taking him out. I put his legs up on the bed and tell him to rest. Good enough for a normal, healthy person but not, as it turns out, for Kenan.

From that day on, Kenan's energy levels dip and the cracks begin to show all over again with unbelievable speed.

The days that follow are an indescribable haze of emotion and activity. I call the hospital and tell them that Kenan has hardly any energy, but they keep telling me that it's fine and that his progress, although slow, is what they expect. But it doesn't *feel* fine. Lev and me are worried out of our minds, because he can't keep any food or drink down, not even his tablets, but even when I tell the hospital this, they still insist that unless he has a fever – he doesn't – I am to keep on giving him his medication until it does stay down. Do what? What sort of advice is that?

But I do as they say, and Kenan continues to throw up his medication. By night time, Kenan is so tired that when he throws up another dose of tablets and it's filled with blood and thick brown bile, I give up. He is not having any more tablets tonight. What's the point if they just keep coming back up? Instead I tuck him in to bed and snuggle in next to him.

"Don't worry, Kenan, I'm not going to make you have more tablets tonight, go to sleep. You'll feel better in the morning."

I know he won't but, as his mother, words of reassurance are the only things I can give him right now. He sleeps at last.

The next day is Eli's birthday. She's having a pool party and Kenan naturally wants to go, but he is so weak I just think it will be too upsetting for him. The other kids will be in the pool and running about and all Kenan will be able to do is sit and watch – and *I* can't deal with that even if he can. It's too unfair.

While Eli is enjoying her party that afternoon, Kenan's temperature suddenly rises. I ring the hospital and, this time, they tell me to bring him in. Lev's taking him and, as we start to pack up his things, he suggests they stop in at the party, but I

persuade him that it might be too upsetting for Kenan
– and Eli – so they don't.

Now I wish Lev hadn't listened to me and had
taken him, if only for a few minutes. *Maybe* seeing
the other children would have given him a boost,
rather than upset him. *Maybe* watching them and
talking to Eli would have given him back the fight –
maybe, maybe, maybe. There are too many maybes.

Lev takes Angelo and Louis to put some stuff
in the car, and I help Kenan sort out his bag. We're
both very calm, which feels creepy. As we pack, he
hands me something to read that he has written while
in hospital, and tells me it's the first part of a story to
go into his memory box.

He started the box a few months earlier after
seeing the idea on some kids' TV programme. The
memory box is private though, I'm not allowed to
peek, but I can't help noticing the old photos and toys
carefully placed in the battered vanity-case that used
to be mine when I was his age.

The story he has given me is based on a time
machine, just like Dr. Who, who he is really into at
the moment.

[sic]

> *One morning, a little boy named Kenan
> walked to school. He would always walk to
> school because his mum was always busy
> doing some paypa work on the computer. His
> dad was a normal floor layer in London. One
> day he was waiting to go to school when a big
> glowing green diamond fell to the ground.
> Kenan looked at it, he picked it up and ran to
> school and hid it in his bag. The class started,*

they where learning about space but in the bush's learked a creatcha.

I am less struck by the story than by his spelling and grammar. It shows how much education he's missed during the last couple of years, especially in English. Spanish is written phonetically and I find his words easier to read that way. Still, I'm amazed how much he's taught himself.

I read on:

[sic]

At lunchTime, Kenan and his best friend Lev where eating when a masife thing came out of the bush's and was heading for Kenan's bag. Kenan grabs the diamond, the diamond glows then Kenan disappears. He finds him self at this house. Kenan looks out side. He sees Alien's and a robot and flying cars. I'm in the futcha. Kenan ran outside and said, "this diamond must be like a time machine." One old woman runs up to Kenan and said, "I've finally found you! Mum in the futcha," said Kenan. "Where were you all this time. I was searching for you but you didn't age," said Kenan's mum. That's because I got a time machine said Kenan, but then two aliens shot his mum into dust. Kenan run into the house and got a knife and threw it but the knife was stoped by the alien. But then he got out the diamond and the alien stopped. Kenan said, "why do you want this?" The Aliens said, "we want power." "Why?" said Kenan. The Aliens didn't answer. They grabed Kenan, he droped

228

the diamond. It glowd and then Zap Zap, the two Alien's turned into dust. Kenan said, "something is protecting me." He picked it up and went outside and run down to the city. He went to a dump to find things but no use, but then the diamond shot out of the bag and started picing together a space ship and then it was done. Kenan said "Wow!" He steped in it, then it started glowing then BOOM it was gone.

I'm stunned by the story. Yes, there are mistakes, but it's not bad. The story doesn't 'mean' anything right now; although later I will consider the words he has written in a different light. I smile as I put the story in his bag so he can finish it in hospital and, when Lev gets back inside, we load everything into the car. Lev will spend the day with Kenan, and Mehmet will stay the night. Standing in the kitchen before he leaves, I kiss and cuddle him, really squeezing him tight. In return I get a pat on my back. Typical over-demonstrative mum! He feels so frail and tiny in my arms that I have to stop myself pressing him too hard, worried he might snap.

Kenan goes down to the car, and I walk out to the naya to wave goodbye. The sun has warmed the tiles beneath my feet – a sure sign that summer is here. I stand looking down onto the road to where the car is parked outside the house and wave goodbye. Kenan is sitting in the passenger seat wearing his green baseball-cap, looking up and waving back at me. He looks so helpless and young. I call out to him,

"Don't worry, Kenan, just a few days and you'll be home again, I promise. I love you. I love you so much." As the car drives away I keep on calling out, "I love you!" until the car disappears around the corner.

Moving off the warm tiles back in to the house, I've a nag in the pit of my stomach again, which frightens me.

When Lev gets back from the hospital he tells me that Kenan is settled and the doctors are monitoring him, but they don't know what's up with him yet. As they don't seem overly worried, Lev is going to go back to England as usual tomorrow and will come back on Thursday.

Unknown to us, in bed that night, Kenan writes the next part of his story.

[sic]

With a flick of light the ship was on a wasteland of dust and rock. Kenan jumped out of the ship and said, "why did you take me here? There is nothing here but stupid rock. But then large sand people came up from the ground and took Kenan down into the ground. When Kenan woke up he was in a royal room. He looked out on the balcony and saw a city of sand, but then he heard a hissss. The alien was here, he said, "are you ... hiss, here to, hiss, help us?" "Why am I here and why do you need help from me?" said Kenan. "Because you have, hiss, the time diamond, hiss, and the great Piefearon will kill us all," said the alien. Kenan said, "So that's why you need me? But how do you kill it?" The Alien said, "we don't." But then the ground was shaking and all of the buildings where falling and the Piefearon was here. The Alien said to Kenan, "use the, hiss, diamond...." "I left it in my ship," shouted Kenan, "take me back there!" "We can't, hissss, because it will kill us all in the time before you come back," shouted the alien. But then Kenan fort of something – "the diamond can listen to my forts! So if I think hard innuf ..." So he did and then in a big glow it appeared. The alien said, "quick, kill the creatcha," "But why is it doing this?" said Kenan. He used the diamond to read its mind and he saw fear of the people. Kenan said, "what have you been doing to that thing?" and he pointed the diamond at them. "The Alien said we took power from its body so we can live on this planet." "But that's not fair on the monster!" shouted Kenan, "why don't you share the Piefearon's power. " "But how?" hissed the alien. "Leave that to me," said Kenan. He got out the diamond and talked to the thing and then it went off in to the shadows. "Your city is safe now" the Pierfearon said. "Yes," the alien said, "thank you." And it rewarded Kenan with a special gold diamond staff that meant on their planet he was the powerful one. He stayed there for a few days and then wondered where the diamond would go next.

The next morning, Lev leaves for England and I take Angelo and Louis to school and nursery before returning home to phone Kenan. But when he answers the phone, I hear immediately that he can't

231

communicate properly with me. Instead he gives the phone to Maureen, who has gone to sit with him. She tells me that Carlos is considering giving Kenan an MRI scan. Immediately I think he must have developed a brain tumour, but Maureen reassures me that it is routine and that Carlos still has no serious concerns about him.

My instincts are screaming the opposite but I keep my fears to myself. I don't want to trouble Lev. My mum is going up to change shifts with Maureen later today, so I'll wait until there's some concrete news before doing anything rash. After all, we've been in these crisis situations many times before.

Instead, I keep busy doing the housework before meeting up for a natter with Tracy. I call Kenan again to tell him how much I love him, but by now he can hardly talk back at all. He manages to tell me that he has almost finished his story.

[sic]

> *When Kenan left he went to bed in the ship and started thinking about how his mum got zapped by those stupid alien's on planet earth. He fort this in his dream but sudenly, Bang! Boom! The ship stoped. Kenan jumped out of the bed and went to check if everything was all right. "every thing's ok. I think I will have a look outside," said Kenan. So he got the diamond and put it in the golden staff and went outside. "WOW. This is massive. There are lots buildings in gold but no one's here. I'm going to see it," Kenan said. So he went*

232

down to these golden gates but they were
guarded by two … …

That's where it ends.

Later I pick the other two up from school. Dad comes by after dropping mum off at the bus station, so I cook dinner for us both, bath the boys and settle them into bed before ringing Kenan again.

"Do you want me to put you on video call so I can see you?" I ask him.

He slurs back, "I don't know." It's as if he doesn't really understand what I am asking him. Instead he passes the phone to my mum, who tells me that he is being given some medication that makes him sleepy. I let out a deep, stress-filled sigh – that probably explains the non-communication bit then.

"He hasn't been given the MRI scan yet," mum tells me "and nothing more has been said about it, but the nurses are checking on him and they keep shining a light into his eyes."

Mum has tried asking why but her Spanish isn't up to it, so she doesn't fully understand what they're saying. I feel very uncomfortable not being with him, so ask Mum if she thinks I should come up. But to her he seems to be OK, the doctors say he's sleeping comfortably for the night, so I leave it with Mum, promising to get hold of Carlos first thing in the morning to find out what is going on.

So much of me wants to be with him, but the other part is reassured that Mum is there and that the doctors don't seem to be alarmed. I spend the evening sitting with my dad and Mehmet, trying to relax, all the while telling myself over and over again that Kenan is fine and will be alright.

Tuesday 19th June, 2007

The day starts like any other. My alarm rings, I shower, give the boys their breakfast and get them dressed for school before dropping them off. I stop for a chat with Joyce and tell her about Kenan. She's a trained nurse, so it is comforting to get a professional insight into what may be happening to him. Then I go round to my dad's house and meet Mehmet there and we all have a cup of tea.

At about 9.15 a.m. Mum phones and tells us that Kenan slept well but that he was unusually restless this morning, especially when they tried to collect his wee in the specimen bottle.

"He's calmed down now," she says, "so I'm just off to have a quick wash and a cup of coffee if you want me."

At 9.45 a.m. she rings again, this time there is panic in her voice. It turns out she'd gone back to Kenan, only to be told not to bother changing into her Isolation robes but to go straight round to the ICU (intensive care unit) because Kenan has been rushed there. Carlos has instructed her to ring me immediately.

"You're to come here urgently he says, Gina."

"What's wrong? What's happening?" I demand.

"They've not told me anything, just get here, Gina."

234

Her voice is trembling now. The next fifteen minutes are a haze, as my dad rushes me home. I grab an overnight bag and we set off for the hospital, constantly ringing Mum. But she is in a right state and keeps repeating over and over that he'd been fine when she'd left for a coffee, a bit dozy but fine.

Half an hour later, driving flat out on the motorway, my mobile rings. It's my mum's number. When I answer, my blood runs cold. I hear Carlos' voice. It is shaking as he delivers the words that change my life forever. He tells me, calmly as he can, that Kenan has had a seizure and has slipped into a coma. He's on a life-support system. My heart almost stops.

"Is he dead?" I whisper.

My dad's hands tighten hard on the steering wheel and I notice them trembling. I can't breathe while I wait for Carlos' reply.

"Yes," he tells me. "His brain is dead and it is now the life-support system keeping his heart beating."

I can't speak to Carlos anymore and, in a daze, I cut the call off. I don't cry. I focus instead on getting to the hospital as soon as possible. I ring Lev, but can't bring myself to tell him the full story, only that Kenan has been rushed to ICU and he needs to get back immediately. The last thing I need is Lev driving like a lunatic, having an accident and leaving me to deal with it all on my own. The less he knows at this point the better – although I know he will not be as shocked as I am.

Lev has always insisted that leukaemia is the biggest childhood killer, but I've always refused to accept that it may take our son. Even now I don't accept it. All I have to do is get there and Kenan will be OK.

I keep busy on the phone and ring Tracy and she offers to come up to the hospital to be with me for support. I don't want Lev's parents there yet. I can't handle any petty bickering and I know Maureen will be in pieces. I only want people there who are strong.

I remember Floria saying to me at Christmas, "If anything bad happens you will ring me, won't you? I want to be there."

I'd found her words strange at the time, but Floria has said things out of the blue or out of context before, that have later turned out to make sense. Maybe she'd had a premonition? I ring her at her office in London. The time is 9.30 a.m. in the UK.

"I'm coming right now," she tells me and walks straight out of work to catch the next plane over to Spain. I think how fitting it is that Floria was with me when Kenan came into this world and how she is going to be there when he leaves it.

My mum meets me on the stairs of *La Fe* hospital, her face drained of colour, a mask of shock and pain. I hug her while she tells me how she's been pacing the ICU for two hours and *still* no one will tell her what is happening to Kenan.

Quietly, I say, "You heard his doctor, he's on a life-support machine, Mum," and with arms wrapped around one another we go upstairs to find Carlos.

He's sitting, waiting in his office, his hands clasped tightly together, resting on his desk. The first thing I see, as we walk in, is the crucifix placed high on the wall. Funny how I had never noticed it before and I look at it with hatred welling in my heart, before collapsing into one of the chairs opposite his desk. I try hard to listen, to concentrate on the chain of unreal events that have led to my firstborn baby now being dependent on a life-support machine.

"Kenan has had a cerebral haemorrhage on the left side of his brain," he tells me "and he slipped into a coma for ten minutes before his brain shut down and died. It was quick and, thankfully, Kenan wouldn't have known anything," Carlos added, trying desperately to offer a thread of comfort.

There are questions I should ask. Why? How? But I don't ask them. Instead, I think only to myself, that Kenan's nightmare is over and our nightmare is just beginning. I must have been crying, but I'm not sure, some button has been pushed and I drift into some sort of trance. I'm trying hard to absorb Carlos' words, but I've heard enough …. I stand up and look down at Carlos and tell him I want to see Kenan straight away. Standing up, he manages to look me in the eye, "Of course."

I link my arm through Mum's and follow Carlos to the ICU, not sure who is holding up who. It's a part of the hospital I've never needed to visit before. He goes in ahead of us and we are shown to a small, antiseptic-smelling room to scrub up in and put on our gowns. What's the use of that now I wonder? But again I say nothing. Then we wait a few minutes before we're taken into another small room, clearly designed for privacy. This one has several alcoves recessed into the walls and four plainly-covered beds. My eyes seek out Kenan immediately. The number above his bed is fifteen – my birth date.

'Funny,' I think. Not significant, but just odd.

There in bed number fifteen is my beautiful boy, my firstborn. His head is still hairless and his pyjamas lie loose on his body. I can see his chest rising and falling in time with the beeps being made by the machine standing close to his bed – the machine that is keeping Kenan alive via a tube in his mouth. I fight the urge to run over and shake him, make him wake up, just in case none of it is real. I'm having a nightmare that's all, I just have to shake him then I'll wake up and hear him calling "Mummy, Mummy!"

But I don't do that. Instead, I walk slowly over to him and take hold of his hand, putting my other hand gently on his chest. I can still feel his heart beating. I then cup his face and notice the whites of his eyes through his semi-open lids. I lift each eyelid.

"Kenan," I whisper. "Wake up, it's Mummy. Please darling, wake up."

I kiss his eyes, his cheeks and stroke his bare head, willing him with every ounce of will I have, to wake up. He looks perfect to me, beautiful, radiant even. Mum stands on the other side holding his hand and stroking his arm, tears in her eyes. I look up and smile – it's all I can think of to do. Carlos comes over then with my dad by his side and pulls up some chairs. Dad literally falls into one of them, his face red and puffy with tears. Carlos stands next to me then and starts stroking Kenan's head with me.

"I'm so sorry," he says and unable to hold it back, he cries too. I take his hand and we all stand there, in silence, around Kenan's bed. I know that Carlos has a soft spot for Kenan and I don't blame him for what's happened even though I don't understand why it has. So I welcome his presence and he stays for a while before leaving us to grieve, kissing Kenan for one last time on his forehead as he goes.

"Goodbye, Kenan," he says.

On impulse, I embrace him and whisper, "Thank you." He couldn't save Kenan, nothing could. His fate was set out from the moment he was born. I have to believe that to get through this.

The three of us sit with Kenan, all trapped in our own hell. The only noise is from the beep of the life support machine. Then I do something crazy. I pull out my mobile phone and say to my mum and dad, "Do you think I'm sick? I want to take a picture of Kenan and I want you to take a picture of me kissing him."

Far from thinking me crazy, my mum says it's a nice idea, so we snap some pictures of Kenan – I want to remember every single moment with him. Every parent films their child or takes pictures when their baby enters the world, and I want the memories of my baby now because I am already so frightened that Kenan might fade from mine. I know that will never happen and that I will think of him every day of my life but still, I have to be sure. The photos will lie undeveloped in the memory of my phone forever.

I don't know how long we stay there, time has ceased to matter, but my dad is taking it really badly, so at some point I suggest we all go for a coffee and a cigarette. My dad looks shocked.

"You can't," he implores. "What if something happens?"

"Dad, he's gone."

Dad is in bits, so Mum gently takes his arm and holds him up as we leave the ICU. A doctor I've not seen before approaches me on our way out of the ward, and asks me a question that even in my darkest nightmare I never thought I would have to answer. He asks if I'm ready to give my consent to turn Kenan's life-support machine off. Somehow, I manage to explain that I am still waiting for my husband to arrive and that we will decide together, when he gets here. I then go and sit with Mum and Dad on the steps outside the hospital with a cigarette.

While we are there, Tracy and Paula arrive, so I take them upstairs to ICU to say their goodbyes. I leave them together and go back to the steps to wait for Lev who I'm expecting to arrive any minute. I want to be there to meet him, to explain what has happened and what the doctors want us to do.

So I sit, suspended in time, with my parents beside me, while people pass up and down the stairs chatting, unaware of our loss, and I chain-smoke until Lev arrives at about 5 p.m.

Lev

I wasn't surprised when I got Gina's call. You better get back quickly she had said, and although she didn't say much, I knew then, knew it was over. Me and the lads were in the middle of carpeting a big townhouse in Hammersmith for an American architect I've worked for a bit, called Derek.

He had a son about Kenan's age – I think they met once – and he was a diamond about it. I thought it kind of weird I should find out while working on his job, but he told me to just down tools and go, which I did, leaving my mate 'Rat Boy' – aka Dave – to finish up. Dave had been with me too on a job when Kenan was first diagnosed which I also thought a hell of a coincidence.

I was reminded of the time he'd come over to Javea with his grandparents and rented a villa near us the first summer we lived there. I remember we all went out on the piss and took Kenan with us. He was only about eight at the time but we had a ball, singing in a karaoke bar until about two in the morning. Kenan had never drunk so much coke in his life! It was packed, but Kenan wanted to sing, so I said OK and offered to get up with him. He turned me down flat, saying he wanted to sing on his own – I didn't know I was that bad!

Kenan got up and sang 'Hound Dog' by our hero Elvis, and got a standing ovation for it. A load of pissed-up, Welsh birds came over then and started trying it on with me (they love a bit of Cockney) and Kenan thought it was hilarious. Dave was on a promise, but I was with my kid, so I told him it was

241

time to get the hell out of there – he was well pissed-off.

We'd lost Dave's granddad as well, who'd wondered off trying to get home but we found him and got him back first before heading back ourselves. I was well drunk and Gina switched on me the moment we walked in the door. Kenan didn't seem to see what the problem was – all I can remember is waking up the next day with my boots still on, as I was too drunk to take them off.

Any normal parent will think this really bad of me, but I don't care now because it's a memory of a good night out with Kenan – our only one together as it turned out – and no one can take that away from me.

In the morning, I remember him saying to me at breakfast that one of the girls had wanted to kiss me, and me nudging him to keep quiet as I was already in the doghouse with Gina. He was winding me up something rotten – just like I would have done too.

Why I don't know, but that night with Kenan flashed into my head when I got the call from Gina. I told her I was heading to the airport to catch the first available flight back to Valencia – and I knew she wasn't giving me the full story.

Chapter Twenty-seven

As Lev gets out of the taxi, I can see from the anxiety in his eyes that he's already guessed the situation is serious. Lev doesn't wait for any explanation, he wants to see Kenan straight away, and so I tell him what has happened as we hurry along to the room Kenan is now lying in. Once inside we stand, side by side, next to our son. Lev asks to be alone with him, and I leave them and go to wait downstairs, fully understanding why he needs his time with Kenan.

Eventually, Lev comes down and says we need to talk about turning off Kenan's life support. I am not ready. I don't want to switch it off yet, even though I know we have to, that it is pointless hanging on. But I am too weak to argue, it won't change anything anyway, and so I walk, defeated, with my mum and dad to give consent to switch the machine off.

My parents say their goodbyes first before reluctantly moving away, leaving me and Lev alone. I don't know how long we stand there before we eventually nod to the nurse, but my composure finally snaps as she starts to move towards the machine.

"Are you sure there is nothing you can do?" I shout, willing her to say yes! Instead, in perfect English, she says Kenan will never be the same boy even if they could do something, because his brain has gone. And then, with an easy flick of a switch she turns off the machine. Its beep begins to slow down and the tube is removed from Kenan's mouth. But his heart is still beating! Albeit very slowly

I look hopefully at the nurse, but she shakes her head. Kenan's body will shut down gradually she tells us. I put my hand flat on his chest, still feeling his heart. Then I notice that his toes are starting to go blue and his fingernails too. It is happening right in front my eyes, Kenan is slipping away from me, and he is dying! Now I lose it.

"*No, No*" I scream, "Please God, *No*! My baby, my baby boy. *No*!"

The nurse asks if I want something, like Valium or some other mind-numbing crap, but I don't want to see any more medication thank you, my cupboards are full of the stuff. And I don't want to be numbed; I want to feel this head on. Lev pulls me away but I pull back, not wanting to ever leave Kenan. I am his mother, I am meant to protect him, I gave him life and this is just too brutal, too cold.

"Why, why, why is this happening?" I keep yelling out loud. I know I'm slipping out of control …. Lev takes me in his arms and makes me leave.

We forsake our old friend, the steps, and go and sit on the grass outside the hospital. The sunshine is glorious today, but what do we care? In a city of almost a million people, we're too alone to notice anything. Neither of us knows what to do. Lev makes himself busy on the phone, ringing a few people in England to tell them.

First Peter, he'd rung Kenan every day he was in hospital, then Mitch and Kelly who I think I speak to as well, and then several other people who we want to know. I feel numb. I can't breathe or swallow – it's as if I'm drowning. I know I have to muster all the energy I have to carry on though, because the day isn't over yet.

Floria rings then and tells us she's here and is on her way from Valencia Airport. One of the doctors comes to find us after that and we follow him back to the ICU. Unbelievably, almost three hours have passed and Kenan's body has finally found peace. Where did that time go?

His face is so pure, so innocent and there is a slight smile to his beautiful lips. His skin looks almost translucent – I search for the faint scar on his face from the bottle that smashed on the floor, but it has virtually disappeared. He really does look at peace and for the first time, in many, many months my baby looks free of pain. At last it is over.

Seeing Kenan like this is killing Lev though, so he goes downstairs, needing his own space. I stay by Kenan's side; I don't want to leave because I am frightened that in some way he still needs me. Then I sense a lady arrive at my side and stand next me.

"Hello," she says. It's Jenny, one of the volunteer nurses. She's spent a lot of time with Kenan over the last two years, reading or playing cards with him. Jenny's English but has lived here ages. She married a Spanish man and has kids of her own – it feels good to have her with me, just to sit and talk with. But our time is interrupted – I don't know how long we've been talking. The doctors need to move Kenan to another room but I can come back in about twenty minutes.

Jenny takes me downstairs now to where Lev is sitting on the steps with Floria. Lev has already told her that Kenan has passed away and she is distraught. She wanted to be here sooner but the fact that she is here at all is enough for me. We have shared so many things me and Floria, her being here now is how it should be.

"Can I see Kenan?" she asks. Eager to get back to him, I practically drag her inside to find him again. I want to spend every minute with him, because I know that our time together is limited and will soon be at an end. Jenny comes with us to speak to the doctors before taking us to a small door round the back of the ICU. We pass a window that looks in to where Kenan is lying on a bed, and I see, just like you see in one of those casualty programmes, the orderlies pulling a white sheet from Kenan's body. The movement stops me in my tracks, because to me he is still alive, not someone who has died. I gather myself quickly.

"Look Kenan, Aunty Floria is here. She's come to see you."

We sit either side of him, each holding his hand and I notice that he is still wearing his blue, hospital pyjamas. I know Floria is holding it together for my sake, giving me the strength that I need. Yet I can see in her eyes that she too is dying inside. We sit for a while reminiscing and laughing, all the while including Kenan in our conversation, as if he is listening. Maybe he is. I hope he is.

246

Jenny helps us talk to the doctors about what to do next and we are told we need to go to the morgue to make the necessary funeral arrangements. It is 10 p.m. now and Mehmet has arrived to take us home.

When I see him, he's sitting with Lev – his son – outside the hospital, smoking, crying and talking. The sky is dark, but the air is still warm as we all follow Jenny to the hospital morgue. We listen to the hustle and bustle of the traffic around Valencia, people going about their lives. It doesn't seem right or fair.

A man in smart trousers and a short-sleeved shirt meets us and shows us inside the modern, stone, brick building adjacent to the hospital, and we sit in chairs as he writes down the details he needs, from his side of a large, wooden desk.

Lev does all the talking through Jenny because the only interest I have is in getting back to Kenan. I want out of the morgue to be with my son, my beautiful baby, who was born on Thursday 9th May, 1996 after a long and difficult labour, weighing seven pounds and eleven ounces.

How can I be here, barely more than eleven years later, sitting in a morgue arranging his funeral?

Life's a bitch.

When we finally leave the hospital, I thank Jenny because I don't think we could have done it without her. Mehmet drives us home and I sit in the back with Floria, exhausted. I just want to be left alone now with my thoughts. When we get home, my mum and dad are there with Maureen and the boys are, thankfully, sleeping in their rooms.

Immediately, I rush downstairs to Kenan's and even though I know in my head he isn't there, my heart cries out for him to be so, safely tucked up in his bed. The ache and pain is so consuming that it hurts physically – really, really hurts. I have no way of controlling the grief; it is like I am going to die. But at the same time, I want the pain and the suffering: to feel what Kenan must have felt, to hurt like he had. I had pushed him and pushed him to get better and now I must pay for that.

Kenan's bedroom is just as we left it. Everything in its place and his things are all tidily put away. Pictures of America are stuck on his wall, including the one of us together riding our dolphin, Coral and one of Kenan on his own with her. He's arranged them neatly around a picture he'd coloured in whilst in hospital one time and then had laminated. It's a picture of a bird in flight and Kenan has written, 'The Bird of Light', which somehow seems symbolic now. I am drawn towards it and I stand there, crying, touching his face in the pictures, feeling somehow that I if I try hard enough I will connect with him again.

I lie on his bed, cuddling his pillows, smelling him deeply on his leopard-print, satin sheets that are part of the animal theme bedroom he'd created and loved.

Oh how I wish I could turn back time, to a place when we are all together and Kenan is well and happy again. So much has died with Kenan today, more than I can take in right now.

"Gina?" I hear Mum and Dad come in to Kenan's room. They try to console me but know nothing can ease my pain. Maureen calls out then that she's made tea – the British cure-all remedy. No surprise there I think, she drinks loads of the stuff. My mouth is parched though and I haven't eaten for ages I realise. I feel too sick for food – a cup of tea would be nice however. I wash my face, taking in my red, swollen eyes in the mirror. The tears just come, no matter how hard I try to stop them. But who cares? I don't, so I join everyone else at the table outside on the naya where the breeze is still warm despite it being almost midnight. I cup my tea, sipping it slowly and draw deeply on a cigarette.

BANG! Fireworks suddenly fill the sky. I look at Lev and he stares back at me as the sky lights up with bright explosions, set off to celebrate the final night of the latest fiesta. We've seen it all before of course, but this time it is different. The smell, the sound, everything is different.

I am suddenly transported back to a time when we were all happy – to our holiday in America, when me and Kenan stood watching the fireworks from our balcony. I can hear the music, breathe the aromas from the food stands and hear people clapping to the big bands playing in time with the displays. It feels so real, it brings me a moment's calmness – perhaps Kenan is making me remember to help soothe away the pain?

I ask Lev if he feels it too, but he looks at me as if I've lost the plot. But I know what I'm feeling is Kenan – his reassurance that he is with me.

That night me and Lev sleep in Kenan's bed, not sleeping but just holding each other, sobbing, crying and talking before exhaustion finally takes over and gives us a few restless hours of relief.

For a split second, when I wake the next morning, I think that yesterday has been no more than a bad dream. But instantly my heart fills with the same excruciating pain as the day before and I know it is real. Kenan has passed away.

It's early and everyone else in the house is still sleeping, even the kids, so I go and sit outside on the naya, appreciating the silence, and watch as the sun rises over the distant mountains. Another glorious, sunny day is coming. I light a cigarette and look at the photos I've taken of Kenan on my mobile. There is a recent video on it as well, from when Kenan was poorly but alive and happy, so I watch it.

Kenan is taking a walk around the hospital grounds with his brothers. I had taken the video because the hospital rarely let Kenan out or let him see his brothers because of the infection risk – I don't know why they had let him go this particular day. Did they know or suspect something then?

Angelo and Louis are arguing for Kenan's attention while they follow him around. Looking at all three of my boys enjoying their time together helps me smile a little.

There are so many people I need to tell still about Kenan, so I finish watching the video and begin texting my friends in Spain and England with the news. I then go back down to Kenan's bedroom and as I start to unpack his things from the hospital, clutching his clothes, smelling him, Lev wakes up. I see in his face, that for a split second he thinks it was all a bad dream too. We say nothing, but hear Angelo and Louis coming down the stairs. Lev is amazing. Somehow he finds the inner strength to take over and get Angelo and Louis ready for their last day at school before they break up for the summer.

I think I try to explain to Angelo that his brother has gone to heaven and that he won't be coming back, but he doesn't really understand. I guess Kenan had been coming and going so much over the past two years that Angelo thinks he's in a hospital now called Heaven. I am crying so much I think I frighten him. I can't deal with the kids right now, so Lev takes them away. In my mind they are healthy and Lev is looking after them, but Kenan has no one to look after *him*, only me – he still needs me.

Lev drops the boys off at school – friends tell me later that I was there with him and Floria – but I don't remember. I don't recall much from the days immediately after Kenan passed away and, in fact, much of what I'm writing now is based on what people have told me. My mind is all over the place. I can only remember sitting in Kenan's bedroom. I sit there for hours, never wanting to lose his smell. I lie on his bed and cry, clinging onto anything I can find that still hold traces of him. Eventually, Floria and Lev manage to coax me out for a few hours.

Funerals happen quickly in Spain, so the day has been set for Friday and we need to go and arrange the flowers. Lev also wants to get some photos of Kenan printed and framed, to put on the funeral table.

Floria persuades me to wash and get dressed. I put on my black shorts with a black, strappy top but no makeup. It isn't worth it because I can't stop crying. We drive to the photo shop and do what we need to do, and Lev gets some for Angelo and Louis, of them with their brother, which he later places in their bedrooms. Lev does everything and I'm grateful to him for giving me the space to grieve. We then order the flowers. All I know is that I want Kenan's name set in an arrangement. Lev, my mum and dad, Mehmet and Maureen sort it all out whilst I sit, numb, in the car outside the garden centre.

We then drive on to the crematorium, a newish building on the outskirts of Javea. I've passed it often on my way to and from the motorway and, sometimes, I've wondered which one of us would be the first to use it, if life worked out for us in Spain. It never ever entered my mind it might be one of our kids.

The morgue in Valencia has made the appointment for us here in Javea and our pool man, Danny has arranged a reverend that speaks English for us. His name is Balbi and he is waiting. Balbi leads us all into a small office inside the crematorium's sand-coloured walls.

We go through the formalities and when I hand over Kenan's passport, I see the sadness fall all over his kind, chubby face when he realises how young Kenan is. Handing over my baby's passport suddenly makes it feel very real. I gaze around the room not wanting to focus on the task in hand, and see above the desk a display of urns on a shelf. Some are plain, some more elaborate but I don't take much notice of them, I'm not looking for an urn. But then my eyes fall upon a bronze dolphin jumping elegantly over waves and I know that this is the one. I turn to Lev – he's seen it too. Price doesn't come in to it; we want Kenan to have his dolphin. We then say our goodbyes having set the funeral for eleven o'clock on Friday.

At home later that afternoon, Floria's fiancé, Antonio arrives which at least gives Floria someone to lean on. The poor girl is burdened with my grief and Lev's too, so she needs someone to support her.

At some point throughout the afternoon I suddenly remember that we haven't arranged the Chapel of Rest for Kenan at the crematorium. I start to panic, because I vaguely recall Lev telling Jenny that we don't want Kenan to be placed there and to close his coffin as we've already said our goodbyes. I can hardly breathe when I remember that. No! No! I haven't said my goodbye – not yet! I need to see my baby again and, frantically, I tell Lev to get Kenan placed in the Chapel of Rest. It takes a fair degree of organising, but Lev and Balbi finally manage to make sure that Kenan will be in an open coffin in the Chapel of Rest, when he is brought back to Javea from Valencia on Thursday afternoon.

That day, I am so excited about seeing Kenan again I can't wait to get to the Chapel of Rest at the crematorium. It's an agonising wait, and I want to rush straight off to see him the moment we. But first, Balbi tries to prepare us by explaining that the morgue in Valencia has prepared Kenan as best they can, given that we'd changed our minds about leaving his coffin open.

I enter the Chapel in a daze and walk slowly to find Kenan, with my mum and dad walking behind me. He is lying behind a huge, glass window. Everything is white I notice; his coffin, the satin robes he's been dressed in, even his skin. He looks beautiful, like a china doll, white of face, full red-rose lips. More than anything I am taken by how peaceful he looks. There is a calmness literally radiating from him that I have never seen before.

I sit staring through the window, my hand lightly touching the glass, my mum beside me. Lev doesn't want to come in – he says he needs to shut out the memory because if he doesn't he'll crack and lose the strength and composure he's managed to muster.

I'm not sure who suggests it, but someone says we may like to write a letter to Kenan and place it inside his coffin along with a few special items. So I sit and write; how much I love him, how much I will always love him and how I wish I could die too so I can be lying there with him. My heart feels divided into three parts, one for each of my children, but Kenan's part has died with him and, right now, I want to die too. I can't shake the feeling that Kenan might be scared and that he needs me to guide him through his passage.

As I write my mum is leaning hard against my dad, hitting the glass and sobbing.

"Why, why?" But I block it all out and keep on writing, barely noticing when Mum calms down and sits back next to me. She is the only person I show the letter to.

Balbi then comes and takes me, Mum and Maureen around the back of the glass and through a small door so we can be inside, with Kenan. The room is cold, but the low temperature doesn't touch me at all. Physically, I feel nothing now apart from an intense longing to touch my baby. He's like stone, but I can feel warmth still wrapped inside his body when I bend over to kiss his lips. I can't believe how good it feels to be this close to him. I tuck the letter down the side of the coffin close to his heart, adding a photo of our family of five and his favourite teddy bear, dressed in a jumper with *Kenan* written across the front that Maureen once gave him. Finally, I place his yellow blanket down his other side, which he'd slept with, along with the teddy, every night. It seems right that he takes his comforts along with him for the last part of his journey through this life.

Over the next twenty-four hours I visit Kenan four, five, maybe six times; I'm not sure how many. All I remember is wanting to see him as much as possible. I fantasise that maybe he'll be OK when I walk in, and will be waiting for me to bring him home. That is how I am coping, by pretending he's out somewhere and I'm going to see him again soon. I'm not ready to face the reality that he has died.

Throughout the day, friends arrive from England for the funeral tomorrow. Paula has taken control of that side of things, arranging where to meet up and organising the sleeping arrangements in a variety of holiday villas. Lev and Mehmet have helped to tidy the places up a bit as I think it helps to divert their heartache by keeping busy. I escape to the crematorium to see Kenan because I don't have the slightest inclination to meet anyone at all.

Lev's refusal to see Kenan really bothers me though. I'm afraid he might one day regret not saying goodbye, so I push him to go and later on he finally relents and goes with Paula. As I watch him cry on her shoulder, I'm grateful she is there for him because he needs to cry; we all do.

Later, I feel obliged to meet some of our friends on the rocky beach. Mitch and Kelly are here as is Pete and Annabel. Although their presence is a comfort, trying to socialise is the hardest thing in the world because all I want to do is hide myself away in the tranquillity of Kenan's bedroom or at the crematorium. I'm aware I still have responsibilities, especially to Angelo and Louis and they need to be picked up from school.

I leave with Lev and Floria. When we arrive at the nursery to collect Louis I'm approached by a lady, who has a child there too. She offers me an impulsive, deep, sincere hug, during which, she whispers in my ear words that later provide me with the inner strength to carry on.

"Do you know that I am a medium?" she asks. "When you are ready I will try to help you."

Her words at that moment leave little impression, but for some inexplicable reason I feel an instant bond form between us, even though I barely know her. Once I too had been a very spiritual person, but my 'gift', for want of a better word, had deserted me. I saw my grandmother the day after she died, clear as day and although I'm not one to thrust either religion or clairvoyance in the faces of others, I have on many occasions told people things about their loved ones I can't have known – usually by holding a piece of their jewellery.

Saying that, my 'faith' in anything is fading rapidly and I'm not sure what I believe in anymore. Kenan had believed in God, although I have no idea why as God certainly didn't help him, so how can I believe?

I am wearing the necklace that he wore in hospital with a crucifix and an evil eye hanging from the chain, but only in the hope that possibly, in some way, his spirit may come through meaning we can connect again. Maybe I am trying too hard because I can't see or feel him, even though I desperately want to.

Little Louis doesn't seem to know what is going on when we pick him up, but Angelo is quiet when we collect him from school. We head for the Arenal to meet some more friends. Lev's brother, 'Big Kenan' is on his way from the airport, even though his wife is expecting their third child any day now. He almost didn't come because Sandra really wants him there for the birth, but I take my hat off to Lev, who kept his cool even though he was saddened when Kenan said he may not make it. Lev simply told him he mustn't hold any regrets, whatever he decides to do and, thankfully, he's come so he can say goodbye to his firstborn nephew. He arrives with Mehmet, shortly after us.

"Hello, Kenan," I say. No sooner do the words leave my lips I break down, sobbing as I realise I'm speaking to Kenan – but not *my* Kenan. The cruel reality that never again will I utter the words, "Morning, Kenan," or "Goodnight, Kenan," to my baby, hits me with such force that I hate Lev's brother's name being Kenan now; it's tearing my heart out. I just want to go home!

But today is also my dad's 66th birthday, and I sense my dad's need to be around us all, so I stay. While we are all sitting at the bar, a large birthday-group come in and amazingly – to me anyway – the guy is 66! When the waiter brings him over a cake, I see the number 66 iced, prominently on the top and I'm convinced it's a sign from Kenan intended for my dad, as a gift. Incidentally Kenan died on my great-uncle Sid's birthday. I'm beginning to read a lot into what is happening around me now and, regardless of whether it's crazy or not, it is helping. A couple of hours later, the day finally ends and I escape back home, to the comfort of Kenan's bedroom.

In the early hours of Friday morning, the day of Kenan's funeral, Sandra goes into labour and having already given birth to two girls, her first baby boy is born – just a few hours before we say goodbye to ours. She sends pictures of herself holding the baby and in one of them there is a small, white circle hovering over the baby. The text message reads: *'I don't care what anyone says, as far as I'm concerned this is Kenan watching over his new baby cousin.'*

For me, Noah's birth is probably the most bitter-sweet moment of my life.

The sun is already up and shining when I open my eyes, but instead of getting out of bed, I curl into a small huddle and wish for the day to simply go away. From the moment Kenan was diagnosed I've refused to accept that this day might come, although I've secretly feared it.

I have to get up of course, so, with Lev's help, I drag myself out of bed and get Angelo and Louis dressed in the clothes I've already carefully chosen for them; shorts, matching shirts and smart sandals. I want them to look good for Kenan and they are indeed a picture. They will be my strength today. I want people to see the boys and not me – the tragic, grief-stricken mother. I don't want or need to attract pity, so I'm going to focus on my two handsome boys, of whom I feel very proud.

Clothes are the perfect defence-barrier for me, because they provide a shield to hide behind. An article in *Grazia* magazine I once read entitled, 'After Him,' sums up exactly how I feel about clothes. It was written by a young woman who had lost her husband, and was about how she wanted to look her best for his funeral. She wrote: '*Never underestimate the power of dressing. Even in your darkest hour, clothes can be the most reliable armour to boost your confidence and hide behind.*'

I've done that all my life, probably because my mum has always been a 'fashion diva'. And at five feet seven and as thin as a stick she always looks perfect and glamorous, even when she used to collect me at the school gate. With my five feet two I don't carry it off quite so well, but I try not to leave the house without wearing a little bit of makeup and a well-chosen outfit. But today, for Kenan's funeral, I don't care how I look. The best I can come up with is black, and with the weather being so hot I opt for black, three-quarter length, linen trousers and a strappy-vest top. No makeup, just dark sunglasses. I want to fade into the background. The boys will be my armour.

Some people can't comprehend why I want Angelo and Louis to be at the funeral, them being so young, but I think they deserve the right to say goodbye to their brother and I know Kenan will want to say goodbye to them. Kenan went to Angie's funeral when he was only six, her own children did as well and, as far as I know, none of them were affected by it. Besides, just like at Angie's funeral, the kids will have a great day afterwards, swimming and playing together and I want their memories of this day to be good ones. Lev has argued with me, but he has accepted that I am not going to give way.

We're ready to go far too early, but I say to Lev I want to get there ahead of anyone else to see Kenan again. Following Lev to the car, I strap the children into their car seats and sit gazing out of the black tinted window while we drive slowly to the crematorium – I can't remember the short journey.

Once there, I go straight to see Kenan in the Chapel of Rest to say my final farewell. Friends have asked if they can add their own items of tribute to his coffin and they are the first things I notice, in particular Eli's and Emily's, who have put in mementos and letters.

I'm only aware other people are arriving when Kenan's headmaster comes in and gently kisses Kenan on his forehead. So many people have been touched by Kenan I realise, but none more so than me and Lev. His strength and courage always amazed us. I don't know how long I'm there, but I force myself to leave his side after a while and go and sit on the steps outside the crematorium and wait for the service to begin.

Lots of people are here now, mingling in a blur above my head. I can't believe how many people have turned up. As I look at the faces around me, I am staggered to see the awful woman from Sandie's party who had proclaimed that it was 'better for a child to die quickly in an accident than to watch a child die slowly.'

In my mind, I walk up to her and knock her out there and then before telling her to 'sod off from my son's funeral' – how dare she turn up? But I have neither the strength nor the willpower. One day I will have my say.

I notice the men mostly, because so many of them are crying. It seems to be the women who are holding it together. One man, whom we know from our Essex days, called Boris, is in tears and not even his wife, Leah can console him. I am transfixed by him as, around our way, Boris is considered a big 'tough' man with a hardened reputation, but today his tears and emotions reveal another side to him. Along with Peter and Simon, Boris was one of the few men that used to ring Kenan whilst he was in hospital. I had no idea and was gobsmacked when he called while I was there one day.

"Is that Boris, Boris?" I'd asked Kenan.

"Yes," Kenan had shrugged. "He rings me quite often."

It means the world to me that Boris took the time to ring Kenan.

I see Balbi talking to Lev – it's time for the service to begin. I'm shaking now, but I stand up and watch, gratefully, as Tracy takes charge of Louis. I found out later that she took charge of a lot of things that day and not all of them for the good. We walk towards the room at the end of the hall, to Eric Clapton's 'Tears in Heaven.' I have no idea why we have chosen that song, I think Lev wanted it. As we enter I see the rows of chairs and fall clumsily into one in the front row, next to Lev. My mum sits on my other side and my heart stops beating for a second when I see Kenan's coffin up on a platform.

Balbi's words wash over me. Mitch gives a speech, but I hear nothing. The only conscious moment I have is when Eli gets up to say a few words. And she is amazing:

"Hello," she starts, *"I'm Eli, Kenan's best friend and girlfriend. He would have loved to see us all here today. I will never forget him – he will be in my heart forever. We had such good times together. I remember our first date at Nanyos, his favourite restaurant – we didn't stop laughing. We will all miss him very much, but we have to be strong. We all love you Kenan. Thank you, bye."*

When she has finished, I notice tears being wiped from a sea of faces, and I want to scoop up this little eleven-year-old girl and hug her tightly for caring so much about my son. She is all I remember of the service. I don't remember breaking down at the end and collapsing on top of Kenan's coffin. I don't remember wailing and refusing to let go, being unable to let go, unable to rid myself of the thought that Kenan needs me with him. But there I am, somehow, hugging the coffin with all my strength and Lev is stepping up to gently try and prise me away. Angelo is by my side too then and it is his presence that brings me back.

"Say goodbye to Kenan, Darling," I tell him and we both kiss his coffin, and I wish I could to stay there forever.

Chapter Twenty-eight

The song playing on the way out of the crematorium is, 'In the Morning,' by Razorlight. It was one of Kenan's favourites and I look around at people wondering if they know that, and if not why not? Relief the service is over is etched onto their faces, but I can't feel anything. I hear little of people's condolences either. I do remember a friend's mum, Marje, taking my hand and saying to me, "There are no words. Just keep talking to him."

I know she understands because she lost her husband quite young, leaving her to bring up three daughters. And you know what? I will *never-ever* stop talking to him.

I sit there with my mum for ages, smiling at the friends and acquaintances that stop to talk to me, before I'm told that Sandy, from the Coastal Bar, and Paula have arranged a wake at a café in Javea. To this day I have no idea who paid for it, but I am very grateful for everyone's generosity. Thank you.

The wake, just like the funeral, is blurred. People begin to relax somewhat and have a drink whilst chatting to friends, but for me it is torture. I take a seat at a table near the doors leading outside and watch everyone mill around. I feel like screaming out, 'Don't you know my son has died?'

I can't believe it – they've moved on already but my life has stopped in its tracks. Even Lev looks normal, although I notice he doesn't touch a drop of alcohol all day, too scared of losing control. I'm battling my urge to just get up and leave. I feel so incredibly lonely even though my family and closest friends are everywhere. Tracy is fussing around me, making herself known to everyone, which is beginning to irritate me, so I move outside with Mum.

"Let's go and check on the boys," I suggest and together we wander outside to where Angelo and Louis are playing in the swimming pool with their mates, under the watchful eye of Kim and Anne. But the scene isn't right – Kenan is missing.

"I want to go back now," I say, unable to endure the laughter of my own children anymore.

"Don't push them away, Gina," my mum tells me.

But I can't deal with that right now. I return to my table and tears roll silently down my face now and again, while people look on, unsure of what to say or if to approach me.

Martin, Paula's husband, suddenly sits down, and to my surprise says gently, "Gina, it's time for change; your life must now change to one that is free of hospitals and medication. You have a purpose, and that is to love your other children."

Those words, spoken by a man who normally says very little to me, even though I've known his wife since I was fifteen, penetrate my shield, for some reason. Perhaps it is the sincerity with which he spoke them.

Before we leave the wake, Tracy approaches the table to say goodbye. She is leaving for England to be godmother to a friend's new baby. She delayed her trip because of today. What an uncanny forty-eight hours for her, saying goodbye to one child shortly before celebrating another's arrival into the world. I expect her to cuddle me goodbye, but instead she says,

"You have my door keys, don't you? Could you just pop round and empty the fridge and maybe give the place a quick tidy? We've had to leave in such a rush because of everything that's happened."

What? I didn't have the strength to clean my own house let alone hers. I'm left speechless by how matter-of-fact her words are. They had an edge to them too. I let it pass though – for now – and say goodbye. We leave shortly after, home to a life without Kenan.

In the days that follow, Lev and I agree that if it wasn't for our other two children, we wouldn't have had the will to go on. What would have been the point?

Chapter Twenty-nine

None of us knew what to do in the immediate days and weeks after the funeral. Kenan's passing had shattered our family and we could only wait to see how, and where, the pieces would land. I would never have predicted, however, that our immediate future would include betrayal or such strange happenings.

We collected Kenan's dolphin from the crematorium the Tuesday after his funeral. Even then, part of me rushed to get there in case he was waiting for us in person, which would mean that the last two weeks had been no more than the cruellest nightmare. I was so excited about being close to him again, and although, of course, he wasn't waiting in person, in a peculiar way I felt as if I was bringing him home.

It was later, when I carefully placed the dolphin in its place in our lounge, between pictures of our other two boys that the truth stared sadly and irrevocably back at me. It was final, the end, all the hope had gone and Kenan's fight was over. It was a massive anti-climax to a long and emotionally exhausting journey, but at least Kenan was finally home, never to leave us again.

The same wasn't true of our friends. Almost all of them immediately escaped the climbing heat of a Spanish summertime and headed back to England after Kenan's funeral. They had to get back to their lives of course, leaving us to cope with ours. But for some reason, I felt angry and resentful they'd left so quickly. I couldn't help but think how false so many of them were. So few of them had bothered to visit Kenan when he was alive, why were they all so quick to flock round as soon as he had passed away?

I felt especially bitter towards those going back to their families and healthy children. I wanted them, more than anyone, to stay and experience my pain. But naturally, none of them could. Only someone who has, like us, lost a child can truly understand the grief. The pain, when it happens at first, is so excruciating, it borders on the horrific, but at least it is physical. You *feel* something.

Afterwards is the real killer, when the mind becomes angry. Irrational and unwanted thoughts crept into my every waking hour, yet life was just expected to go on. That surprised the hell out of me! How fast we were meant to simply move on without Kenan, as if everything that had happened had been no more than an episode from '*EastEnders*'. Somebody dies, they have a funeral, and then what do you know? The following week everyone has forgotten about it. That's not how it is in real life. The torment goes on forever and the ache and longing never leave your side.

Close friends did try to be kind and sympathetic, telling me that I'd see Kenan in the things that Angelo and Louis did, but none of it helped. In any case, I was scared to throw much of myself into Angelo and Louis in fear that something happened to them too.

When I did start to venture out again, a couple of weeks after the funeral, there were some people who pretended they hadn't seen me, or they crossed to the other side of the road, even though they knew me. Summer sunglasses hid people's stares, but I knew that among our small expat community, I had been labelled as 'tragic' or 'the poor woman whose son has just died from leukaemia'. In a place the size of Javea, there was no escaping from it.

The thing was, I *wasn't* tragic – I was hurting and I was upset. If only people had approached me, then they would have realised that all I wanted was for them to remember Kenan. Ignoring me meant they'd already forgotten he ever existed. I wanted to talk endlessly about him and yes, to *anyone* who'd listen.

I understand that people didn't want to be embarrassed by my ramblings or weeping. I realise they were apprehensive in case they said something 'wrong' – but to be shunned by people was a terrible feeling.

What they didn't grasp was that I *had* to talk about him, because I couldn't consciously cope with losing Kenan in the immediate days after his passing, neither my head nor my heart could even begin to come to terms with it. I know it's selfish, but I couldn't stop thinking that the days we'd spent traipsing back and forth to the hospital were the good ones even though Kenan was ill and in pain, because he was here at least. And I wanted him to be here, whatever the price, even in hospital miles away from home.

I struggled daily to complete even simple tasks like changing Louis or getting him dressed, because my mind wondered, constantly thinking about Kenan. I broke down in tears all the time because I missed him so much.

Lev and the boys were suffering too, of course. Angelo became very quiet and never left Lev's side, which in many ways helped Lev, but being so young he was very confused about where Kenan had gone to and he didn't understand why he wasn't ever coming back again.

As a family, we sat together and watched films of us all with Kenan, thinking it might help. But unlike me and Lev, Angelo didn't find comfort in them. One afternoon while we were watching a film of Lev messing around with Kenan in their own version of, 'Cribs,' the MTV programme about celebrities' houses, Angelo disappeared to his room as soon as Kenan came on the TV screen. I followed him and our conversation made my heart ache even more.

"Don't you want to watch Kenan?" I asked him

"No." Angelo replied.

"Why?"

"My stomach hurts."

"Angelo, do you feel sad?"

"Yes."

"Do you feel like crying?"

"I don't know."

I gave him a cuddle, then let him be and joined Lev to watch the rest of the film. A while later Angelo

asked me if he could ring Kenan. I didn't know what
to say.

"No, Darling, you can't," I sighed,
"Why not, don't they have phones in heaven?"
"No, Darling. They don't." I wanted to cry for
him.
"Then can I go and see him?"
"No, because if you do, you can't come back"
"That's OK, because Kenan can look after
me."

Angelo tried desperately to get to grips with why he
wasn't able to see or speak to Kenan, but he was only
five years old and it was simply beyond his years to
comprehend why Kenan couldn't return from heaven.
And no wonder he was confused, because when
Kenan was alive and I'd left home to visit him at the
hospital, I'd always promised Angelo that his big
brother would be home again soon; now I was telling
him that Kenan wouldn't ever be home again.

Angelo missed him more than he could
express, but crazy as I was at the time, I was aware
enough to know that he needed to feel comfortable
talking to us, in his own way, about Kenan. So, as a
family we answered his questions and did the best we
could.

Louis' mood was very different to Angelo's.
He was 'distracted' a lot of the time, and his actions I
can only describe as 'odd'. I can't explain why but,
during the first week after Kenan's funeral, strange
things started to happen and they usually involved
Louis.

At first I thought Louis' strange behaviour
was his way of coping with my constant crying,

because at only two and a half he didn't know why Mummy was so upset all the time. But thinking back, Louis had begun to act differently as early as the day after Kenan had passed away.

When Lev and I got back from the hospital, late on that heartbreaking, surreal night, Lev panicked because he couldn't find his camera, which held pictures of Kenan that he'd taken in America. He frantically searched all over the house for that camera but it was nowhere and Lev's a typical bloke where gadget stuff is concerned – he can't find a pair of socks, but a camera or an iPod has its 'proper' place. The camera was always kept in the kitchen cupboard away from where the boys could get hold of it, especially Louis who was into everything. But it wasn't there.

The next day, I was sat in the garden with Floria and Mehmet when I heard Lev asking Louis, "Where did you get that from? Gina! Come and see what Louis has got!" Rushing in, I saw Louis, his arms outstretched towards Lev holding the missing camera in his hands.

"For you, Daddy," he said. Lev was trying to get Louis to say where he'd found it and his reply stunned us. "Kenan give it me, for you, Daddy," Me and Lev just stared at each other before staring back at Louis. I ran upstairs to where Louis had been playing but found nothing out of place in his bedroom or Angelo's. Then me and Floria took Louis up to his room and she asked him to show her where he'd found the camera, but he couldn't. Instead, he climbed on his bed and, as me and Floria watched, started jumping up and down saying, "I love you Kenan," over and over again, all the while looking above his head. Eventually I had to calm him down and make him stop. The whole episode left us unnerved to say the least.

The following day, Louis again seemed peculiar somehow. He'd taken a red hat with 'Support Leukaemia' printed on it from Lev's dad, and although it was usually impossible to make Louis wear a hat, he'd put it on and point-blank refused to take it off again. Mehmet tried to coax it back, but Louis was having none of it, so Mehmet gave it up, deciding to wait until he got bored with it.

Later on, Louis found a toy car that my friend Mandy had bought him. He'd never shown any interest in it, but Kenan had the same toy at a similar age and I was standing by the pool on the phone, when Louis ambled out with the red hat on his head and the red racing car in his hands. I called out to him, but he didn't hear me, so quickly hanging up my call, I stood watching him, not saying a word. Mehmet came out too and commented on how out of the ordinary Louis was behaving. We watched him play with the car for at least ten minutes before he even noticed we were there. In a flash he took off the red hat and abandoned the red car on the floor. He never picked up either of them again.

Whilst changing his nappy one day, Louis suddenly became spookily silent, as if he was in a trance and he started staring at me, in a really penetrating way. In a soppy, baby-style voice, I tickled his tummy and said, "Love you," because usually Louis would smile and say, 'Love you,' back, but that day he said nothing.

For some reason I then said, "I love you so much," in my normal voice, which is what I used to say to Kenan.

Louis said, still staring. "I love you too," in a voice that didn't belong to a two and a half year old.

It freaked me out, but when Lev walked into the room the trance was broken and Louis reverted to his normal toddler-self again. Real, or imagined? Who knows? I'll never forget it however, because it was from that moment on, that I began to believe that Kenan must be communicating with us through Louis.

For weeks after that I asked Louis what he was doing, because nearly every day something happened that would half freak me out and half comfort me. He might take two yogurts from the fridge and say one of them was for Kenan, or pat his hand on the rug for Kenan to sit down next to him. If I asked him where Kenan was, he'd point to an empty space beside him or say that Kenan was in his bedroom. He'd say this quite matter of fact, so I never questioned him. I have no doubt that Louis believed he was seeing Kenan.

If it had been Angelo telling me these things I'm not sure I would have believed him, but Louis was only two – he couldn't have been making it up. Was he imagining it? I don't know, but I hope in my heart that it was Kenan, somehow letting us know he was still around. In any case, strange happenings weren't going on only with Louis. In the weeks to come, my belief in life after death only grew stronger; even Lev was forced to question his totally opposite belief, because no matter how hard we tried to dismiss it, inexplicable things started to happen.

Chapter Thirty

Lev had to get back to England for work a couple of weeks after the funeral and I felt so alone, even within my own family who were still struggling to put personal feelings aside and get along. There was so much anger in all of us, now Kenan had gone, and we were so lost and without direction, that I should have seen the row I had with Maureen, coming.

It happened the night after Lev had left for the UK, during dinner at my house. Maureen and Mehmet were there, ignoring each other as usual, and my mum and dad had joined us as well.

Maureen, by this time, was living back at my mum and dad's having moved out of the studio apartment – 'temporarily' she said. I cooked a pasta dish, Mum laid the table outside on the naya, and despite the fact that my appetite was still practically non-existent, we all got stuck in.

I can recall it being wonderfully tasty, for some reason. The chirping crickets in the garden, supplied the background music, and we chatted amiably on and off until my mum asked me what Lev was doing that night. I told her he'd gone to visit his brother, 'Big Kenan' and Sandra, to see his new nephew, Noah. It was hard for Lev emotionally, I said. He didn't really want to go, but felt he ought to. We both knew it wasn't the baby's fault he had been born on the same day as Kenan's funeral, but his birthday is a date that will sadly always remind us of what we have lost.

Maureen took all this in sitting next to me, and then turned around and said, "Why is it hard for Lev?"

"Well, it would be wouldn't it," I told her. "After all he's just lost his first-born son and Kenan is celebrating the arrival of his. It's going to be tough for Lev."

"Why?" Maureen pressed. "It's not the baby's fault."

"Yes, I know that Maureen, but it is still hard to deal with. How can you not see that?"

"I don't see why it's tough for Lev – it's a baby."

I gave up trying to make her see, "Oh just leave it Maureen …. "

"Yes, but …"

"I said just leave it!"

My dad had started kicking her under the table in an attempt to get her to shut her stupid mouth. Mum tried changing the subject, while Mehmet just carried on eating. Either he agreed with her or, more likely, he knew how futile it was to try and get Maureen to drop it. She kept on and on about how it wasn't the baby's fault he had been born on the same day as Kenan's funeral, until I could stand it no more. I pushed back my chair, stood up, leant right over her and she started to push her chair back as well.

"No, you wouldn't understand would you?" I screamed. "You've got your sons and your grandchildren. But we've lost our son and you just don't get it!" Still she didn't back down.

"You're overreacting, Gina. I simply mean that it's wrong to blame the baby."

Even as she stood up to face me, she didn't shut up. But that's the thing about Maureen, in all our many rows she has never once shied away. She comes across as sweet and mild, but her skin is as tough as a buffalo's balls. I snapped and pushed her backwards, shouting at her to see it from mine and Lev's point of view, but she kept harping on and on about her new grandson. The red mist came down fast, I put my hands tightly around her throat, and squeezed until she started choking. Dad pulled me off but I was too far gone then.

"Get out of my house, get out, get out, get out!" I screeched. "You are nothing but an evil old cow; it should have been you that died. Fuck off!"

Somehow we'd managed to move during the course of the row from the table on the naya outside the house, to the entrance gate down below. I sensed we were being watched and looked up to see Angelo and Louis staring at me horrified, their mummy completely out of control. And I started to cry, ashamed and angry with myself for losing my temper and, even worse, for allowing my children to witness it. I needed help, so I rang Lev at Kenan and Sandra's.

Ironically, he was coping fine, but I demanded he book the first flight back to England for his mum; I wanted her gone. She wanted to go anyway she said and as far as I was concerned, the sooner the better.

276

My mum stayed with me that night; unable to bear the thought of going back home with Maureen, as she knew that she probably would end up in a row with her as well. Maureen *never* let things drop.

Lev realised how close to the edge I was, and rang my friend Kim who came round with a bottle of wine to keep an eye on me, which was greatly appreciated. I'd managed to settle the boys again by the time she arrived but I felt awful. They had been shocked and scared by my outburst. When they were sleeping again, the four of us, me, Mum, Mehmet and Kim went and sat on the naya, wrapped in the warmth of the evening, not saying much, just drinking the wine. That was when the 'things' began to happen again.

My phone beeped suddenly, interrupting our comfortable silence. It was a text message from the woman I had bumped into at the nursery, the one who had told me to contact her when I was 'ready' for a reading. I've called her Molly, because she doesn't want anyone to know who she is. The text read, '*He wants you to put on 'Love me Tender,' by Elvis Presley.*'

I stared at my phone, not quite understanding what the message meant. I knew nothing of Molly before that night. In the past we had chatted briefly, as one mum to another, when we dropped our children off at the nursery, but our backgrounds and friends were totally different. She had never been to my house or into my confidence and knew none of my likes or dislikes, as I knew nothing of hers. Her contacting me so suddenly, and on a night that I felt especially vulnerable and wretched, took me by surprise.

She had suggested we play something by Elvis Presley. How did she know Kenan loved Elvis, just like Lev did? I'd even arranged an Elvis impersonator for our wedding as a surprise for Lev, and he and Kenan used to play Elvis CDs every Sunday morning whilst they cooked breakfast together. The phone, still tightly gripped in my hands, beeped a second time. It was Molly again. *"You must play it now,"* read the message.

I wasn't sure if I could even find the CD let alone play it, as over the time we'd been in Spain, Lev had taken a pile backwards and forwards to England with him. I showed the messages to Kim and to my mum and then went to search for the CD. I found it straightaway. 'Love me Tender' was the first song listed on the back of the box, however, not realising, when I took out the CD, it said on the front, 'Are You Lonesome Tonight.' It had obviously been put back in the wrong box.

Nevertheless, I put the CD on and pressed play. Instead of 'Love Me Tender', 'Are You Lonesome Tonight' came through the speakers.

"This isn't 'Love me Tender'," I exclaimed to my mum, "I'm turning it off." But Mum didn't let me.

"No," she said. "It is the right song, just listen." So I sat and I listened, as Elvis asked if I was lonesome tonight and, for a moment, I didn't feel so desperate or lonely, as the music and the words took over the emptiness. Yet the pain in my chest burned worse than ever, because the song expressed everything I was feeling. If only Kenan *was* standing there. Only he could ease my agony.

'Love me Tender' was wrong, but 'Are You Lonesome Tonight?' was so, so right – the right song, in the wrong box.

We all looked at each other and we cried, really cried. Mehmet had to get up and go and wander around the garden and after a while I rang Molly and told her what had happened. She said that Kenan was very anxious and worried about me. I decided not to tell her about the argument with Maureen that night, but made up my mind I would have a reading with her. Anything that brought me closer to Kenan had to be good. Molly also said that Kenan wanted me to put his things back and leave his wallet alone. That did make me laugh, because Kenan was always fretting about hiding his wallet from me to stop me dipping in it while he was away! I'd always put the money back again – eventually – but he always knew that.

That night, Molly made me feel as if I was really connecting with Kenan again, and I craved more. I wanted as much as I could get, even though deep down I knew it would never be enough. That was the start of my relationship with Molly and she has been a wonderful friend ever since.

I can't listen to Elvis anymore these days, or the two songs that were played at Kenan's funeral. If they come on the radio, I switch them off.

The day after my row with Maureen she left for England, but her leaving broke the spell that had bound us together for so many months, and Mehmet announced too, that it was time for him to go home. He needed to get away from the sadness and emotional outbursts, but it still felt like rats leaving a sinking ship. Where could we go? I wanted to run away too from all the pain, but I had no choice but to face the grief head-on.

With the benefit of hindsight, I now realise that it was better for me that way, because now the torment can't haunt me for evermore.

But when Mehmet left, I was honestly distraught. Me and Mehmet had formed a bond over the time he'd lived with us. It was Mehmet who was around for me while Mum and Maureen were at the hospital with Kenan. It was Mehmet who had prepared the dinner for me and the boys and it was him that I had sat alongside in the quiet of the evening, sharing a cigarette and chatting into the early hours, after the kids had gone to bed.

We were easy in each other's company and were able go about our routines without upsetting the other. I missed him when he left. I missed that time we had together, when Kenan was alive and when hope was too. But that was then. Our lives had been changed forever, and we all had to move on.

Chapter Thirty-one

Eli and Emily struggled too, at coming to terms with Kenan's passing. They were so young to have experienced the loss of someone their own age – Eli had lost her first love and Emily a life-long friend.

Me and Lev started to spend a lot of time with Eli and her parents, Karen and Simon, and her lovely sister Alice, and somehow it felt the natural thing to do. Their friendship helped us begin the move forward.

Lev found solace chatting over a beer with Simon, who listened endlessly to his memories, all the while offering him support as Lev was hurting. As a result they are now, and always will be, very good friends. The same was true of me and Karen, who also had Eli's feelings to take care of.

As Kenan's girlfriend, Eli was privileged to know about his memory box and she asked me one day if she could come and see it. Me and Lev were more than happy for her to, so along with Emily and Alice, we all sat in the cool of Kenan's bedroom and looked through the box.

Lev asked Eli and Emily if they wanted a teddy bear off Kenan's bed and they jumped at the chance of having something of Kenan's to take home. This was hard for me, because Kenan's bedroom was exactly as he'd left it. Even the clothes he was wearing on his final trip to the hospital were hung over the back of his chair, so that I could breathe in his scent, at night. They are still there today – I couldn't ever bear to wash them. But I thought Kenan would want the girls to have the teddies, so I let them go.

We fingered through the items in the box – the photos, souvenir coins, letters between him and Eli. Alice was particularly engrossed in the stories he'd written, and part way through broke off to ask me,

"Have you read these, Gina?"

"Yes." I replied.

"No, I mean have you *really* read them. Listen." She looked me straight in the eyes, and started to read out sections of Kenan's story.

'I saw my mummy again as an old woman ... ...''

She said, "where have you been Kenan? I've been looking for you. You haven't aged!"

Then she read from the final page, the part he'd written the day *before* he died,

"And I walked up to these two golden gates, guarded by two ... ...'

That's as far as Kenan had managed to get. He knew. Kenan had known his fate. Had he been trying to tell us too? Was that why he had shown me the story? We sat in silence trying to absorb this possibility until Eli broke in.

"Who's this?" she demanded.

I had to laugh. The look on her face was pure jealousy. She was holding a picture of Kenan and his friend, Abigail, with whom we had spent a day at Aqualandia, the water park in Benidorm, the previous year. Abigail's parents – Gail and Eddy – are long-time friends of ours and had a holiday home in Alicante. Kenan and Abigail had spent the whole day together, riding down the waterslides.

The unusual thing about that day was that me and Gail had let them go round by themselves while we played with the younger ones, even though they were only ten years old. We felt relaxed enough to give them the freedom, happy that they knew where we were. But we've often asked ourselves why we did that. Some things are obviously meant to be. Anyway, hence the picture of Abigail, and Eli's subsequent worried reaction to it. It was a good memory I told her, that was all, and was therefore worthy of a place in the memory box. I'm not certain she was convinced!

With regards to Kenan's story, I wasn't sure what to make of it, but a while later I read in *Grazia* magazine (again), a story about sixteen-year old, Ben Kinsella who had been murdered in a despicable, unprovoked attack in London. In the article his sister had written:

'In an essay we found in his room, Ben describes being attacked by an imaginary killer and of being cradled by an imaginary girlfriend. His story includes the words, "I've been stabbed. Three times in the chest." He also wrote that he was

surrounded by loved ones in hospital, but how his world turned black, and suddenly he is in heaven.'

After reading that article it made me think. Is our death written into our sub-conscience? Or is it all a coincidence? And why do we, the ones left behind, never get to realise it, until it is too late? Is there life after death? I don't know, but I do think that most of us need to believe there is something.

Years ago, when I was 'spiritual' I did readings for people, usually by holding a piece of their jewellery, and somewhere between my own psychic experiences and the things that had happened since Kenan died, meant I did believe, and still do believe, there is at least a window of time after a person dies, that we can connect with them again.

Now after re-examining Kenan's story, and following Molly's text messages, I was eager to get a reading done as soon as possible, so the day after Eli and Emily's visit, I went round to Molly's with Mum, leaving the kids with Dad. I was desperate to keep Kenan close to me – above all I wanted to know he was OK because no matter how hard I tried, I just couldn't reach him myself.

Chapter Thirty-two

We sat out in Molly's garden, in the shade, away from the warm sun, drinking tea and smoking cigarettes, while Molly channelled the 'energy' she picked up. She did this through writing – and my God did she write.

Before, during and after the reading I cried hysterically, unable to control my torrent of tears.

Did the reading help? Yes and no, because the more I believed and the more I heard the more I wanted the real thing. And I wanted Kenan, alive and happy and healthy. Molly wrote quickly and there is no other way she could have known what she did, other than from Kenan.

I hadn't told her about the argument with Maureen, or about the girls taking Kenan's teddy bears, or mine and Lev's late-night debates about moving to America, or about a watch of Kenan's I'd been searching for, or the letter that I put in Kenan's coffin. But she knew it all, even my feelings about some people at the funeral. Here is a small part of what she wrote that day:

Mummy, do you know anything about the circle of life? You have to understand birth, death, life are connected. I love my nan and I love you so much. But other people have their lives too. Don't be so angry about everything, they don't mean to hurt you. Daddy took me to the park, other babies need to have this experience as well. Be happy for them Mum. Don't be angry about other people. Giving birth is a part of life. I am happy for them.

.....I am with you all the time. It is over but I am not over yet. You did your very best. I did my very best. ....Hello Grandma, you are there too? I am with you all the time. It has been a big shock to me as well but it is okay now.

You've too many questions Mum. Take your time. Love comes first with everything. Why are you so bothered about this watch? It is in the bedroom, okay?

.....I am here with lots of nice people. Very different from the false people around you Mummy! I know you feel shocked....You'll never get over the first shock and I am okay.

.....I am not ready for Eli yet. She has my little heart and for now that's enough. I am okay, really. I can tell you 1000 times the same thing, but I know you will ask me this question over and over. I knew I was dying. I chose for you not to be there Mum. Don't look for me. Don't give all my teddies away! They were mine!!!!!!!

......Why did you write you wished you were lying next to me? You're alive! It's my time not yours. Lots of people need you like Dad, Louis and Angelo. Open up and feel me!!!! I don't want to go back – this is much better for me.

.....Tell Dad I will come for a visit one of these days. He knows I am with him since he came back to Spain. He knows our friendship was good.

.....What else do you want to know? I am with lots of people I know – will tell you later. Can't open any doors so don't need the keys.

....Don't go to America, I want to stay here. We can't stay there – we had to come back. I want more time with you wherever you are. Fishing – would like to do this again with Dad. With Daddy I was a big boy, with Mummy I was a little boy. You let me go, you've given me the chance to go. I've had enough – more than enough.

.....I loved going out, I really loved going out with Dad. Dad is like me – we are one!!!! ....I need a rest. We will meet again.

It was difficult for me to listen, not only because of what Molly had furiously written, but because Kenan obviously felt that he could talk with her, but not to me. Relying on someone else to hear from my own son was one of the hardest things I've had to do. I wanted to talk to him; I wanted to see him, to tell him everything was a nightmare, and that this wasn't how it was meant to end.

But to date, I have never been able to 'contact' Kenan myself.

I'm aware that some of what Molly wrote could be relevant to anyone in our situation, but so much of it meant something only to us. The watch she talked of was the one Lev had bought Kenan not long before he died, and he'd been anxious to find it. She told me about Angie, of whom she knew nothing, describing her exactly, from the colour of her hair to her bubbly personality.

It all made perfect sense to me because who else would Kenan be with other than Angie? She would take care of him and protect him, laugh with him. By coincidence, a few months after Kenan died Angie's parents, Kath and Brian, had contacted me. They lived in Spain, a few miles south from us and had heard about what happened to Kenan through the grapevine, so we went to visit them.

They later came to see us in Javea and brought Angie's children with them. I hadn't seen the kids for a long time and it was a very surreal experience. Olivia was then nine years old and the absolute image of Angie. It took my breath away when I saw her. Harry was twelve and very tall but still a child. I felt so much joy at seeing Olivia and Harry again; joy at how well they were growing up, but the reunion left me with sadness too. Angie should have been there with them and Kenan should have been playing with Harry. But we kept our own individual sorrows buried deep in our hearts, and the day was a happy one.

Chapter Thirty-three

As the days passed and the summer reached its peak, Tracy encouraged me to get out more with Angelo and Louis. Even though Tracy had her own place, she was virtually living at my house with her kids, so often we'd go out together to one or other of the local beaches. I hated leaving the house, but it was the summer holidays and I knew I had to trade the security of my home for the benefit of everyone's sanity.

I was vaguely aware that Tracy was keeping me close to her, although I didn't feel she was deliberately keeping me away from other people. However, unbeknown to me, other friends had started to question her motives and found it annoying that whenever I met them, Tracy came too. But Tracy made me feel safe and I didn't have any real reason to question her behaviour so I continued cooking meals for her and her children, and let her come and go more or less as she pleased.

I was conscious that Tracy didn't like my growing friendship with Molly however, so it surprised me when she got herself a job cleaning her house. Later, it transpired that Tracy had tried hard to stir up trouble between myself and Molly, because I saw Molly a lot after the reading and it wasn't long before she knew me inside out.

I might be standing in the kitchen, thinking of Kenan, perhaps even shaking with grief and my phone would beep with a message from her. *Are you OK? What's wrong?*

It was as if we had some strange kind of telepathy and she knew my feelings before I did. Sometimes she might ring to tell me something Kenan had said, like the time he wanted to remind me that his rock collection was still under his bed, and often she would speak the exact same words I'd be thinking in my head.

It was really freaky and it happened a lot. She even picked up on Lev's dreams. She knew I wasn't able to dream of Kenan, but at that time Lev was seeing him often in his. She called to tell him she'd dreamt about Lev and Kenan playing in the snow. The night before Lev had dreamt of the two of them skiing. Even Lev, a *complete* non-believer, was gracious enough to at least think it peculiar, although he prefers to believe that all things 'odd' were just coincidence.

Yes, Molly had become a big part of my life and Tracy wasn't happy about it. It became obvious how desperate she was when, one day, she announced that she too was psychic. It was the first I'd heard of it in thirty-five years.

"But don't you remember?" she'd said. "From when we were young I was like that."

I honestly didn't remember, but not wanting to upset her I agreed. In hindsight, perhaps I should have been more honest, because her new, 'psychic' skills were in part responsible for our friendship ending.

For reasons I will never know, she took it upon herself to tell my mum that she had seen Kenan and that Kenan had something or someone with him that was evil. My mum stopped her and refused to let her go on, but what kind of woman tells another woman who has just lost their grandson something like that?

Tracy knew too that my mum felt terrible about being the one who was at the hospital the morning Kenan passed away and that she was already battling with her nerves, guilt and depression. When my mum told me, I said the only 'evil' around, was Tracy herself, but I wasn't able to explain why she'd said it.

She also started to call my friends, Karen and Paula, forcing her company on them, gossiping about me and insinuating that I'd been talking about them behind their backs. She told Paula to be careful who she trusted as people use people in Javea, then she said the same to Karen and then she said the same to me! Talk about stirring, but my real friends protected me and never let on to how they really felt as they knew I needed Tracy. Kenan's words, 'All the false people around you, Mummy,' did ring in my head, but I never believed it was referring to my childhood friend.

I still spent so much time with her. As I said, she was round my house constantly, so often in fact that my neighbour thought she'd moved in. Sometimes I'd just wish she'd go home and give me some space, but generally I was happy to have her with me.

I put what she said to my mum down to a moment of madness, but I realised how rocky our friendship was becoming when she refused to help me out, after I fell into a spot of trouble with the police a short while later.

We'd arranged to treat the kids to a train trip from Tracy's sleepy home-town of Gata, to the brighter lights of Benidorm, but driving to the station the police stopped me. My own car had broken down, so I'd borrowed my dad's old, Mazda convertible. It didn't have much space in the back, and the kids didn't fit in safely so, annoyingly but quite rightly, the police pulled me over.

Luckily, a friend who spoke fluent Spanish stopped to help when she saw me in trouble, and obviously explained that I'd just lost my son and wasn't thinking straight. The Spanish police aren't known for their leniency, but they let me off, although they wouldn't let me leave in the Mazda. I had to arrange alternative transport, so I called Tracy to let her know what had happened, thinking she would come and pick me up. Instead, she said she'd made her plans for the day and was going to go to Benidorm without me. I was astounded as I honestly thought she'd come and get me and we'd catch a later train. I still remember the conversation:

"But the kids are looking forward to it," she said.

"Mine are too. We can still go, but later."

"Don't worry about it. You go home and we'll go."

"What? Why can't you just come and get me?" I must have raised my voice because she started to shout at me then.

"Don't expect me to just drop everything, I'm not your slave and don't you dare talk to me like that."

"Not your slave!" I shouted back, "What does that mean? I thought we were going to have a day out together."

And then she cut me off, leaving me stranded in the high street, in the scorching heat, with two kids and a car I wasn't allowed to drive. I rang back but she cut me off again. I was fuming. I had rarely rowed with Tracy in all the years I'd known her, but who the hell did she think she was?

I calmed down eventually and called my dad instead, who, of course, collected us and took us home. An hour later, Molly called me to ask what had happened. Unbelievably, Tracy had phoned her, slagging me off. Then Paula phoned. Tracy had called her too, again spouting the same rubbish. These were my friends she was calling. What was the matter with her?

Molly refused to tell me what Tracy had said, but suggested instead that as we'd been friends for such a long time we ought to try and make it up. We were both under a lot of stress. So with Molly's words in my mind, when Tracy called later, we both apologised and made arrangements for her to come over the next day. We were fine, but the cracks were there and, without really realising why, I had started to question our friendship.

We grew further apart when, one late, crazy night, she accompanied me and Molly to Kenan's room. Now that she was 'psychic', Tracy wanted to be included whenever me and Molly got together and again, not wanting to upset her, I let her, even though I had my doubts about her psychic sincerity.

The 'strange' things involving Louis after Kenan's death had started to slow down, leaving me now searching for other ways to connect with him. Hence the visit, that night, to his bedroom. Molly had been encouraging me to delve into my spiritual side again and it had started to work a little. Standing in the pitch black of Kenan's bedroom that night, I saw a figure. It wasn't Kenan, but an older woman who began to tell me about things she had given Tracy. It must have been her grandmother, but as I spoke the words she was telling me out loud, Tracy completely freaked out. She frantically started scratching at the door to get out. But I was standing in front of it... and I couldn't move.

"Get out of the way!" she screamed at me.

"Gina, open the door!" said Molly. When I moved aside, Tracy flew past me and ran upstairs to the safety of the light. I looked at Molly, shocked by Tracy's response and my own. I was more shocked by that, than by the figure I had just seen. Molly and me 'believed', so what had just occurred didn't surprise or scare us. We weren't playing some stupid game of attention-seeking bullshit like Tracy obviously had been. I was *desperate* to see Kenan and if it meant seeing others again first then so be it.

Why had Tracy gone into the bedroom of a child that had just died, with a medium and the child's mother if she didn't truly believe? There was always the chance that something might happen.

Floria interrupted us, by ringing to ask me what I was doing because 'odd' things had suddenly started to happen at her house. The TV and lights had started flickering, even though they were all switched off. You see, there are always three and Tracy was never meant to be part of the three. Perhaps you might be reading this thinking I had lost my mind and maybe I had, but what I saw was significant to me.

I didn't get to see Kenan, but the fact that I had seen somebody that night, left me with hope that I may one day be able to communicate with Kenan again.

Tracy never talked about what happened, and I never pushed her to. We were a little awkward together for a while, but as these things do, it passed. We continued pretty much as we'd been before and then she made plans to go back to England for a holiday. I asked her if while she was there she'd make a copy of the video her boy, Jack had taken of Kenan, two weeks before he died. It's the last video we have of him. I'd asked her to make me a copy when she'd gone back to the UK after the funeral, but she told me that she had forgotten to do it, so this time she promised.

Tracy also warned me to be careful of Molly whilst she was away and not to trust her. When I pressed her why, she told me that Molly had said some things to her that she couldn't repeat. I begged her to tell me. Apparently Molly had said that Kenan hadn't liked my mum being with him, nor did he like where he was now. Here she was, again, spreading what I suspected must be a pack of lies, but she was my friend and her words crushed my self-belief and confidence. Tracy was at times being so spiteful, that deep down I was beginning to sense that there must be something else going on here – which there was.

On the day she left for England, we had lunch, even though she'd been reluctant to see me. In a roundabout manner she told me she was going back, not for a holiday but to live there again. Life in Spain wasn't as she'd imagined, and Mike, like Lev, had to work mostly back in England, so she wanted to go home. She said she'd be back to pack up the house, and that she'd send me the video of Kenan.

I can't really describe how I felt about her decision to leave, I hadn't expected it. Needless to say, the video never did arrive and I didn't hear a dicky bird from her. In August, on my birthday, I found out just how bitter Tracy had become towards me. I was out with Paula when she suddenly received a text from Tracy. It said she was coming back at the end of the month to tie-up loose ends. Why hadn't she texted me I wondered? I asked Paula what the hell was going on.

Tracy had been talking about me behind my back for some time and had been calling Paula and my other friends, although they never returned her calls. I then rang Molly to ask her if what Tracy had said about Kenan was true. Of course if wasn't and Molly was livid. She called Tracy there and then. Text messages raced back and forth between all of us, but that was the end of it. Our friendship was over.

Had I been in my normal state of mind, I'd have phoned the bitch myself and had it out with her once and for all, but my confidence was low and I didn't know who to trust anymore. If I couldn't trust my friend of thirty-five years, then who could I? I felt so dumb that people, who'd only known her two minutes, had worked her out and had never liked or trusted her.

But what bothered me more than anything, was that I didn't know why she had turned against me. When Lev came home he called Mike and during their heated discussion, the truth finally came out. What was really eating Tracy, the reason she had grown so nasty towards me, was this.

I'd not stood up at the funeral and thanked her for all the hours of help she'd given me.

"It was a funeral, not a wedding," I heard Lev rightly point out to Mike. "What planet is she on?"

No-one was 'thanked' that day. Real friends don't need to be thanked; they help each other through hard times knowing it is always appreciated. They do not go around saying hurtful, horrible, untrue things because they haven't been 'thanked'.

She never sent the recording of Kenan either. Lev managed to get it after weeks of upset and pleading with Mike, but only because their son, Jack, Kenan's friend, agreed to meet with him and make a copy.

About a year later, Tracy contacted me via text. As far as I knew they hadn't been back and had just abandoned their house in Spain to the bank, unable to sell it quickly. The text said that she often thought about me and Kenan and that time was a great healer. If I ever wanted to contact her, I could. Well, I did want to and I didn't. I was ready by then to face her, to hear what she had to say, but Lev asked me if I wanted to be friends with her again. No, no I didn't. I would never have been able to trust her, so what would have been the point? She'd only have lied anyway.

Everyone had said the same thing about Tracy – Paula, Karen, Molly, Floria – none of them had trusted her, and they had all been right. But it still hurts, because I will never understand what possessed her to act the way she did.

Chapter Thirty-four

Despite everything that happened between us, losing Tracy from my life, like losing Kenan, was never meant to happen. I felt like closing myself off from the world again, but just before the summer holidays ended, Lev suggested going away. He needed to escape from what had happened to Kenan and to get away from everyone who knew us, but I didn't want to leave Javea. He persuaded me it was the right thing to do for Angelo and Louis; they still needed a holiday. So I duly booked a family hotel for a week in a resort called Mojacar, about three hours south of Javea. To everybody else we were just another happy family enjoying ourselves, playing in the pool, building sand castles on the beach, frequenting the children's play areas. No one guessed that one of our children was missing.

I took a family picture of the five of us along with me though, which was my way of taking Kenan too. Lev was great with the kids as usual, playing and messing about, giving me the space to just be.

Louis started to behave oddly again while we were there. When I was reading one day next to the pool and Lev was attempting to teach Angelo how to play pool, Louis pulled up two chairs to the table I was sitting at.

"Who's that one for?" I asked him, pointing at one of the chairs.

"That's for Kenan," he said, just as Lev came back with Angelo.

"Where is Kenan?" I asked him, glancing at Lev to try and gauge his reaction.

"He's sitting there!" Louis said and pointed to the empty chair. Lev was staring at me now. He thought I'd made Louis say it.

"I've said nothing, don't blame me." But nothing would make Lev believe that it was anything more than Louis' imagination.

On the surface Lev had coped with losing Kenan fantastically, strong and there for me and the kids, but I knew he was suffering badly. He laughed at me throwing myself into searching for Kenan, but I knew that he'd turned to the numbing effect of 'the bottle' to help him. He had started to drink quite heavily by this time and his moods changed frequently depending on how much alcohol he'd had. He'd start happy, get a little more chilled, then talkative until the drink finally took him over and he became aggressive and argumentative.

He was fine, always, with the kids, but angry with me. He belittled my beliefs about Kenan even though I never pushed them on him, screaming at me on occasion, "He is dead, gone and that's it!"

It was the drink talking, not Lev, but I was so mad with him at times.

When the holiday ended we came home further apart than when we'd left. Angelo and Louis had enjoyed it, but being away from Javea had changed nothing of course. What it had done for us was to get us through another week. And that we realised was the only way forward now, one day, one week, one month at a time – it was the best we could do.

Lev

Not many people realise that alcoholism is a progressive disease and I find it hard to talk about, but Gina thinks I need to, so here it is.

I was always a heavy drinker like most blokes I know. Work hard, play hard was the motto I grew up with and being a piss-head was par for the course in the industry I worked in. Floor laying is that kind of job. Like many trades, it's a big drinking culture and you show your worth on site and in the bar. That's OK in your youth, but it doesn't work when you get a wife and a family.

I started overdoing it when Kenan was having chemo first time round. It was a conscious thing too – if he was being poisoned, then I was gonna poison myself as well. Then it was, if he can't eat, then I'm not gonna eat either.

I became a master at hiding it, like all alcoholics are, saying I was going for a coffee and necking six beers instead – no one even knew.

Alcoholics can handle booze well, but that doesn't make it less of a problem, and one that is likely to kill them in the end.

For a long time I told myself I was in control of it, because the line between heavy drinking and alcoholism is a fine one, that once crossed is very hard to come back from.

Maybe it was worse because I was on my own a lot, travelling back and forth from the family, or maybe that was only the excuse – whatever, after Kenan died, I crossed the line and went over.

Chapter Thirty-five

Between my 'searching' for Kenan, and Lev's growing dependency on the drink, our relationship started to falter. We just stalled really, unable to understand each other or to communicate with one another. We talked and rowed about splitting up, but we stuck it out and almost without us noticing it was suddenly December and our first Christmas without Kenan loomed.

With that milestone on the horizon, I decided it was time I went back to *La Fe* hospital in Valencia. I'd been putting it off, but I knew I needed to take one final trip back to get what we like to call these days 'closure'. Also, I still hadn't given them the money that had been raised at the sponsored head shave that spring. We gave half of the five thousand euros to a children's orphanage in a nearby town, Gandia, and because of hospital rules over cash donations, we spent the rest of the money buying loads of new toys and electronic gizmos for the children undergoing cancer treatment at *La Fe*.

Molly came with me and did all the hard work, packing the car with Playstations, DS consoles,

DVDs, CDs, colouring pens, toys, games … loads of stuff to try and make the kids' stay a little less gloomy.

I had butterflies in my stomach all the way to the hospital. As always whenever I went any place that Kenan had spent his final days, I felt excitement going back. I *still* imagined I might see him again, still wanted to believe his passing had been one long bad dream, even though it had been months ago.

My memories of Kenan were still so fresh, that I was no closer to accepting that he had been sent to some other place, than I had been the day he died. My heart longed for him, although the pain was less intense. But as soon as we walked in, I knew Kenan wasn't there. Why would he be? The hospital held few good memories for him; it's the last place he'd want to be.

We asked for Carlos when we arrived at the *Ingreso* and appeared at his office with two trolleys, full of toys. Nothing had changed on the ward. The smell of cleaning products, the furniture, and the sense of hope, sadness and anxiety was exactly the same. There were a couple of nurses I hadn't seen before but that was all. Carlos came and cuddled me like we were long-lost friends, which in a way I suppose we were. It was surprisingly good to see him again and I felt so proud handing over the gifts we'd brought, because it was thanks to Kenan we'd managed to buy them. I knew Carlos would make good use of it all.

We didn't stay long; there was no need to do so, but the visit, emotionally, was an important step for me and I think it did help to bring about a small amount of 'closure'.

People often ask me if I could turn back the clock would I do anything differently. No, I don't think so. My only regret is that Kenan had to go through all that pain second time around, only not to make it, but I didn't have a crystal ball. If I had known the outcome, then perhaps we wouldn't have put him through it. But we didn't, so we had to give him a chance.

I used to ask why him? Now, I ask why anybody? I have to believe that it was his life path, that it was all just very, very bad luck.

Saying that, neither me nor Lev had any desire to put up the Christmas tree that year, but for Angelo and Louis' sakes, I laced the tree with twinkling fairy lights, placed decorations around the house and shopped for presents. Christmas still held all the excitement and promise it always does for Angelo and Louis, as let's face it, nothing can ruin Christmas when you're little, but for me and Lev, it marked one of a number of significant dates we would have to get through.

Lev was in a very bad place by this time, his drinking was heavier than ever, and it was not only dividing us, but his family as well, as none of us knew how to reach him. In England he spent most of his time at work, then drinking at night, and in Spain, well, he stayed in bed mostly, nursing yet another hangover.

Louis' third birthday on 18th December was a difficult day too. We held it at a playhouse we'd been to many times before, and although Louis had a great time with his friends, I wanted to crawl under the covers at home because Kenan wasn't there to join in. But one of the great advantages of having kids is that they need you, and my duties as a mother got me through the day as they always did.

Christmas that year was actually fine. My mum and dad came over and we ate, drank, the kids played with their new toys and we watched Christmas shows on the TV. Our mood at times was sombre, but by now we had started to accept that there was a great, big, gaping hole in our lives and feeling sombre was OK. It didn't stop me wishing I could turn back the clock to a time when Kenan was with us, healthy and happy, but that is a wish that will never leave.

On New Year's Eve, Eli and Emily came round with Karen, Simon and Paula. Mum and Dad were there too. We wanted to wish Kenan a happy New Year, so we stood on the naya and after writing on our own personal messages, let off helium balloons. It felt right looking at the tear-stained faces standing around me that night, because their sadness meant they *remembered*, just like me and Lev did.

Then the season changed again from winter to spring, and another landmark date came around. This time, Kenan's birthday on 9th May. I woke to the sound of rain outside my window and I didn't want to do anything. Not get up, not see a soul and for most of the day, me, Lev, my mum and dad, walked around not bothering to say too much, for fear of upsetting someone.

Eli however, was mortified when she found out we were effectively 'forgetting' Kenan's birthday. "Kenan loved birthdays!" she reminded me on the phone. "Why do you remember the day he left, but not his birthday? He'd rather you remember his birthday."

She was right of course. Birthdays are a big deal when you're a kid, so later on, we all gathered together, me, Lev, Mum, Dad, Maureen, Karen, Simon, Eli, Paula and Emily, this time on the beach and let off helium balloons, again covered with messages for Kenan.

I'd love to say it all went off movie-like, balloons floating up high all the way to 'Neverland', but Eli had attached a letter and a card to hers and her balloon got caught on a flagpole. She never knew, but the letter fell. Lev picked it up, soggy and ink-run, and gave it to me. I slipped it quietly into my pocket so as not to upset Eli, and later put it in Kenan's memory box.

I thank Eli for having the balls that day to make us celebrate Kenan's life and not just focus on his death. Releasing balloons has become our way now of remembering Kenan, of keeping a bond with him, and it helps Angelo and Louis, especially, to 'talk' to their big brother. I know why Kenan loved Eli, she was a true friend, his soulmate and their paths I believe were destined to cross. Still, for me, Kenan's birthdays are the hardest days I have to get through, because with each one that passes, I wonder what my baby would be like now. How tall would he have grown? What he'd look like. What he might be doing. Would he have ever driven himself through the West End of London shouting 'Oi Oi, Saveloy!' out of a van window like Lev?

These are things that I will never know.

Chapter Thirty-six

For two hellish years after Kenan passed away, each one of us battled privately with our guilt and demons. Grief is gruelling, and my mum, in particular, struggled with depression, troubled by frequent nightmares about her last day with Kenan, and Lev struggled with his alcoholism. But slowly – '*poco a poco*[8]' as they say in Spain – we all started to move on, but not to forget.

Lev carried on commuting to and from the UK for work, and I got on with looking after Angelo and Louis, and generally running our life in Spain. As the credit crunch hit, good friends started to return home to England, unable to find enough work to sustain them. Those that didn't leave Javea talked about doing so, and the mood hung pretty low around the place. That was one of the downsides to living abroad I'd discovered; new friendships came and went all too easily.

Lev too, stayed away longer and longer to drum up business. With his 40th birthday approaching

---

[8] '*little by little*'

that May, I decided to throw a big, surprise party for him to cheer everyone up a bit. Lev was adamant he didn't want any sort of party, but I was just as stubborn, insisting he was going to have one.

Immersing myself into 'projects' I'd found, was a useful way of stopping myself thinking about Kenan all the time. Besides, Kenan would have wanted his dad to have a party. We also needed help uniting as a family again because we were drifting, and I was hoping a fun-night out together might help.

Organising the party was a full-time job over a period of several months. I started after Christmas; nicking Lev's mobile and writing down a list of friends to invite – many of whom had been at Kenan's funeral. Then I set about ringing and texting everybody. Maureen helped, tracking down friends Lev hadn't seen for years – one didn't even know we'd lost Kenan.

Between us we got together a guest list of about a hundred and fifty people. I booked a great venue overlooking the beach, with a bar and dance floor. The sumptuous, comfy sofas on the terrace outside would be perfect for chilling out on later. I sent off the invites then threw myself in the task of booking flights and arranging accommodation for the guests and, for a time, I was wonderfully distracted from the day to day reality of my life.

Mehmet flew over a week before the big day to help with collecting people from the airport and the day before the party, Maureen flew over, with Lev and her niece and nephew, Jade and John. Lev clearly smelled a rat with both his parents back in the house, but I managed to convince him they were here only because it was his 40th.

Peter and Annabelle also came over early to help with airport runs, and in settling people into their hotels and apartments. So far so good, but hiding everything from Lev started to get a bit stressful.

First thing on Saturday morning, Lev decided to go for a run, even though I reminded him it was his birthday. I had to quickly call Peter to make sure no one went for an early walk on the beach and bump into him. All morning I played cat and mouse with people as I tried to keep Lev away from the Arenal.

Finally we managed to coerce him into going to another beach, a few miles in the opposite direction, for lunch and as it was such a lovely warm day, I said I wanted to stay at home and hang out around the pool during the afternoon. It was then that the bad luck monkey paid us *another* little visit.

I know I've had a fair old dig at Maureen throughout this book, but it gives me no pleasure to say that when disaster struck, it yet again involved my mother-in-law.

It was about three o'clock, five hours before the start of Lev's big surprise party, when Maureen stepped out of our pool and slipped badly on the wet tiles. She landed with a heavy thump, which is when I heard the scream. Running from the kitchen, the first thing I saw was Lev, totally frozen to the spot, his face white with shock. His gaze was fixed firmly on Maureen, who was lying on the tiles writhing, in what I suspected then, exaggerated agony. I shouted at Lev to go and help his mum up, but each time he tried, Maureen yelled out with the pain. Even Mehmet tried to help her up, but she just couldn't move. Eventually I said we'd have to call an ambulance, thinking that the threat might shift her, but she agreed! I knew then that it was bad, and *today* of all days.

The ambulance arrived fifteen minutes later and took Maureen away, wrapped in a towel and still wearing her swimsuit. Angelo, bless him spoke to the paramedics and explained what had happened, because my Spanish wasn't good enough. I quickly grabbed her some clothes, fetched her passport and most importantly the form which sorts out the 'free' healthcare.

Louis stayed with Mehmet, while the rest of us all followed the ambulance to the hospital in Denia. I rang Mum and Dad on the way, to tell them what had happened, who in turn rang Peter and Annabelle, to ask them to take care of things. By this time it was five o'clock … just three hours before Lev's party. Angelo again took command of the Spanish at the *Ingreso*, even though, in fairness, I could have handled that part having been through it countless times with Kenan, but he was enjoying himself, telling them all about his nanny, so I let him carry on. The doctors went about doing what they needed to do, while my phone rang off the hook.

By now, Lev was sure something was going on; too right there was, and it wasn't meant to be this! I had to tell him something because he wanted to cancel whatever restaurant we were going to that night, but I was damned if I was going to let months of planning go down the drain because of Maureen. I knew it wasn't her fault, but two years of built-up resentment came flooding out and I was furious with her.

I told Lev that friends would be waiting at the restaurant, which he only got angry about. He answered back by saying that he was pissed-off with me for organising something he didn't want, anyway. I was so annoyed, fuming in fact, that everything I tried to plan seemed to go wrong.

It was seven o'clock when my mum and dad arrived at the hospital and I was itching to get out of there. Maureen had had an X-ray and had broken her hip. She needed to have an operation to insert two metal rods. It was a bad break and, when Lev found out, he said he insisted he wasn't going anywhere.

For once, Maureen picked up on my mood and thought about someone other than herself, and pleaded with Lev to go and celebrate his birthday. He still wasn't too sure, but my mum and dad came to my rescue, just like they used to when Kenan had first been diagnosed, and offered to stay with Maureen for as long as she needed them.

For all the upset Maureen was causing, I felt a hint of consolation that, at last, the family was pulling together again, and I hugged my mum and dad in a big thank you. Lev was reassured that Maureen wasn't going to be alone and we finally left the hospital with the kids at half-past seven. Lev was still upset with me for dragging him off though and I was pissed with Maureen for causing all of this in the first place, so the drive home was in stony silence. Soon after, my mum called to say that the operation was going to be done on Monday, and that Maureen was settled so they'd be able to see us later at the party after all.

Rushing around now, I showered, flung on the clothes I'd spent ages carefully choosing, stuck on my make up and left, still cross because I hadn't had time to get ready properly.

The evening light was just going down when we bundled into the car at about nine o'clock – Mehmet, Jade, John, Lev, Angelo, Louis and me. Any excitement about the 'surprise' had long left me, and Lev sat sulking and quiet, unable to enjoy his birthday because he was worried about his mum. I felt a bit bad for him then, and really hoped that seeing his friends would cheer him up a bit. He didn't have a clue where we were going, so when we pulled up outside the party venue he said, "Why are we here? I thought we were going to a restaurant."

"We are, but we're stopping first for a drink."

When the automatic, glass doors leading to the party pulled apart, over a hundred friends inside called out, "SURPRISE!"

Lev genuinely didn't know what to say. He had had no idea, and looked on in stunned silence at the colourful scene that greeted him. At last, after a miserable few hours, he smiled as he spotted friends he hadn't seen for ages. Most of them were drunk! We'd put a bit of money behind the bar, but I'd say nearly all of it had gone by the time we arrived, so we quickly decided that after the day we'd had, we'd just get on and join them.

A whirl of happy, well scrubbed-up people, stopped to ask me in disbelief about Maureen.

"It could only happen to you!" they all said. After a while, I found a quiet corner to gather my thoughts and to watch everyone from. I watched Lev finally relaxing with friends and, as he caught my eye, he smiled a silent 'thank you', before turning away again to carry on drinking and chatting.

I watched Angelo and Louis dancing with their guardian angels for the night, Eli and Emily, and I watched Mehmet trying to get up close and personal with every available woman that passed his way. It was midnight by the time my mum and dad arrived, and I felt a surge of gratitude towards them.

Despite the arguments and estrangement of the past couple of years, we were still solid – children, parents, grandparents, all happy together under one roof. My mum waved across at me, so I went to join her and Dad. Everyone chatted about Maureen of course, and in spite of the bad start, it was just what we all needed. The party turned out to be terrific and lasted well into the early hours. I vowed never to plan anything ever again!

Afterwards, Maureen turned down the chance to fly back to England and decided to have not only the operation in Spain but also her aftercare and recuperation time. I know it sounds bitchy (again!) but I'm sure she stayed because she knew my sister-in-law would never look after her like I did. I waited on her hand and foot for almost two months.

True to form, once Lev knew his mum was going to be alright he, miraculously, had loads of work on in England and buggered off for three weeks. Life came full circle when I had to ring Kenan's old nurse, Carin, to come and look after Maureen who needed her dressings changed and help in the shower ... which is where I drew the line.

Having Carin back in the house again was incredibly hard. It reminded me all over again of the time she had spent with Kenan and my pain of loving and losing him was at the forefront of my mind again. I resented Carin being with Maureen. I wished it was Kenan's dressing she was changing, not Maureen's, Kenan she was helping in and out of the shower, but I suppressed those feelings so I could deal with the now.

I'd love to say Maureen and I grew close during those weeks and in some ways being forced together for such a long time did help our relationship recover. I hold no real grudge towards her, and I hope she doesn't towards me, because I know we were all under a lot of stress during Kenan's illness. But we are like we are and we will always have our ups and downs.

As for life now? Well, we're lucky that we have two other children, Angelo and Louis, even though it hurts me to know that Kenan, their beautiful, brave, kind, sensitive brother will one day become a distant memory to them, no matter how often I talk about him. They are my strength and my reason for living.

Losing a child challenges one's beliefs about the world like nothing else, but Kenan, Angelo and Louis have taught me more than they'll ever realise about the human race and how a mother's love will keep her fighting for her child.

Lev is in AA and although he still has his setbacks, he is trying and I am proud of him for that. Time, for me, doesn't ever 'heal', but it does go on. Both me and Lev find it easier if we have goals to achieve, projects if you like, to focus our minds, but we get on with life just like everybody else.

Above all, as a family unit we are solid. That is the East End way. We have pulled through and I hope in my heart that we always will. We remain constantly challenged by what life has dealt us, but as my grandma always used to say, 'What doesn't kill us makes us stronger.'

It's hard, but I try to remember those words.

Lev

I can admit now that I am an alcoholic and although I swore blind that AA wouldn't help, I went and they are good people. A lot of them are lonely and I would do better if I spent more time there, but I have a business to run and a family to look after, although I'm aware I need to try and sort my problem out before it gets the better of me.

To anyone in my situation with drink, my advice if they want it, would be to give AA a try. It's hard for Gina because we've had enough to deal with, and her strength overwhelms me. She was there with Kenan 24/7, but gets on with life, because Angelo and Louis need a mum and a childhood.

I have to beat my addiction for their sakes too – they've already lost a brother, they don't need to lose a dad as well.

When I think now about my three boys, I realise how much Angelo loved, and looked up to, Kenan and I feel heartbroken that Kenan has been taken from them both.

Kenan was such a sensitive boy, a perfectionist, a thinker and I remember how Angelo and Louis used to stand to attention, like his little foot-soldiers, when he insisted we do the recycling.

"We have to recycle to save the planet," he would announce, using up all of Mummy's bin bags.

Things like that I remember with a smile now, although at the time it used to do my head in! I remember too how he used to call me from the hospital whenever I was in England because he worried about me. There he was having chemo, pissing acid and continuously vomiting and we'd speak on the phone and he'd say he was scared I'd get blown up on a flight or stabbed whilst working in London. You had to laugh; this kid was fighting for his life and still worrying about his silly, old dad.

My relationship with Angelo is very different to the one I had with Kenan. Like me he's a control freak, and likes to get one over on me. I love and admire his determination, even though it drives me crazy at times too. Louis reminds me of Gina – kind and loving but with a sting in his tail. All my boys are different from one another and from them I have learnt a big lesson. That is, as parents we worry if our kids don't get along and we try to get them to be friends.

But there is no need, because it's only when you lose one, you realise how much they loved each other all along.

END

Acknowledgements

I would like to thank my parents and my in-laws for allowing me to be so honest and to disclose so many personal facts throughout the book. I know at times my honesty may have upset them but it was never, ever, meant to offend. I love them all dearly, and I admire them all individually. I would also like to say a personal and heart felt thanks to all of my friends mentioned and not mentioned in these pages. All of you helped me to pull through. A big thank you goes out to Joyce and Philip from Rainbow Nursery – they know why, so no need to say more. I must also thank my husband Lev, who I have driven mad throughout this project. The staff at La Fe hospital deserve a special mention too for their wonderful support as does Lucinda Greasley, Managing Editor at Grazia, for allowing us to quote from the magazine. I would also like to say a massive thank you to Karen Mullally. She has relentlessly slaved over pages and pages of scribble to create this book from our memories. On that same theme, thank you Gaile, Sidney and Sandy at U P Publications for extracting 'Oi Oi, Saveloy!' from my laptop and turning it into something real.

Most of all, I would like to thank my precious boys, Angelo and Louis. Without them, life would have had no further purpose. We love you more than I can ever say and I cherish you both dearly.

English Glossary

Cockney

1	Drum	drum and bass	place (house/home)
2	oily	oily rag	fag (cigarette)
3	ruby	ruby murray	curry
4	barney	barney rubble	trouble
5	kettle	kettle on the hob	fob (watch)
6	dicky bird		word

English slang

1	Babe	A term of endearment, i.e. 'Love'
2	bollocks	testicles
3	gutted	disappointed
4	karzy	toilet
5	leccy	Electrician
6	totty	good looking girls, sexually desirable
7	knackered	tired, worn out, exhausted
8	twat	Idiot, crude connotations

For further information about Leukaemia the following websites may be of interest:-

http://www.beatbloodcancers.org/

http://www.leukaemia.org/

http://www.anthonynolan.org/

http://www.leukaemiacare.org.uk

http://www.clicsargent.org.uk/

http://www.leukaemiabusters.org.uk

http://www.leuka.org.uk/

http://www.cureleukaemia.co.uk/

http://www.cancerindex.org/clinks2g.htm

http://www.elfcharity.org.uk/

http://www.pontins.com/charities-leukaemia-and-lymphoma-research/

There are many more sites around – so we apologise to any charity or information site that we have neglected to mention. The book's website www.oioisaveloy.info not only has links to the sites listed above but it also includes others we have found, since publication.